We Were
Dreamers

SIMU LIU

We Were Dreamers

An Immigrant Superhero Origin Story

WM

WILLIAM MORROW

An Imprint of HarperCollins*Publishers*

Photographs in the inserts are courtesy of the author unless otherwise noted below.

Second insert: page 4 (top) photo courtesy of the Canadian Broadcast Corporation (CBC); page 4 (bottom) photo by Dylan Hewlett; page 5 (top) photo by Emmanuel Raif; page 6 (top) photo by Sean William O'Neill; page 6 (bottom) photo courtesy of the Chinese Canadian Youth Athletics Association; page 7 (bottom) photo by Alberto E. Rodriguez/Getty Images; page 8 (top) photo © 2019 Eric Charbonneau; page 8 (bottom) photo © Marvel.

HarperCollins books may be purchased for educational, business, or sales promotional use. For information, please email the Special Markets Department in the U.S. at SPsales@harpercollins.com or in Canada at HCOrder@harpercollins.com.

A hardcover edition of this book was published in 2022 by William Morrow, an imprint of HarperCollins Publishers.

FIRST WILLIAM MORROW PAPERBACK EDITION PUBLISHED 2023.

Library of Congress Cataloging-in-Publication Data has been applied for.

Library and Archives Canada Cataloguing in Publication information is available upon request.

ISBN 978-0-06-304650-4

ISBN 978-1-4434-6061-3 (Canada)

23 24 25 26 27 LBC 6 5 4 3 2

For 妈妈, 爸爸, 爷爷, 奶奶, and Barkley, with all my love

CONTENTS

We Were
Dreamers

PROLOGUE

The call that would forever alter the course of my life came on a hot July afternoon in Toronto, as I was lounging around in my underwear eating a bag of Nongshim shrimp crackers. I had flown to New York and screen-tested for Marvel Studios just two days prior, and was desperately trying to pass the time until they made their decision. This particular day, I had finished my scenes for *Kim's Convenience* early in the morning and then gotten some shut-eye after returning home. I had barely woken up and cracked open the bag of crispy fried treats when my phone lit up:

UNKNOWN NUMBER
Burbank, CA

Ordinarily, I wouldn't have batted an eyelash; it could have been a friend I'd forgotten to save into my phone, or my manager calling from a remote office, or a "Nigerian prince" searching desperately for a place to stash his money.

But this day is different.

This day, I know exactly who is on the other side, and I know exactly what he is calling to tell me. My heart pounds furiously as I grab my phone and yell/shriek the most unattractive *"HELLOOO!?!?!"* you could ever imagine.

The divine voice of Kevin Feige answers back.

"Hello, Simu, this is Kevin from Marvel Studios calling. I'm here with some folks in the office who want to tell you something!"

My head is spinning so fast I want to fall over and puke my guts out. Far off in the distance, I hear our director Destin Daniel Cretton's jovial voice:

"We want you to be Shang-Chi, man!"

"OH MY GOD OH MY GOD OH MY GOD OH MY GODDDDDDDD!"

I collapse to the floor with tears already streaming down my face. My entire body is on fire; I want to thank Kevin a trillion times over, but also to get the hell off the phone before he changes his mind. Kevin tells me I'm going to be at the San Diego Comic-Con in four days, where I will be announced to the world as Marvel's newest Avenger.

"Now, Simu—it's imperative that you not tell *anyone* before we break the news. We don't want any leaks. Just hold it in for four days. Sound good?"

"No problem, sir. I won't let you down!" It's the first and only time I will lie to Kevin Feige.

I hang up the phone and drag myself to bed, where I sob and convulse into my pillow for what feels like forever. I have just fulfilled a dream so inconceivably far-fetched that I may as well have wished for a pet unicorn, or a treehouse made of rainbows. As this impossible reality begins to set in, I repeat these words to myself over and over again:

I'm going to be a superhero.

A minute later, unable to hold my secret in any longer, I call my best friend Jason to break the news. He was one of the only people in the world who knew that I was up for this role.

". . . Yo."

Jason's voice is monotone and blasé, almost as if he's annoyed that I've taken him out of whatever Nintendo Switch game he'd been playing. As per usual for our relationship, I decide to troll him a little bit.

"So, the thing is . . . I can't tell you anything," I say, trying to match his detached demeanor. "So here I am, calling you and not telling you anything."

"Uh ... okay ..."

"I am *definitely* not going to tell you who just called to offer me a job."

"Dude, I have no clue what you're talking ab– wait. WAIIIIIT."

"Yup."

"Are you serious? ... ARE YOU FUCKING SERIOUS?!!"

We both scream in unadulterated joy after I assure him that I am, in fact, fucking serious.

After Jason and I hang up the phone, he races over to my apartment and we hatch a plan to record my parents' reaction over FaceTime. He stands just out of my camera's view as I dial my dad's cell, anxious to break the news to the people who raised me. Like me, I know they've probably had a bit of trouble eating and sleeping these past few days. I want this call to bring closure not only on this movie, but to their entire lives spent in the pursuit of a better life for our family.

I want to tell them that their better life has finally come.

The call connects: *"Wei, Máomao! What's going on?"*

The moment I see my dad, a slender fifty-nine-year-old man with more salt than pepper in his hair, I feel my throat begin to close up. It's been thirty years since he left his home in China to eventually settle in a suburb outside Toronto—over twenty of which he has been a working professional with dental coverage—and yet, the man has never bothered to fix his horrendously crooked teeth. I think he was too busy paying for my braces, my education and my apartment to notice that he looked like a jack-o'-lantern whenever he opened his mouth. I should also mention that he cuts his own hair—don't ask me how.

"Hey, is Māma home? Can you put her on, too?"

Mom hates when people know her real age, so let's just say she's not exactly a spring chicken anymore. You'd never know it looking at her though—she's got a smile that radiates youthful energy and a flawless complexion that owes itself to religious use of Estée Lauder's Night Repair Serum. A white man mistook her for my wife many years ago during a family ski trip, and she hasn't shut up about it since. I don't have the heart to tell her that he was probably just trying to hit on her.

"Máomao! What's wrong?"

"Nothing's wrong, I, uh . . ." I take a deep breath.

". . . I just wanted to tell you that I got it."

It feels like eons before my parents respond. When my dad finally speaks, it sounds like someone's just told him his dry cleaning will be ready on time.

"Oh . . . okay! That's good!"

Four days from now, after watching a livestream of me walking out on stage at the San Diego Comic-Con to the thunderous applause of eight thousand die-hard fans, my parents will finally understand the significance of landing a role like Shang-Chi. For now, though, they are simply happy that I have a job. We talk for a few more minutes about stupid things like money when I see Jason motioning for my attention. *Say I love you*, he mouths.

I nod, already knowing what my parents' response to this will be. Exchanging *I love you*s was a uniquely Western custom, and I had long ago come to terms with the fact that my parents expressed their love in a very different way—by telling me to put on a jacket, asking if I had eaten yet, or yelling at me when they felt like I wasn't studying hard enough. The actual words were not a part of our family's vocabulary at all.

Still, it would've been pretty nice to hear them say it.

"I gotta go, so I just want to say goodbye, and of course, I love you."

"Yeah, yeah—stay calm," my mother says.

"A new day has begun," my dad adds, wistfully.

Maybe they just didn't hear me? Just to be sure, I double down.

"*I love you.* Bye."

There's a short pause. Jason and I look at each other, wondering if one of them is going to prove us wrong . . .

"Yes, go go go," my mom says. *"Thank you for letting us know."*

"Yep," my dad chimes in the background. *"Bye-bye!"*

BEEP. The call ends, and we both burst out laughing.

That fateful day, the 16th of July in 2019, a single phone call would change my life forever. On that day I became more than just a comic book character—I became a part of an idea that everyone deserves to see themselves as superheroes, as the leads of their own stories, or simply, just as multifaceted beings with hopes and aspirations and flaws.

At this point, some of you are probably wondering how I got here. At least, I hope that's the case—I mean, you did buy the book after all.

Being *here*, and making history with this movie that we should have had a long time ago, was a product of more than my own personal struggles; it was also the culmination of everything my parents had fought for. Our stories are one and the same, our destinies forever intertwined and defined by our sweat, our sacrifice and our unyielding dedication to defying the odds and achieving the impossible.

That is why I'm writing this book. *This* is the story I want to tell—a story about our little family of three that crossed the ocean from China to North America in the relentless pursuit of a better life. A story about the obstacles that nearly tore us apart, whether it was a clash of cultures, a gap of generations or simply our own stubbornness. A story about an imperfect family that made mistakes, often hurt one another and nearly imploded on many occasions, but held on, survived and even thrived.

Most importantly, this book tells the story of an immigrant dream that is shared by the tens of millions of families who made the same journey as mine, and who continue to fight every day for their happy ending.

This book is for all of us.

ACT ONE

CHAPTER ONE

MADE IN CHINA

Every epic cross-generational tale of perseverance and triumph has a beginning, and ours begins in China—specifically in Harbin, a modestly sized city in the country's northeastern tip known for its brutal winters and its famous annual ice sculpture festival. I was born on the 19th of April, 1989, in this Chinese Winterfell, to a working-class family that possessed neither money nor influence of any sort. My family was neither House Lannister nor Stark; they were innocent villagers in the background, whose simple lives were unencumbered by any political aspirations whatsoever.

I spent the first four and a half years of my life with my dad's side of the family in Harbin, sans Dad—or Mom, for that matter. My father left China when I was eight months old to do a PhD program at Queen's University in Canada, and my mom joined him a year later, leaving me in the care of my 爷爷 (yéye) and my 奶奶 (nǎinai), my paternal grandparents.

My parents named me 思慕 (sīmù), from the Chinese characters 思想 (sīxiǎng), meaning *introspection* or *ideation*, and 羡慕 (xiànmù), meaning the envy or longing for something one doesn't have. My name was meant to be a reminder of my parents' journey and the sacrifices that they made along the way—I would always be envious of the other children whose parents never left their side.

So Sīmù wasn't exactly a name that evoked the happiest of memories; luckily, I had two! In China, it is extremely common for loved ones and close family members to give you a nickname, or "little name." I was only ever called Sīmù if I was in trouble–刘思慕 (liúsīmù) if I *really* messed up. Otherwise, I was known to my family as 毛毛 (máomao), which roughly translates to "little furry caterpillar." It was much less depressing than "introspective envy" . . . and *way* cuter.

To be honest, I never really noticed that my parents weren't around. I was far too young to have formed any lucid memories of them before they left, so there was nothing for me to miss. I knew that my 妈妈 (māma) and 爸爸 (bàba) existed, but to me they were more like abstract concepts that I spoke with on the phone every now and then. I was told that my folks were a part of a very small group of people who had been given the opportunity to study abroad, and that one day I would join them on their worldly adventure.

Of course, I didn't understand what any of that meant; I was content to just live my life.

My grandparents and I lived in a charming little ramshackle apartment on the fifth floor of a cement building, tucked at the very back of the university campus where my yéye taught chemistry before he retired. The place would have been out-of-date ten years before I ever set foot in it, but it had character. The paint on the walls was chipped and faded, the wooden doors aged, and our rickety mismatched chairs always seemed like they were on the verge of collapse, kept alive only by my yéye's tinkering. Our home was full of little DIY "improvements" that he dreamed up, like water pipes wrapped in newspaper and plastic bags, or wooden sticks strapped to table and chair legs to reinforce them. It was an ingenuity that would've made MacGyver jealous.

The kitchen was effectively a series of open flames, next to a sink made of blackish-brown concrete, surrounded by a jungle of exposed pipes. My grandparents didn't get a refrigerator until after I was born, and it was stored in a separate room because the kitchen had no power.

Our water—which was unfit for drinking and only came cold—ran for roughly half the day, which meant that we had to keep reserves around the apartment. A good chunk of every morning had to be spent boiling the water over the fire and then storing it for cleaning, cooking and bathing, the latter of which was an art form of finding the perfect ratio between scalding-hot boiled water and the water pumped from the depths of the earth's cold body. As far as I can remember, my grandparents always got it just right.

My grandmother—my nǎinai—was my primary caretaker, a strong-willed woman with wavy gray hair and joyous eyes hidden behind thick, horn-rimmed glasses. As a former pediatrician, Nǎinai would follow me around tirelessly, removing my thumb from my mouth, stuffing food *in* my mouth or forcing me to put on a sweater. In Eastern medicine, there was no greater enemy than the cold—I was always tucked under layers and layers of covers before I went to sleep and scolded for leaving my hands or toes exposed. If I was sick in any way, the number of layers would double. Leaving the window open overnight was strictly forbidden; Nǎinai had a brother who passed suddenly when they were both children, and their entire family was convinced that it was because he had slept too close to an open window during a particularly breezy night. The many hardships she endured in her life made her ever more vigilant as my guardian—she was very adamant that I not suffer through the same things she did.

My yéye—my grandfather—was my teacher, a balding man with startling athleticism for his age and a generous smile punctuated by teeth of silver and gold. Whether it was explaining all his fixer-upper projects around our home or quizzing me with English flash cards, Yéye always had something to impart to me. There were the essential life lessons like good manners and living frugally, but also fun ones like learning to play table tennis or Chinese chess. I'd spend many afternoons with my yéye playing games with him or just watching him work; it seemed like he possessed all the knowledge of the universe. He radiated self-assuredness; a man of infinite patience and understated wisdom.

The combined salary of a university professor and a pediatrician would have afforded my grandparents a vastly different lifestyle if they had raised me in North America, but China in the nineties was far from the global superpower it is today. Nobody was rich; if there were exorbitantly wealthy families out there, I was certainly not aware of them. But so what if we weren't the Chinese Kardashians? My childhood memories in Harbin were filled with love and laughter—I didn't need anything more.

I used to sit on the back of my yéye's bicycle as we rode through the street markets on Héxìnglù near our campus, marveling at all of the delicious treats and shiny toys on display. Yéye would often buy me a candied hawthorn-berry stick, cumin lamb skewer or frozen yogurt Popsicle to satisfy my cravings, but he obviously couldn't do it all the time. Being the little brat that I was, I'd often throw a tantrum when he told me no. I'd lie down on the pavement and cry loudly, punching and kicking the ground and refusing to move until I got tired or my yéye relented.

Thankfully, he never did. Can you imagine the kind of overly dramatic, attention-seeking diva I would have become if he had?

As the tantrums persisted, my grandparents began to wonder when the terrible twos would finally be over—which definitely did not speak well to my maturity level, seeing as I was almost four by that point. Eventually my yéye had had enough; I was way too old to be acting out like that, and it was time to grow up.

But rather than yelling or threatening to hit me, Yéye sat me down in our apartment before we went shopping and told me about the importance of keeping your word.

"Máomao, when two people speak in good faith with each other, it means they *promise* to hold up their end of the bargain."

As he explained it calmly and patiently, the concept of what a promise was slowly began to take shape.

"I will take you to Héxìnglù to do groceries with me, but you have to *promise* me that you will not throw any tantrums. If you break your word, I'm afraid I won't be able to bring you with me anymore. Do you understand?"

"Okay. I promise!"

The next time I rode through Héxìnglù on the back of my yéye's bicycle, I instantly felt the pang of desire as I cast my eyes across those shiny toys and books, and smelled the delicious aromas of the street food—but then promptly kept my mouth shut. Yéye was so surprised that he would recite this story for many years; even he had no idea whether the lesson would stick!

Harbin winters were epically cold, with temperatures often dipping to as low as -30°C (-22°F for you Americans). My grandparents would bundle me up in layers upon layers of cotton and wool (we didn't have the luxury of goose down) and ushanka hats with earflaps, an inheritance from our Russian neighbors to the north. Still, we never let the cold rain on our parade—one of my favorite wintertime activities was making bīngdēng, or "ice lights," with my whole family. It was a simple process, really, beginning with eating a lot of yogurt and saving the packaging. We'd put the colorful foil that sealed the top inside the containers and then fill them with water so that they'd freeze and harden. Finally, we'd take the ice out of the containers and hang them on the balcony, where they would glitter against the soot-soaked sunlight.

Rain or shine, summer or winter, I was visited often by my 姑姑 (gūgu, aunt), 姑夫 (gūfū, her husband) and cousin JingJing, who lived just a short walk away. We celebrated most holidays together, a family of six making dumplings or noodles from scratch. Despite being six years my senior, JingJing was my closest friend and playmate. When she came over I would gather all of my toys and knickknacks onto my bed, which would become my makeshift bodega. She would pretend to peruse my merchandise, asking me questions about the products and haggling on the prices. JingJing always drove a hard bargain, but I always cut her a good deal. What choice did I have; she was my only customer, after all!

One time, with everyone in a nostalgic mood, my grandparents brought out one of JingJing's old dresses. It was lightly worn because she had quickly outgrown it, but it was just right for me. It was so pretty and shiny—a long white dress with frills on the side—that I knew I had to try it on. I was initially confused when everyone told me that girl clothes were different from boy clothes. *What was the big deal?!* I refused to take no for an answer and proceeded to wear the shit out of that dress, heteronormativity be damned. I even convinced my grandparents to do a little photo shoot (and yes, of course we put the photo in the book).

My gūgu and gūfū were also professors, making my entire family practically the embodiment of Asian excellence. Like my parents they possessed no desire for political power, or material wealth beyond the bare necessities. That said, they always found a way to spoil me, often buying me toys against my grandparents' wishes and treating me as if I were their second child.

When it was just me, I would entertain myself with my favorite picture books and TV shows. I had a particular affinity for *Jīngānghúluwá–Calabash Brothers*, a series about a group of young color-coded superheroes with special abilities to match the calabash gourds on their heads. The Calabash Brothers books were the subject of many a tantrum, to my grandparents' chagrin. I just couldn't get enough of the superpowers, the fantastical monsters and the eternal battle between good and evil—you know, childish superhero stuff that I've totally, 100 percent outgrown.

When I say that I was a happy child in Harbin, I definitely do not speak to how difficult I may or may not have been for the ones tasked with taking care of me. Despite the best efforts of those around me, I still found plenty of ways to get myself into trouble. One time, I got salmonella by drinking the water from our fishbowl. Another time, I nearly electrocuted myself poking power outlets with my finger. Finally—and I have racked my brain trying to solve this mystery—there were even some instances where my grandparents and I awoke to discover that someone had pooped in my pants overnight.

(Would now be a good time to mention that I was named one of Canada's Hottest Bachelors in 2018?)

Regardless of whether I threw a tantrum, pooped my pants or drank dirty fishbowl water, I knew beyond a shadow of a doubt that I was loved unconditionally. It didn't matter what destruction I had wrought during the day—at night, I would always take my place in between my grandparents and we would fall asleep in one another's arms.

They were my safe haven.

Now, when I picture our old home in my mind's eye, my heart yearns to go back and curl up in bed with my yéye and năinai one more time, so I could listen and doze off to the sound of Năinai's soothing voice as she reads me my favorite bedtime story. Both she and my yéye passed away in 2021, shortly after my thirty-second birthday, while I was in the middle of reshoots for *Shang-Chi and The Legend of The Ten Rings*. I had planned to take them to the premiere of the movie, to hold their hands on either side of me as they watched their grandson on the big screen for the first time. There's not a thing in this world I wouldn't give to be able to see the both of them again, as they were back then.

In the summer of 1993 I noticed that my English flash card lessons were starting to pick up, along with talk that my departure date to Canada was drawing ever nearer.

I didn't like that one bit.

My whole family—my yéye, năinai, gūgu, gūfū, even my cousin JingJing —spoke of this "Canada" as if it were some sort of idyllic paradise, a place of abundant snacks and endless affection.

"You can eat whatever you want," Năinai would say, as if I didn't already have pretty regular access to all of my favorites on Héxìnglù.

"You will finally reunite with your parents," my gūgu added reassuringly, as if I didn't already have five amazing people around me who loved me.

Looking back, it felt kind of cult-y, like gospel from the Church of Canadology that I was supposed to just accept. I played along, even though I was still rough on the exact terms of this proposition. Sure, I welcomed the thought of meeting more members of my family . . . but

I had no idea that said new family members would come at the cost of everyone that I knew and loved.

So, with about as much agency as any four-year-old possessed, I kept on, ever the obedient child, dutifully memorizing my English flash cards. 苹果 (píngguǒ)–Apple. 猫 (māo)–Cat. 香蕉 (xiāngjiāo)–Banana. 爸爸妈妈 (bàbamāma)–Parents, whom I would meet in the winter.

An air of excitement permeated our household in the days leading up to my father's arrival in late December. Word had come to us that Bàba would fly over to pick me up and escort me back to Canada, while Māma would meet us at the airport once we landed in Toronto. If my grandparents were dreading letting me go (they were), they went to great lengths not to show it. We made a big WELCOME BACK sign in giant letters and hung it on our door. I wore my nicest clothes on the day, an outfit of absolute fire consisting of a collared rugby shirt with blue and purple stripes, a pair of brown overalls with yellow polka dots and a vest that looked like a burlap sack. That's right, I was pattern clashing way before it was cool.

My gūgu and gūfū came over and we prepared a feast that filled our little round table: white mushrooms with sliced pork, large tail-on shrimp, bean curd, soy-sauce ribs and Russian-style red sausage–my father's favorite, apparently.

The food is starting to get cold when we hear a little knock on our door. I perk up anxiously as my yéye answers, opening the door to reveal a scrawny, square-faced man with bowl-cut hair wearing a big cozy sweater along with the bleary glaze of exhaustion that comes after an eighteen-hour train ride from Beijing. This man who resembles an Asian Eric Forman from *That '70s Show* is my bàba, the man who I had waited my entire four-and-a-half-year life to reunite with.

This is the man who is going to bring me to the promised land of Canada.

"Máomao! It's me!"

I freeze.

I had imagined this moment in my head many times, as I'm sure my father had. I want to run to him, embracing him enthusiastically and without any reservations, as any child would run to their own father—but I just . . . *can't*. Everything about this man is foreign to me, from his voice to his smell. I had only seen his face in photographs, only heard recordings of his disembodied voice. He feels almost like a celebrity, someone I recognize from somewhere, but who is himself unknown and unknowable.

I scurry to my nǎinai's side nervously. I'm sure my father was a little disappointed, but he respected my space, taking only a small step toward me.

"Do you know who I am?"

I ponder this for a moment.

"You . . . you are Zhenning Liu."

Everyone around me bursts out laughing. The ice is broken, and I laugh along, even though I don't get the joke. "Zhenning Liu" is exactly who this man is to me; not "Dad," not "Father," not "Bàba" . . . but a stranger, an acquaintance at best.

Slowly, over the next few days, it dawns on me that this stranger is going to take me away from my family, my home and everything that I have ever known.

CHAPTER TWO

BACK IN TIME

I have to pause at this highly climactic moment to bring you back in time to tell you the story of my parents.

Trust me, it'll be worth it—we're going to take a much deeper look at the circumstances of their upbringing, paying special attention to how they came to view the world as they did. When we do pick back up in December 1993 in Harbin, you'll have a much better sense of who my mother and father are, and why they made the choice to risk everything and leave the country they called home.

If you *are* feeling a burning impatience to pick up chronologically from where the previous chapter left off, you can skip the rich family backstory that pays off beautifully at the end and advance to chapter seven—just know that you'll miss some juicy insights that will definitely move you, and may even affect the way you view your parents. Also, you'd totally be committing the cardinal sin of immigrant families: wasting money.

Still there?

Good.

Our literary DeLorean will take us to the year 1960, when a still-fledgling Chinese government was just beginning to realize its vision of becoming a global superpower. Eleven years earlier, Chairman Mao Zedong led the Communist Party to victory in the Chinese Civil War that saw the defeated Nationalists—the Kuomintang—fleeing to Taiwan. For the first time, the entire country was united under one single banner: the People's Republic of China. I hope you weren't expecting flower power, the Beatles, or William Shatner on *Star Trek*—the '60s were very different in the Middle Kingdom.

Now, if you live in the West, chances are that your impression of China has been heavily influenced by what you've heard in the news. Most dangerously of all, you might get the sense that people from China are a fundamental threat to your existence and your ideals of freedom, capitalism, bald eagles and cheeseburgers.

Look, I'm not here to lecture you about Eurocentricity or media bias; I just want to put forth the idea that maybe China has been the punching bag of the West for a very, very long time, and that nothing is gained from the continued demonization of its people . . . of *my* people. If you can accept that a single country can give birth to both a Donald Trump and a Donald Glover, a Steve Carell and a Stone Cold Steve Austin, you shouldn't have any difficulty accepting that the 1.3 billion people who call China home are just as varied in their ideologies and philosophies. There are the party officials, the pure-of-heart idealists, the Crazy Rich Asians, the activists, the social media influencers (smash that subscribe button!), the internet trolls and every conceivable thing in between—but perhaps most of all, there are the families like my parents, who simply did their best to stay out of trouble and survive from one day to the next.

For the sake of the story, I want to start with my dad, whom I technically met first and whose side of the family played a much more active role in my upbringing.

This will, of course, upset my dear mother, whose hyper-competitiveness is matched only by her son's. I can already hear her now, reminding me that *she* was the one who had to carry me to term while I incubated in her belly for nine months, leeching off of her like a parasite, only to then exit her body in the most painful way imaginable. Then again, I feel like she would also be mad if I wrote about her first—*I don't like all this attention, why did you put me front and center right away?!*

As you will discover later, my mother is a very difficult person to argue with.

My father was born in April of 1960 in the middle of a very tough time for all of China. After unifying the country and bringing about an era of peace, stability and healthcare reform—all objectively good things—Mao had hoped to reform the economy as well. This included the collectivization of agriculture and industrialization of rural communities across the country.

As it turned out, this proved way more difficult in practice than in theory; the government's insistence on high export quotas for grain meant that they weren't storing enough for themselves. The country was deeply vulnerable to a natural disaster such as a drought . . . which is exactly what happened in 1959, resulting in severe famine in many rural parts of the country.

Whenever we talk about my dad's childhood, though, he's always quick to remind me not to paint him as some sort of victim.

"My life is not a sob story," he'd say.

He would always remind me that while his childhood was by no means glamorous, he wasn't an unhappy kid at all. Looking back on my own upbringing in Harbin, I can definitely see where he was coming from.

Despite being born at a time when the country was plagued with food shortages and declining birth rates, my dad somehow made out okay. Harbin was by no means a developed city at that point, but it was still an important one in the Northeast region. As such, it was relatively well supplied. Nobody was dying on the street, but nobody was feasting either—rationing was heavily enforced, leaving each family member with just a half pound of meat each month, in addition to other foods and household items. It was common practice for a family to combine their rations into one big feast, ensuring they could have at least one good meal each month.

My yéye would often scour the vegetable markets of Héxìnglù for discarded cabbage stems and other produce that you and I would deem inedible; after a rinse and a boil, drizzled in soy sauce, they were a nice addition to a meal that would otherwise have been painfully bland (e.g., a bowl of rice).

Dad lived in a tiny apartment with my yéye, năinai and gūgu (his older sister) just down the street from the similarly tiny apartment I would grow up in twenty-nine years later. My gūgu and I shared similar experiences in our formative years—she, too, was separated from her parents at an early age, and raised by her grandparents. When my năinai found out she was pregnant in 1953 while preparing to go to medical school in Shenyang, she knew right away that she and my yéye wouldn't be able to manage the workload. She made arrangements to birth the baby in Shanghai, where my yéye's mother had agreed to take care of the baby. My gūgu wouldn't be reunited with her parents until she was six, after my grandparents finally settled in Harbin with another baby on the way—my dad.

While it may have made sense at the time, the decision was not without consequence; Gūgu's relationship with Yéye and Năinai never reached the same level of intimacy as my dad's. She fought with her parents often, and always felt like the outsider of the family.

In retrospect, my father can't help but feel a pang of guilt—he always knew that he was the favorite child, the young prince who my yéye and năinai had raised from birth. Naturally, I can't help but wonder how much closer we'd be if I, in turn, had never been separated from him.

My dad had barely started primary school when, having just recovered from an era of sweeping countrywide reform, China went through . . . well, another era of countrywide reform. The Cultural Revolution, or wénhuàdàgémìng, would span the next ten years and drastically alter the lives of an entire generation of Chinese youth.

Bear with me as I attempt to give you a crash course here:

In 1966, Mao set out to purge China of anti-revolutionary ideals that he claimed had polluted the population. In an effort to reform the education system, primary and middle school hours were reduced to half days, universities and colleges were shuttered, and the National College Entrance Examination, or the gāokǎo, was placed on an indefinite hiatus.

As a result, kids like my dad were pretty much left to their own devices.

"It was awesome!" he explained.

Huh?

"Yeah; we got to do whatever we wanted!"

Too young to understand the political implications of what was happening, my dad proceeded to skip enough school to put Ferris Bueller to shame. He and his friends would roam around the Songhua River, racing each other and getting into all kinds of tomfoolery. One summer, he challenged himself to run ten kilometers every day, because . . . well, why not?

It was also during this time that I'm convinced my father attained godlike ping-pong skills. He would pass on only *some* of this knowledge to me, withholding just enough so that his son would forever be his inferior. *Curse you, Dad!*

Meanwhile, my yéye began to seriously fear for his own safety. As an academic, he felt that he was in imminent danger of being branded as a "stuck-up intellectual" by the Red Guard, a militia of radicalized Chinese youth that harassed, beat and sometimes killed in the name of the revolution. Not willing to put himself and his family at risk, Yéye effectively became homebound for much of my father's childhood, while my nǎinai continued to work as a pediatrician, a job that was still highly regarded at the time.

"Sometimes, it is good to keep a low profile," Yéye would say to my dad.

Despite his self-imposed house arrest, my yéye was determined to instill in my father the same curiosity for science and knowledge that he had. He would sneak into closed-down libraries and bring back whatever books he could for them both to read.

That's right—while the Americans were experimenting with marijuana and LSD, my father was fighting the system by dabbling in . . . *learning*?

What a nerd.

When my dad was eight, the government introduced shàngshānxià-xiāng—"Up the Mountains and Down the Countryside"—an initiative that required millions of Chinese families to send their children away from home to work in mountainous areas or farming villages to learn the value of hard labor and proletariat life. By the party's decree, each family had to send their able-bodied children once they either graduated from or dropped out of high school, with one exemption allowed per household.

The mass exodus of millions of Chinese teenagers resulted in a brain drain of massive proportions; without the ability to advance their education, many were deprived of the opportunity to reach their full potential.

My grandparents were spared from making an impossible choice between their children when my gūgu, at age fifteen, volunteered to be the one to leave. She had never fully felt like she fit in anyway, and so this seemed like a natural opportunity to leave home and go on an exciting adventure—at least, that's how it was being sold. And so, she packed her bags and hopped on a train to the village of Raohe on the Sino-Russian border, some 750 kilometers away, where she would work in the fields for eight years alongside the rest of China's lost generation before finally returning home.

Dad went on to attend the affiliate high school of the university that my yéye taught at. The three-story, Russian-style brick building had a full-length running track outside, which my father would use very frequently. Still, despite being a well-equipped institution, the school—like all schools—was not exactly a bastion of learning. Kids ran the rooms rambunctiously, talking to each other and ignoring lesson plans. There was no passing or failing, and barely any homework; the teachers understood that the majority of these kids would be headed for the countryside anyway.

Fortunately for my dad, the universe would intervene in his favor.

On September 9, 1976, Mao Zedong passed away and left behind a legacy that was as remarkable as it was complicated. While his portrayal in the West is oftentimes that of an unsympathetic dictator, he continues to be revered in China as a great (if flawed) leader who uplifted a nation and brought its people to global prominence. Following the Chairman's death, de facto successor Deng Xiaoping reopened China's universities and reinstated the gāokǎo exam.

Great—now everything could return to normal! Problem solved, right?

Well . . . not so fast; when the government reopened the universities and reinstated the gāokǎo—their version of the SATs, if you will—they announced that anyone who would have been able to take the test in the last ten years was eligible to apply. Many of these people, like my gūgu, had already been working in the countryside for years at this point, without having so much as thought about complex mathematics or Chinese literature. How could they be expected to have a fighting chance? The opportunity to go to university was seen as a ticket to a better life, and it *was*—but there were only as many tickets as seats in the classroom, and there was a backlog totaling ten *years'* worth of applicants clamoring for their shot.

This is where my dad's exceptional fortune came into play.

When news of the gāokǎo came, my dad was seventeen and halfway through his senior year. Although he wasn't necessarily getting a top-tier education, being in a school was infinitely better than being out in the fields working. One day, the entire student body was ushered into rooms and given a mysterious exam with writing and math questions. My dad took the test and aced it, completely oblivious as to why it had been administered in the first place. A few days later, he was informed that he was one of eight students selected out of over three hundred to train for the historical gāokǎo.

As it turned out, the school was trying to pre-screen for students that had a legitimate shot at getting into university a half semester early. These teenagers would be considered the country's best and brightest, a pace car for the older applicants to be measured against. These kids certainly had their work cut out for them though; they would be held to a higher standard than their more senior counterparts, who were at an educational disadvantage because of their gap in schooling. Only the top 1 percentile would be accepted into a university or college.

Siri, play "Eye of the Tiger" and cue the most *epic* study montage ever known to man!

Over the next few weeks, my dad and his seven compatriots would study for the gāokǎo in their principal's office, which had been converted into a makeshift classroom complete with desks and a chalkboard. Dozens of students crowded at the principal's door during lunch and recess to catch a glimpse of this Elite Eight, none of whom would ever take a break.

Around the Eight, teachers rotated in and out, filling the chalkboard in their classroom with math, physics, chemistry, literature and political theory. As the weeks went on, the fans at their door slowly began to dissipate, but the laser-eyed focus of the Eight would not break. This was their time—their *destiny*.

On the morning of the exam, in the middle of Harbin's lethal winter, my father and his seven anointed classmates took a public bus to a remote testing facility where he saw hundreds of other hopeful students who had come from across the city, eager to try their luck.

With limited preparation, a high-pressure deadline, and the determination to secure a better future for himself, he would crush the gāokǎo.

A few weeks later, an acceptance letter would arrive in the mail offering my dad a spot at Beijing's Jiaotong University to study electrical engineering—his last choice, ironically, not that beggars could be choosers or anything.

In total, 5.7 million candidates from across China would take the gāokǎo exam that winter, whereas tens of millions more decided to forgo their eligibility—the less academically inclined who knew they had no chance. Universities around the country would extend offers to just 4.8 percent of the total applicants, most of whom had already been pre-screened in some way, like my dad. The Elite Eight would fare significantly better than the national average; four would end up receiving offers, while four would not.

Against all odds, my gūgu (who had never gotten the chance to attend high school) also did well enough on her gāokǎo to be accepted into the College of Electrical Motor Design in Harbin. Once resigned to live out her days in Raohe, she was finally able to return home.

My dad still fondly recalls all the attention he got in the six weeks leading up to his exam:

"I was like a celebrity," he jokes wistfully. "It was the proudest moment of my life."

"Prouder than when you found out your son was a literal superhero?"

"Oh yeah. For sure."

CHAPTER THREE

THE FROG AND THE SWAN

My mother would hate me revealing anything about her childhood or her upbringing.

I think it's because she's so good at hiding her age; on any given day walking down the street you'd never think that she lived through so many chapters of Chinese history just by looking at her. She works out, dyes her hair and dresses simply but elegantly, carefully curating the image of a sophisticated and ageless woman with a radiant smile. If you ever meet her, you might even get the idea that she was born into privilege; she speaks deliberately, with eloquence and grace, reflecting a poise that is not often seen outside of bourgeois circles. Just one peek behind her eternally youthful shell, however, and you will find a scrappy and unrelenting woman who came up from abject poverty and battled impossible odds to become the strong and distinguished mother she is today.

(She was also the absolute bane of my adolescence, but we'll get to that later.)

As far back as my mother can remember, she was in charge of something. As the eldest sibling to my jiùjiu (uncle) and my yímā (aunt), she cannot recall a time where she was not constantly looking out for her brother and sister—dressing them, changing them, making sure they had done their homework and fighting off their playground bullies.

Often, she was also their disciplinarian, barking orders and reprimanding them when they fell out of line.

My mother never had the luxury of being naughty, mischievous and young—she was a full-fledged adult by the time she was eight. When she wasn't busy helping to raise her siblings, she would be helping her parents with various chores around the house, cleaning and mopping and making sure the charcoal briquettes were properly heated and ready to cook with by the time they got home. Jiùjiu and Yímā often regarded her like a third parent; with respect, admiration and even fear of getting on her bad side.

My parents had drastically different upbringings, which affected how they developed into adulthood. Whereas my father grew up as a de facto only child, and was subsequently coddled like a little prince, my mother was a part of a much bigger family in the capital city of Beijing. With three hungry little mouths to feed, as well as family back in Hunan to support, the salaries of my 老爷 (lǎoyé; maternal grandfather), a mechanical engineer, and my 姥姥 (lǎolao; maternal grandmother), a blueprint drafter, were stretched incredibly thin; every single penny was carefully budgeted and allocated, with zero room for excess. Clothes and toys were inevitably shared among all three siblings. Sometimes, if they ran out of toilet paper for the month, my mom and her siblings would tear the pages off their old notepads and repeatedly crumple and un-crumple them to soften the texture of the paper on their skin.

There was no shame in doing what you had to in order to make ends meet; it was just life.

At school, my mom was constantly reminded of her family's financial shortcomings compared to her peers. Her long-outgrown shoes were tattered and frayed with her toes practically sticking out, while most of her classmates sported newer, more comfortable shoes. Her pencils were the cheap three-cent kind without erasers on the tops, whereas the others all sported the premium versions with erasers attached, which were a whopping five cents each. My mom coveted these pencils so much that she would save up all the pocket money that

Lăolao gave her each week—it was only ever one or two cents to buy a Popsicle or something—so that she could afford them.

I don't know about you, but I've never been a delayed-gratification kind of guy; I definitely would have taken the Popsicles.

Nice pencils or not, my mother never let any insecurity or embarrassment get in the way of her studies. If anything, it had the opposite effect; she was self-motivated, totally brilliant and downright impossible to outwork. When students' test results were very publicly posted to the classroom wall, regardless of what the subject was, everyone would crowd around the sheet of paper to see who got *second* place . . . because they already knew that my mom was first.

Coming home after parent-teacher interview nights, Lăolao and Lăoyé would always be in incredibly high spirits.

"The teachers just could not say enough good things about you," they would say incredulously. "They keep asking us how we managed to raise a daughter like you!"

But my mother is very adamant that, unlike her siblings, nobody ever had to teach her how to be studious; it came as naturally to her as procrastination or Xbox did to me. She was a scrapper through and through, tirelessly absorbing whichever books she could get her hands on, doing all of her homework and never skipping school no matter how sick she got (this sounded a lot more heroic before the pandemic happened; now, it just seems irresponsible). Those words of praise from her parents and teachers meant everything to my mom, and it seemed that there was no limit to how hard she would work to hear them—consequently, it was a not-so-hidden secret in the family that she was the favorite child.

My mom had a particularly close relationship with her dad, my lăoyé. Born in the southern region of the Hunan province in a family of ten children, he was one of only two to complete a high school and postsecondary education. Lăoyé was a kind, patient and brilliant man, whose long legs and handsome features bestowed him with an undeniable charisma when combined with his intellect. He would often bring my mother to his workplace, a research institute just a few minutes' walk away from their home in the same suburb. Watching him in his lab coat, commanding the attention of his staff, she saw the person she herself wanted to become—a distinguished scientist who worked hard and earned the respect of peers and superiors alike.

Things with her mother—my lǎolao—were a bit different. Unlike my lǎoyé, whom my mother describes as a thoughtful listener and a good confidant, Lǎolao was just not that easy to talk to. She was incredibly hardworking and career-driven, which often made her blunt and impatient with her children. Much of their relationship consisted of Lǎolao admonishing my mom for not working hard enough, not taking good enough care of her siblings, or being disobedient. Suffice it to say, there was always something that my mother could get yelled at about. And if she ever approached Lǎolao with any sort of personal issue—an argument with a teacher, a bad day at school, a problem with a friend—Lǎolao would seldom respond in any helpful way.

"It's all your fault," she would bark dismissively, regardless of what my mother was talking about. Lǎolao always seemed too preoccupied to truly listen to my mom, and their relationship never evolved as a result. Ironically, I had that exact same issue with my mom growing up—if they had just taken the time to get to know each other, they'd have realized that they were much more alike than they could ever imagine.

During the Cultural Revolution, when landowners and intellectuals were persecuted and harassed, Lǎoyé experienced the misfortune of being both—a mechanical engineer whose parents had owned farmland in Hunan prior to the liberation of China.

When my mother was just twelve, Lǎoyé and many of his colleagues were ordered to attend a cadre school—an education camp that consisted of hard labor and "cultural studies" in the countryside. He was shipped off to the Henan province, some 900 kilometers away from home, and given only twenty days a year when he could visit home.

While this was a tough time for everyone in the family, it was especially difficult for my mom. After all, Lǎoyé wasn't just her dad; he was her best friend. Each year, when his twenty days elapsed, she would go to the Beijing train station to bid farewell to him, with his bags in her hands.

"It's not so bad, kiddo," Lǎoyé would always say to console her. "I grew up in the country, so it's easy work for me."

But my mother wasn't convinced—she would cry and refuse to let my lǎoyé go every time, and Lǎolao would have no choice but to forcefully pry her hands off him.

Both my lǎolao and lǎoyé viewed all of this as little more than an inconvenience, having both been around for long enough to know what the new government had saved them from. To them, the hardships and ordeals they were experiencing were incomparable to living in a constant war zone where bombs from Japanese fighter planes could end your life in an instant.

Even though they had taken Lǎoyé's family's land, my mother's parents abided by the rules of the regime faithfully and without protest . . . even if it meant sending their favorite daughter away.

As you might remember from the last chapter, the Cultural Revolution had brought about shàngshānxiàxiāng, the mandate that forced Chinese families to send their children away to rural camps and factories to experience the ordeals of the working class. As the firstborn daughter, my mother had always expected that burden to fall on her. In her final year of high school, however, her teachers and principal were so impressed with her academic performance that they implored my lǎolao and lǎoyé to figure out a way to keep her away from the fields. For many students who were otherwise subpar academic achievers, going away to the countryside was more or less a best-case scenario; for my mom, the star student, it would be a massive waste of potential. They even offered to make her a teacher's assistant after she graduated, which would have excused her from having to go away. Barring some sort of special political connection, this was an exceedingly rare circumstance—but my mom's teachers clearly saw something in her that made them intervene to save her from a different fate.

So, problem solved, right? No harm, no foul, and my mother gets to stay home and work her way up the ranks of the school to become a schoolteacher?

Well . . . not exactly.

In my mother's final year of high school, Lǎolao and Lǎoyé came home from work one day and immediately barricaded themselves in their bedroom to discuss something urgent. Listening in from outside, my mother could only guess at what they were talking about—actually, she thought it meant that she was in trouble. After an eternity, Lǎoyé finally opened the door and addressed his prized daughter:

"Zhèngzheng, could you please come in?"

My mother nervously obliged, thinking she was about to get a scolding or a slipper to the butt. But something was different as she joined her parents in their bedroom—Lǎolao and Lǎoyé were solemn and resigned, their faces fallen and drained of color as if they had just learned that a friend had passed away unexpectedly.

"Bàba, Māma, what's wrong?"

"Zhèngzheng . . . we want you to turn down the job offer."

As she stood there, stunned and confused, her parents explained the reasoning behind their request. According to the government's policies, if my mother didn't go to the countryside, then my jiùjiu would surely have to go in her place. Compared to her little brother, my mother was far more independent and resilient, which meant she would take more easily to the long hours and the hard physical work.

In the end, knowing that they were asking the impossible, Lǎolao and Lǎoyé left the decision to my mother, who had already spent her whole life doing everything she could to make her parents happy, including giving up her whole childhood. This was the daughter who would rather bear the embarrassment of wearing tattered shoes to school than ask for money to buy new ones, who stared longingly at her classmates who played the violin or the piano but never dared ask to take lessons of her own. My mother had never made a selfish decision her entire life; of *course* she agreed to volunteer herself as tribute to go away to the countryside. Of *course* she chose to protect her younger siblings. Of *course* she sacrificed her own aspirations for the good of the family. What else was she supposed to do?

Graduating from high school is supposed to be this amazing coming-of-age transition to adulthood that feels ripe with endless possibility and wonder. Will you go to college? Pick up a trade? Take a gap year to backpack through Southeast Asia and get your heart broken by the cute Australian staying at your hostel?

As the perpetual big sister who grew up too fast because she was busy taking care of everyone around her, school was the only place where she could actually be a kid. She had practiced tai chi, learned Russian, played on the volleyball team and gossiped about boys with her classmates. For my mother, graduation would hit a little differently; it meant being sent away to a life of hard labor in the fields of Changping, a rural county on the outskirts of modern-day Beijing.

It may not have been as far as she could have been sent—students in the past had been dispatched to places like Gansu or Yunnan, some 2,000 kilometers away—but getting to Changping took nearly a full day of travel that required transferring between three buses, followed by an hour-long hike on a sandy dirt path. While bushy-tailed young people brought some reminders of home—clothes, or books, or big bags of treats and food from their parents—with them as they trudged down that last leg, my mom watched as many of them slowly abandoned their cargo over the course of the arduous trek, unable to carry on with the weight of their baggage.

My mother shed something on that journey as well. Somewhere, in the midst of all the discarded luggage, lay her hopes of ever becoming a scientist like her father.

Life in Changping was every bit as tough and exhausting as you'd imagine. There were no sick days from this full-time job; after a hard day's work, with your hands thick with calluses, you'd retreat to your clapboard dorms—where seventy-odd people were crammed in each building separated by gender, and four to eight people were crowded into each room walled by thin plywood—and get ready to do it all again the next day.

Lǎoyé had worked in the rice paddies during his time in a cadre school, which had the upside of being at least productive and fertile; Changping's soil by comparison was dry, sandy and completely not conducive to growing crops. The commune tried to farm melons, sweet potatoes and peanuts in addition to wheat, but this was backbreaking for digging through, and rarely fruitful. During the busy season, work began before the crack of dawn and ended sixteen to eighteen hours later, with only a short break at lunch when the sun beating down overhead was deemed just too dangerous to work under.

The worst tasks, in my mom's eyes, were on opposite ends of the seasonal spectrum. In June, when the sun beat down at its fiercest, the wheat fields needed to be threshed and harvested in full before the rainy season came and spoiled the entire crop. To make sure it was all collected on time, the youth—their skin dark and tight under the sun—had to work day and night. It wasn't a rare occurrence for kids to sneak off to where the wheat was piled up and effectively go missing for a couple of hours, falling asleep in the dried straw because of how hot and tired they were. The other was the wintertime, when planting and harvesting weren't quite possible, so the youths instead had to prepare food for the horses and pigs to eat.

Nearly two *years* passed, during which my mom had grown so thick and muscular that she was barely recognizable to Lǎolao and Lǎoyé when she came home to visit. Ever the overachiever, she had even found a way to excel at farming and harvesting crops—her daily output was by far the highest of any woman in the camp and was higher than even a lot of the men. The constant hours spent under the sun had made her skin leathery and her eyes tired and sunken.

Gazing upon the hardened woman who had once been his little girl, Lǎoyé was racked with guilt. Had he made the right choice to send his daughter away? Would she collapse from heatstroke and exhaustion one day, after overworking herself? Or, perhaps most frightening of all, would she simply work until she grew old, her skin cracked and peeled from the punishing sun, never to fulfill the potential that her teachers saw in her?

Had my mother not gone to college, she would not have married my father, and I would not be playing Marvel's coolest and most handsome superhero (just kidding, Evans). But in 1976, history would toss my mother a lifeline—a chance to reclaim her destiny.

Not long after Mao's death, while walking back to her dorm after another exhausting day, she overheard two girls gossiping about the new government's plans:

"I hear Deng Xiaoping is reinstating the gāokǎo," one said, immediately piquing my mom's interest.

"What do you mean?" my mom asked. "There's been no gāokǎo for years."

The girls stared back at her incredulously.

"Haven't you heard? Deng just reopened them," they said. "What does it matter, though? There's going to be so many people trying out; it's not like any of us are getting in, anyway."

But my mom refused to dismiss her chances so easily. To her, getting into a college wasn't like making a varsity softball team—it meant getting a second chance to pursue a dream that she had long abandoned on that hike to Changping. Although the odds were heavily stacked against her, she was determined to try; she resolved to spend every waking minute of her spare time studying for this test. She had one shot, one opportunity, to seize everything she ever wanted.

Would she capture it . . . or just let it slip?

On her next trip back home to Beijing, my mother dug up all the high school textbooks she could find—suffice to say that she was not throwing away her shot.

Okay, so this may not sound as badass as an aspiring rapper making a name for himself in the streets of Detroit—but studying for the gāokǎo was every bit as difficult as the freestyle battles of *8 Mile*. It had been two years since my mother had last opened a textbook, and she only had six weeks to brush up on all of the subjects. Additionally, while everyone at the camp was permitted to take the gāokǎo, nobody would be allowed any time off to prepare. She would have to study on her own, after those grueling days of work on the field. Back at the dorm, lights went out at 10 p.m., or even earlier if any one of her several roommates wanted to go to sleep. The walls were made of thin plywood, too, and if you made a peep, people would complain to the dorm master to check in on your room and give you a harsh scolding.

But now was not the time to be discouraged or afraid. This was a make-or-break moment that would define her life for decades to come. My mother had been making sacrifices her entire life, living in the servitude of other people to make their lives easier. It was time to be selfish for once.

Somewhat surprisingly, studying for the gāokǎo exam wasn't particularly cool among her peers, many of whom knew her from high school and had witnessed her academic prowess. Most of the young men and women in Changping seemed content to simply live their lives, singing and dancing and hooking up with each other after a long day's work. For them, getting into college was a pipe dream, and anyone stupid enough to think they had a legitimate shot deserved to be knocked down a peg.

In order to justify their own complacency, my mother became their tall poppy.

"Zheng's a frog who wants to eat a swan!" they teased, using a Chinese idiom that cautioned against having unrealistic dreams.

My mom believed that it was her ambition that bothered them. Maybe that was true; but the reason didn't matter as much as how she responded. Every trip back home, she'd truck a load of textbooks on that three-bus ride and that arduous hike to the camp. Instead of hanging out and flirting with boys, she'd go back to her room to read after work, despite the snickering of her peers. When everyone went to sleep, she'd crawl under her bed—a door-size wood board propped up on two benches—and, with her blanket over her head, she'd study by flashlight until she just couldn't keep her already bleary eyes open anymore.

Gāokǎo game day came on a freezing December morning. As it turns out, my dad actually had it pretty easy, hitching a ride on a bus; my mom, along with a few others from the camp, had to travel by *tractor*. Completely exposed to the biting cold and traveling only marginally faster than a brisk walking speed, she wound up arriving fifteen minutes late with her hands so frozen that she could barely hold her pencil.

Feeling the golden opportunity beginning to slip away between her icy fingers, my mother immediately began to tear up. But instead of crumbling under the pressure, she bit her lip until the tears went away, warmed her hands with her breath until they were warm enough to write with, and got to work.

Weeks later, my mother received official notice that she was one of the select few who had met the cutoff score. It was a dream deferred, but she was finally going to university—one of just four people (and the only woman) in the whole camp to be accepted.

When she finally told my lǎoyé, he broke down and cried, overwhelmed with the guilt of what he had put her through. Because the shàngshānxiàxiāng mandate was abolished after Mao's death, my jiùjiu never would have been sent off to camp anyway—my mother had essentially sacrificed two of her best years for nothing.

"I'd never have forgiven myself if you hadn't gotten in," he said, sobbing. "I would have failed you as a father."

On her last day in Changping, her fellow peers gathered outside their clapboard dorms to watch as she and the three boys loaded their luggage into the back of the tractor and headed away from the camp forever, toward whatever bright futures lay ahead. The rest of the boys and girls, many of whom had openly ridiculed her for studying, could only look on with envy, admiration and perhaps a sense of regret for not believing more in their own abilities.

My mother, in turn, watched as they disappeared into the horizon and became just a memory. With her ultimate dream renewed, a new life awaited her at Beijing Jiaotong University, where she would study to become an engineer just like her father.

I'd like to think that the folks in Changping continued to speak of her for some time afterward, as a symbol of hope and inspiration—the frog so strong and so determined that she gobbled up an entire swan.

CHAPTER FOUR

AN IMPOSSIBLE DREAM

Classes at Beijing Jiaotong University—a school so serious in its reputation that its motto was "The Unity of Knowledge and Action"—began on March 5, 1978, with its classrooms and student dorms filled for the first time in over a decade. It wasn't the most creative or inspired slogan out there, but at least it was clear and concise, unlike Dartmouth's "A Voice Crying Out in the Wilderness," which sounds more like something you'd chant on a Joshua Tree trip or in an ayahuasca circle than the official motto of a top-tier school.

(For the record, I would have *killed* to have gone to Dartmouth.)

Section 77-5 of the electrical engineering school was comprised of thirty-four of the best and brightest students from all over the country who, like my parents, had defied the odds by acing their gāokǎo. The students ranged in age from seventeen to thirty and had come from equally scattered backgrounds. The lucky ones like my father came straight from high school, but most were already working jobs as middle school teachers, steam engine stokers, or sanitation workers. Others came from camps similar to Changping. There were no electives or add/drop periods—everyone took the same courses, lived together, and ate at the same meal halls every day for the entire four-year program.

In stark contrast to your stereotypical weed-vaping, Coors-guzzling, poor-decision-making college freshmen of today, the new students at

Beijing Jiaotong took their studies *extremely* seriously. This was a generation of Chinese youth who witnessed their dreams and prospects essentially vanish; they would've sooner worked themselves into the ground than wasted their golden opportunity. The university actually had to institute a curfew prohibiting students from studying after 9:30 p.m. because they were beginning to develop very unhealthy sleep habits. When even *that* did not discourage them from studying in secret, the school simply cut all electrical power to all the classrooms when the clock struck half past nine.

It was in this highly sexy climate that my parents met.

There wasn't a spark—at least, not at first. Everyone was simply too focused on their grades to care about things like hormones. My mom was actually pretty envious of my dad in the beginning, being one of the young'uns who had been spared the hardships of working the fields. The fact that my dad and his friend Liuchen consistently scored at the top of the class only further fueled her jealousy.

It seemed at the end of their first three years together that love was the last thing on either of their minds. But eventually, fall in love they did.

Midway through my parents' fourth year, the two of them were paired up on a three-month-long thesis project on optimizing the controls of positioning systems. Over the endless days and nights spent working together and talking, my parents would develop feelings for each other. Unable to resist each other's charms, they started a relationship soon after.

Dating and relationships, however, weren't encouraged at this time. It wasn't a hard rule on the part of the university, but it was certainly implied that any distractions that resulted in a dip in their grades would negatively affect the job assignments they'd receive from the government after graduation. My parents had no choice but to keep their relationship a secret from their classmates and *especially* from their professors, who they were sure would not react well. So, they began a steamy love affair, sneaking around under cover of darkness to empty classrooms and abandoned portables, so that they could do nothing but hold hands and *occasionally* kiss—and no, I refuse to think about anything else that may or may not have happened.

So successful were my parents at keeping their romance a secret that a year after they all graduated, one of my mom's friends pulled her aside and flat-out asked her, "Zheng . . . do you think you could set me up with Zhenning? He's fine as hell!"

(I'm paraphrasing slightly, of course.)

"You better back the hell up, ho!" is definitely not what my mother said to her thirsty friend, but I don't care—I'm writing it in anyway.

My parents' fledgling courtship would face its first major test after graduation, when their paths would diverge. My mother was assigned to work at Beijing Locomotive and Rolling Stock Inc. as an electrical engineer, for which she woke up at 5:30 a.m. six days a week to endure an hours-long commute to the office, taking three buses. My dad, following in the footsteps of my yéye, chose to pursue higher education—he was accepted to a master's degree program at the Harbin Institute of Technology back in his hometown, nearly 2,000 kilometers away from Beijing. Almost as soon as they had gotten together, my parents would be forced to continue their relationship from a distance.

My parents' standard of living was very different from that of their American counterparts in the early eighties; home telephones were a luxury reserved for high-ranking officials, and train rides between their cities were long and prohibitively expensive. The only way to keep in touch was writing each other letters, which my parents did every week. My mom would run to her department's mailroom every Monday at precisely 3 p.m., eagerly waiting for the mail to come, and without fail, there was always a letter from her beau. The mailroom workers even learned to recognize the envelopes he used, with distinct red-and-blue borders, and started setting them aside for her. Through their letters my parents would share their lives, tell each other about work, ask the other for advice about their colleagues and bosses, and discuss the movies they'd seen and books they'd read. For me, a textbook commitment-phobic millennial raised in the era of Tinder and disappearing Snapchat nudes, it's so romantic I want to cry.

It's at this point in our interview that my mother interjects to make sure I know that *she* was the better writer of the two of them. It's very much in alignment with her "needlessly competitive about very inconsequential things" brand, which I am ashamed to say that I have inherited.

On June 28, 1984, two months before my dad graduated from HIT, my parents got their marriage license. This was a bit more like the Mom and Dad I knew, which is to say unfussy and businesslike; their marriage was registered in an office of the civil affairs bureau in Harbin solely for bureaucratic purposes, in an effort to convince the university to assign my dad to work in Beijing so he and my mom could be together.

"The decision to get married was the result of a combination of factors that pointed us in that direction," my dad would say later.

"Yes," my mother agreed. "A natural progression."

Real steamy stuff, I know.

A few months after their very bureaucratic marriage, Dad was reassigned to the Beijing Institute of Electronics Systems Engineering, under the Ministry of Aerospace Industry. After two and a half years, my parents would finally be together again.

A year later, at my mother's family's apartment, my parents finally had a wedding ceremony. It was an intimate gathering of no more than ten, with none of the pomp and circumstance of what you'd expect today. Nevertheless, it was a declaration of their commitment to each other. My parents cooked their favorite dishes for their guests, and they all talked and laughed long into the night. I can't imagine anything more beautiful, to be honest.

After their marriage and subsequent honeymoon to the Yellow Mountains, my parents moved to a communal apartment nearby, with only a hundred-square-foot room to call their own; they had to share the washroom and kitchen with another family.

My mother loved her job, even though it required many arduous, transfer-filled hours of sitting in packed buses in each direction. She found that she could apply what she'd learned from school, in an academic atmosphere of mutual respect and admiration. Dad, in turn, had been assigned to work in his dream field of aviation and aerospace research. All in all, life was pretty good—my parents had already achieved the unthinkable at the time, landing extremely prestigious jobs with opportunities for upward mobility based on their technical qualifications. They were, by all measures of the word, *successful*.

For my parents, though, neither of whom had been raised to be complacent, it wasn't enough. It was only a matter of time before they would cast their gaze upward yet again, toward another nearly unattainable goal: North America.

Sometime in 1986, my parents' former classmate Liuchen told them that he had been accepted into a PhD program in electrical engineering at Queen's University in Canada. This immediately piqued my mom's interest—actually, the idea of leaving to study in the West quickly grew inside her mind to the point where she would not stop bringing it up with my dad.

"If Liuchen can do it, why not us?" she would say. "His family has no special connections—he's common folk, just like you and I."

For decades, opportunities to study abroad were mostly reserved for those who had influential ties or had family living abroad. Even then, it was an extreme rarity. But Liuchen's success story meant that the tides of favor were shifting; China was beginning to open itself to the world, and people like my parents were becoming curious about what lay beyond its borders.

My dad admits that it took a little convincing to get him on board with my mom's plan. They were both competitive by nature and were indeed jealous of Liuchen's accomplishment, but my dad had essentially just moved heaven and earth so that he could relocate to Beijing to be with my mom.

"And now you want to leave *again*?"

"We don't know how long our borders will stay open," my mom reasoned. "This might be our only chance to see the outside world. Don't you ever wonder what's out there?"

In fact, my dad *had* wondered—even as a teenager he would find ways to sneak into the cinema whenever an American movie was playing, just to catch a glimpse of what life was like *out there*. Even though the films never played with subtitles, the imagery of pictures like *The Sound of Music, Casablanca* and *Futureworld* nonetheless made a strong impression on him; it didn't take much to change his already curious mind. My parents had spent the better part of the last decade reaching for an impossible dream and then willing it into being. If anyone could beat the odds yet again, it was them.

My parents' monthly salaries as engineers amounted to the equivalent of twenty American dollars each. While that was considered to be quite comfortable at the time, they both knew their station in life: influential family backgrounds or connections in China remained hugely important, and they weren't about to earn their way into any of those.

With Liuchen's help, they formulated a game plan: my dad, who was on more of an academic track than my mom (and the stronger English speaker), would apply to PhD scholarship programs in North America, and then obtain a student visa. Once he had settled in, he would bring my mother over on a spousal visa, after which she would begin to apply to postgrad programs. Easy peasy, right?

There was only one small problem: the Test of English as a Foreign Language (TOEFL) was a notoriously difficult exam that all international postgrad students had to pass. Back in their freshman year of college, my parents couldn't even identify all twenty-six letters of the alphabet when tested by their professor. While my dad did improve his English in his four years of undergrad, it's not like he was using it every day; he was nowhere near the necessary level of fluency to pass the TOEFL, which required him to know the difference between words like *adamant* and *adequate, cumbersome* and *curriculum*.

It just so happened that around this time, the ministry that my dad worked at was actively looking to send its people abroad to gather knowledge and bring it back home. He was selected, through a ministry-wide English test that was much more forgiving than the TOEFL, to receive one year of English training at a management school in Nanjing. And so, in late 1987, my parents were separated yet again as my dad left home for Nanjing to brush up on his English.

Returning again to student life, my dad was put into a shared dorm upon his arrival. He and my mother continued their letter-writing tradition; actually, it was in one of her letters that my father would read the three words that would change his life forever:

Zhenning . . . I'm pregnant.

As my parents were in the middle of telling me the story of how they were able to leave China, I couldn't help but ask, "If you were trying to leave, why would you decide to have a baby? Why not wait?"

I often wondered this during my teenage years, when our relationship was contentious and acrimonious, but never outright asked them. What if they, not my yéye and năinai, had raised me? Would we have been closer? Would our bond have been stronger? Would my shortcomings have been forgiven a little bit more?

"The truth is, we didn't really have a plan," my dad explained. "We had no idea whether we would be able to stay in the West, or for how long. We didn't know if I would be able to bring your mother over, or you; it could have taken two years, or three, or longer. But we figured that having a child would solidify our family bond and keep us together no matter what."

My parents also knew that their child would be better off in the care of my grandparents. It was a difficult and heartbreaking decision, but ultimately the one that made the most sense. On top of that, my năinai had recently retired, which would free her up to take care of a newborn baby. Looking back, I have to agree that it was the path of least resistance.

The universe, however, had other plans for our family, and my mother's first pregnancy would end in tragedy. In the winter of '87, she suffered a miscarriage while hauling a bicycle up a flight of stairs. My father, who was still in Nanjing studying English at the time, received the news by telegram and hurried back to Beijing a few days later after taking a leave of absence.

Bad news always came in waves, and my dad would suffer a disappointing blow of his own soon after. There had been an opportunity to leave the country on a fully paid scholarship courtesy of the ministry, and my dad was sure that he would get it—all he had to do was ace a standardized test similar to the TOEFL. As he was already at the top of the class, he never doubted his chances.

When the results came, he was shocked to discover that although he scored third in the entire class, he had been edged out by a man who had worked with him at the ministry. The ministry had designated only a single scholarship to be awarded to its highest-performing employee—in this case, not my dad. This was a significant setback, because my parents simply didn't have the money to support themselves in North America; they were not wealthy to begin with, and the exchange rate at the time was absolutely abysmal. A full-ride scholarship was a golden opportunity, and my dad felt incredibly guilty for having squandered it. He was going to have to apply to schools on his own and hope that one of them would be willing to offer him one.

Heartbreaking as the whole ordeal was, my parents were determined to push through. My dad finished his studies in May and took the TOEFL soon after. The fee to take the test was the equivalent of a month's salary for my dad, so he knew he had to make it count. With a sufficient TOEFL score to certify his proficiency in English, he was able to apply to PhD programs in schools all over North America. Despite every obstacle that was written into his blood and his history—his humble upbringing, his hardships during the Cultural Revolution, and the uphill battle he now faced—my dad managed to get not one but *two* offers from American schools: the New Jersey Institute of Technology and Arizona State University in Tempe.

No offense to the people of New Jersey . . . but it wasn't exactly a tough decision.

When my dad finally returned to Beijing in the summer of 1988, he took my mom on a date to celebrate. They went to a newly opened amusement park in the city, riding a Ferris wheel and a roller coaster for the first time, laughing away all their worries and past hardships. It was the dawn of a new era—one of infinite possibilities and endless wonder . . . which meant it was the *perfect* night for Kentucky Fried Chicken.

Yeah, my father's idea of fine dining was eating at the restaurant that would give us the Double Down sandwich.

In his defense, KFC had just opened in China, and it was absolutely *crushing* the fast-food market with its impeccable service and mind-blowing efficiency. It was an immediate hit for the Chinese locals, who were used to long wait times and meandering service.

My parents waited excitedly in line and paid a week's worth of salary for a two-piece meal and a Coke each. Even though nobody in the West would consider KFC anything more than a cheap and greasy fast food option, everything imported from America was viewed as an immense luxury in China—the prices there were still prohibitively expensive for most households.

"Was it worth the hype?" I asked.

My dad shrugged his shoulders—*meh*. "The chicken was pretty tasty, but there was this side dish called coleslaw that was absolutely disgusting. I couldn't believe that white people ate that stuff!"

But going to KFC was about more than getting that *finger-lickin' good* chicken; it was an acknowledgment that they, like Colonel Sanders, would soon cross international borders and lay down roots in a completely foreign land. When my parents bit into those eleven mouthwatering herbs and spices, they were tasting *America*—land of opportunity and home of assembly-line cooking—where you could make just about anything happen through imagination and sheer force of will ... even a sandwich made of a slice of bacon wedged between two pieces of battered chicken. It was probably the most meaningful meal ever shared in a fast-food establishment.

"And *that*, Máomao, was the night you were conceived."

TMI, Father. TMI.

When my mother had almost carried me to term, she took a train to Harbin and shacked up with my yéye and năinai (her in-laws) while my father continued to work in Beijing. As a former longtime pediatrician at the Heilongjiang Provincial Hospital, my năinai could vouch for the quality of the facilities and the staff who worked there. At her behest, my parents made the necessary arrangements with the hospital.

All that was left for me to do was introduce myself to the world.

On the afternoon of April 19, 1989—a few days earlier than expected—my mother went into labor and was rushed into the maternity ward. She would like you to know that although it was the worst pain she had ever felt in her life, she never screamed. Instead, she listened to the cries and sobs of the other expectant mothers and told herself she would be different—she would be stronger.

At roughly 10:45 p.m., while my dad was still on the train to Harbin, I exited the womb without making a peep, taking after the woman who birthed me. My mom stared at me, then back at the nurses in a panic.

"Why isn't he crying?!" Crying meant breathing, and silence ... meant stillbirth. My mother's greatest fear, understandably, was losing another baby.

"Hang on a sec," one of the nurses said as she cut the umbilical cord. "We see this all the time."

The nurse dangled me upside down by the leg and proceeded to give me a thorough spanking—*WHACKWHACKWHACK!*—after which I promptly broke out in a loud wail. All things considered, not a bad way to be brought into the world.

The next morning, my totally oblivious father arrived home from the train station only to be told that the baby had already been delivered. He dropped everything and rushed straight to the hospital to meet his son for the first time, the drowsiness and fatigue from his overnight commute evaporating in an instant. After reuniting in the maternity ward, the new parents spent one more night at the hospital and then were discharged the following day. As the nurse brought me out, an adorable eight-pound baby with a big ol' head and healthy heartbeat, she turned to the other couples in the ward and jokingly proclaimed:

"You see this one? This is how they all ought to look!"

This harmless comment from my parents' sassy nurse would color their expectations of me for my entire life. I was the "perfect baby," the torchbearer of my family name, and—per the government policy at the time—the only child; my tiny shoulders would bear the weight of all their combined hopes, dreams and ambitions.

April in Harbin was far from a fresh and balmy spring. I had to be smothered in every available blanket in the apartment in order to not freeze to death. Even though my parents were able to borrow an electric heater from a neighbor, they could not afford to use it unless absolutely necessary, like during baths and diaper changes. Electricity was incredibly pricey, and the risk of blowing a fuse was also very high. Still, under the watchful care of my mom, my dad, my yéye and my năinai, I pulled through.

Barely a month after I was brought home, my father once again packed his bags and prepared to leave for Beijing, where he would return to work for a few months before heading to America.

"Of course we would have preferred for us all to stay together, but it just wasn't feasible," he said.

My parents, like many in their generation, were willing to sacrifice greatly so they could provide financial stability for their children. The decision to leave me was not born of indifference or a lack of parental love; I was, in fact, the most important thing to both him and my mother.

"The scholarship money provided to me was barely enough for me to live off of," my dad continued. "It would have been no life to bring a child into; better that you were raised in Harbin, where you could be properly taken care of."

And so it was settled: on May 20, 1989, my dad kissed my adorable little one-month-old head and boarded a train to Beijing. He would fly to Arizona seven months later, emptying what life savings he had and leaving behind his family, his job, and everything he knew. As his plane took off from the runway, perhaps carrying the hopes and dreams of many families like ours, he looked down at his home and wondered when he would get to see his son again.

Over three decades later, the average standard of living in China has increased dramatically, and immigration to North America is much more commonplace. Journeying to the West is no longer seen as a pursuit of a "better" life; after all, China is the country with the sprawling megacities and bullet trains that travel more than 300 miles per hour. Although issues like income inequality still exist, China's rapid modernization has been truly staggering; an estimated 800 million citizens have been lifted out of poverty, and the country's economy has become the second largest in the world, projected to surpass the United States by 2032.

Although this is something that my parents are undoubtedly proud of, they express an equal amount of disappointment that this growth seems to have caused a rift between East and West. Today, they find themselves torn between two vastly different ideologies, perspectives, and media biases . . . and they worry the rift is only growing wider. As uncomfortable as they feel reading some of their Chinese colleagues' texts over WeChat that demonize the West, they feel equally unsettled watching CNN, Fox News and the rest of Western mainstream media lambast a villainous, straw-man version of China over and over again. Like many immigrants who left their homes, they acknowledge that theirs wasn't perfect—but home was home, and always would be. For my dad, China was kicking a soccer ball around with his best friends on a hot summer day, rowing along the Songhua River, making dumplings at home with his sister and his parents, and sneaking out of his dorm at night to see my mom. To attack "China" as a whole would be to attack all of those moments he held so dearly in his heart. He wouldn't tolerate that any more than someone disparaging Canada, a place that has become equally meaningful to him.

As I listen to my father reflect on his journey, I begin to understand just how much pressure he must have been under. Dad had emptied his life savings and still had barely enough money to cover his course fees and a few months' rent. It was a *gigantic* leap of faith with no safety net to catch him—but for my mom and me, he was determined to make the jump. My parents never thought of themselves as heroic or courageous, and they certainly never believed that anything they did would be worthy of being written into a book. But their determination and quiet resilience are a part of the canon of every starry-eyed immigrant family who has ever dared to journey across an infinite ocean in search of a better life. As the beneficiaries of their courage, we in the next generation are responsible for keeping their stories alive so that our great-great-grandchildren will know their roots and, in the face of adversity, will remember that they are descended from wide-eyed dreamers who never gave up on their goal.

CHAPTER FIVE

WELCOME TO AMERICA, JERRY LEWIS

After nearly twenty-four sleepless hours in the air with multiple layovers, my father touched down at Sky Harbor Airport in Phoenix, Arizona. Stepping off the plane, he was instantly hit with a blast of hot, stuffy desert air. It was a fitting welcome for a country not exactly known for its subtlety.

Clutching his small, worn-out luggage and an envelope containing all the money he had saved up—barely two thousand American dollars—my dad walked through the airport and marveled at this strange and foreign land he had just entered.

After clearing customs, Dad wheeled his luggage over to a pay phone and called the one phone number he had taken down, which allegedly belonged to the president of ASU's Chinese Students' Association. This was a moment of great anxiety for him, as there were no iPhones or caller ID in 1990. If this mystery man was not home at this exact time, my dad would have to find his own way to campus. Even though he had spent countless hours studying English, actually having to speak it in a real-world setting still felt extremely daunting.

Thankfully, the man picked up after one ring.

"*Hello?*" he said brusquely, in accented English.

"Uhh . . . nǐhǎo," my dad responded in Mandarin. "My name is

Zhenning Liu, from Beijing. I was told to call the head of the Chinese Students' Association when I arrived at the airport in Phoenix?"

After clocking the Mandarin, the man's tone softened considerably. *"Just wait at the luggage claim, and I'll come to pick you up."*

I just want to point out that even I, a notorious non-planner, would have called ahead.

Thirty minutes later, a rail-thin Chinese man in a baggy varsity-gray T-shirt approached my dad and extended his hand.

"You Zhenning Liu?"

"Yeah, that's me!"

"Great," the man said, reaching for my dad's luggage. "If you were from anywhere else, I wouldn't have come."

The scrawny CSA president brought my dad home and showed him to his lavish accommodation: an old couch in the living room of a shared three-bedroom apartment. For my father, it didn't matter whether he had a king bed or a spot on a cold floor; he promised himself that he was going to make something of himself in this new world.

Maybe, if he was lucky, he could even get fat off of junk food!

The next few months felt like wave after crashing wave of abrupt new life changes. Walking around in Arizona's dry heat was like stepping into a kiln for baking clay. It was a massive adjustment from the frigid winters that Harbin and Beijing were known for, and my dad quickly realized he should have packed fewer down jackets, and more cargo shorts and Birkenstocks.

And then, there was the language barrier. Arizonans were friendly, but the American English they spoke was different and far quicker than the Received Pronunciation my dad had learned in Nanjing. Thankfully, the university offered a free class in English syntax and pronunciation for all international students. My father jumped at the chance; the engineering classes that he had enrolled in were extremely expensive, so it was an absolute godsend to be able to take a course without paying out of pocket. It was here that my father's English was able to improve beyond a conversational level; some three decades later, his language skills are still a step above my mother's and miles ahead of almost all of his colleagues'. He speaks with near-perfect grammar and a very impressive vocabulary, and still retains just a tiny hint of that BBC newscaster accent that he picked up in Nanjing.

Hilariously, the professor of this English syntax class once tried to give my dad an English name, because she figured nobody would be able to pronounce "Zhenning."

"I think you're a Jerry. Like Jerry Lewis. You're always smiling and laughing, just like him!"

True to his description, my dad laughed and said he'd give it a shot.

A few weeks later, the professor spotted my dad on the street and tried to get his attention.

"Hey, Jerry! Jerry!!"

My dad was completely oblivious. It was a kind gesture, but it just didn't stick. Which is really too bad because it would have opened up a world of *Jerry Liu-wis* puns.

Aside from the language barrier and the cultural differences of America, there were also the fun little discoveries; my dad still vividly remembers the shock he felt walking into a supermarket for the first time. He had never seen such perfect-looking fruits and vegetables, in all their vibrant colors. Even though he was far too poor to be able to afford them, he loved to just look at the rows and rows of beautiful fresh produce. As for what he would actually buy, it pretty much came down to some eggs, a head of Chinese cabbage and whatever happened to be on the discount rack.

Eventually, my dad moved from the CSA president's couch and into an apartment of his own. While this greatly increased his quality of life, it also meant that he was dipping further into his savings.

The fear of running out of money was very real to my dad at this time. He had no lifeline to fall back on, not even enough to fly back home if things went sour. He needed a way to make money. He picked up a part-time gig waiting tables and washing dishes at a local Chinese restaurant called the Red Lantern that specialized in cooking bastardized Chinese food that white people liked—chicken balls, General Tso's chicken and a number of other dishes in which chicken is completely drenched in batter, deep-fried into oblivion and drowned in sugary syrup.

That's right, white people; if you've ever complained about getting a "Chinese food coma," I hope you know that you did it to yourselves. Lemon chicken, orange chicken . . . it's all the same thing!

After a long shift for which he was paid $3.50 per hour, my dad would sit down with the other staff and enjoy *actual* Chinese food—a simple bowl of steamed rice and lightly stir-fried vegetables with an occasional braised meat, just like he'd make back home. The Chinese couple that owned the restaurant took an immediate liking to him, having themselves immigrated eight years ago. They soon upped his hourly pay to $4.00 and expanded his duties to include making bike deliveries to dorms and frat houses. I can totally see my poor thirty-year-old father at one of ASU's famous pool parties, timidly stepping over passed-out frat bros on the ground, clutching a bag of chow mein and spring rolls and trying to figure out who was going to pay him while Run-DMC blasted from a boom box in the background.

Having a job meant having a means to survive, which my dad was extremely grateful for. He had been bleeding money ever since he arrived in the country.

Despite taking a full course load, holding down a part-time job and subsisting on a diet of rice and boiled cabbage, my dad remembers his time in Tempe fondly. It was, after all, a period of unlimited freedom and discovery. He had made new friends, even road-tripped to the Grand Canyon with a roommate. After eight months, he was even beginning to think of Arizona as home.

After his first semester at ASU, my dad's supervising professor offered him a scholarship in the form of waived tuition and fees for the remainder of his studies. It was a fine gesture, and one that he would surely have taken in the absence of other options . . . but my dad wasn't looking to simply survive; he wanted to *thrive*, with his whole family in one place.

What he *really* needed was a scholarship that covered tuition *and* living expenses, so that he didn't have to continually dip into his savings. His gig at the Red Lantern was great for a little extra pocket money, but he could never convince US Customs and Immigration that he was capable of supporting a spouse, let alone a *child,* on four dollars an hour. Maintaining the status quo meant that he'd have to continue his studies by himself until he graduated, after which he'd have to return to China if he couldn't find a job.

If only I'd chosen to go to New Jersey, he thought. Yeah . . . things were *that* bad.

Around this time, my dad's old roommate Liuchen—the one who had initially inspired my parents to move to North America—called to catch up.

"To be honest, I'm pretty stressed-out," my dad confessed, and proceeded to tell his old friend about his situation.

Liuchen listened intently, and then responded:

"Zhenning, I think I can help you."

Liuchen was in a PhD program at Queen's University, a Canadian school situated in a little town called Kingston three hours east of Toronto, and knew that his lab supervisor was looking for more students.

"My scholarship at Queen's covers my tuition and my living expenses," he reassured my dad. *"If you submit an application to Queen's, I can put in a good word for you. You've got a strong resume and a stellar TOEFL score; trust me, you've got a really great shot."*

This wasn't an easy decision for my dad to make. On one hand, getting a full ride to Queen's would be a phenomenal opportunity that would likely allow the family to be reunited more quickly. On the other, he really didn't know anything about Canada aside from its cold weather and its geographical proximity to the States. As China's borders opened up, my parents saw the States as the golden land of possibilities and new opportunities. Canada was like a little cousin—it was fine, but it wasn't *America.*

In the end, the promise of financial security was too great to resist. My dad applied to Queen's and was quickly accepted—in the fall of

1990, he would pack his entire life up yet again and head north, across the border to the land of maple syrup and double-doubles.

Mid-1990 to 1991 was a chaotic time for not only my father, but our whole family. My dad was working hard to be able to bring us over—but there was also my mom, who was back at work in Beijing, eagerly waiting to join her husband.

Then, of course, tucked away up north in Harbin, bundled under a million blankets, there was me—a handsome little baby destined to disappoint both of them.

My mother would return to Harbin at every possible opportunity to see her son again, often bringing back gifts and trendy clothes from the capital city. She used whatever vacation time she was allowed at her workplace to take the long train ride up north to where my grandparents and I were. She could only afford to buy the cheapest ticket, in the sitting area.

Initially, her office was very sympathetic to her situation, as she was effectively a single mother whose child was very far away from home. But as time went on, some of her coworkers grew to resent her. In their minds, she was getting preferential treatment, since I was already in my grandparents' care.

"It must be nice to have a husband abroad trying to bring you over, and in-laws to take care of your son," a colleague sneered at her one day. "And still, you have the nerve to take *this* much time off of work."

For my mother, though, life was anything but easy. Her family was spread out all over the world, and there was no indication of when they would all be together. Through my father's letters, she learned that his supervisor at ASU did not have the resources to offer him a full scholarship that covered living expenses. For all she knew, she wouldn't even get the chance to see America. Every day was uncertain, and full of doubt. To top it all off, she had a little boy that she missed terribly.

"You were a very cute baby, Máomao. Everyone that saw you would say it," my mom says lovingly, before miming the rigid posture of an overly muscular man. "Now you're just a big giant meathead. What happened?"

Clearly, she has never heard of The Rock. If I was a meathead, then what was he? A turducken?

On a warm July afternoon in 1990, my mother was at work when her supervisor approached her.

"Zheng? Phone call for you!"

This was peculiar for her to hear, as phones were still prohibitively expensive at the time and nobody in her family owned one. Without any idea of who would be calling her, she followed the supervisor into the designated phone room and picked up the receiver.

"Wei?"

"Hey, it's Zhenning," came my dad's familiar voice. It had been months since my mom had last heard it.

"What?! How are you calling me right now?"

"One of my TAs snuck me into the faculty office. Listen, these long-distance calls are pretty expensive, so I'll keep it quick. I got a scholarship at Queen's University in Canada. Full ride, plus eight hundred bucks a month for living expenses. I'm leaving in a week!"

"WHAT?!"

"You know what this means, right, Zheng? I'll be able to bring you over! You're coming to Canada!"

CHAPTER SIX

OH, CANADA?

For the second time in a year, my dad packed his whole life up and moved to a city he had never seen before. Although he remembers that the in-flight meal wasn't as good, he was grateful to see his friend Liuchen waiting for him at the end of the arrivals terminal at Macdonald-Cartier Airport in Ottawa. Together, they drove south toward the next chapter of my dad's life.

Kingston was nothing at all like Tempe, and yet in many ways it felt like home. Like Harbin, it was a city of hot summers and harsh winters, situated next to a large body of water. Driving along the lakeshore and looking out at Lake Ontario, my dad imagined instead that he was staring at the Songhua River. He couldn't help but feel a pang of homesickness as he wondered when he would get the chance to see the river from his youth for real.

After staying on Liuchen's couch for a week when he first arrived, my dad began to house hunt. He finally found a room after an exhausting day driving all over town with Liuchen, in a house close to campus for just $150 a month. In the process, he made a most unlikely friend . . . in Mary.

Mary was a spry elderly woman in her nineties and the owner of the house my dad had found in the newspaper. She had retired from her job as a department store clerk decades ago and, having never married, had been on her own ever since.

Mary's only house rule was "don't come home late," which my dad would come to understand was more for her worry of him than anything else. On the rare occasions that he would break the rule, he would come home to find Mary wide awake and perched on a chair facing the window, like a disapproving mother waiting for her teenage son to stumble home after a house party. The two formed a bond that was much closer than just a landlord and tenant—to that end, Mary never increased the rent, which was already insanely low. I think she was just happy to have some company.

In return for her kindness, my dad often helped Mary with chores around the house, from sweeping and dusting to raking leaves. He even offered to make her Chinese food, which she was initially wary of because of her limited diet of cheese, bread and cold cuts. Never one to give up so easily, my dad pushed her to try new foods and expand her horizons, with such wildly adventurous delicacies as eggplant, or watermelon. So exotic, right?

While Mary was an absolute joy to be around all hours of the day, my dad had no concept of just how lucky he had gotten with her as a "landlord." Other people that he dealt with in the country were not nearly as kind.

Sure, he doesn't remember any distinct moments in which he experienced overt, virulent racism—no one yelled "chink" out of a car at him or told him to go back to China—but there were subtler ways he felt the sting of discrimination in Canada. He'd seen it in his dealings with bureaucracy, like when immigration office employees would look down at him for filing his paperwork incorrectly (because nobody ever makes mistakes on paperwork, right?), or when people at the DMV would roll their eyes and sigh impatiently when he stumbled over his words or strained to understand their instructions. I witnessed this subtle prejudice firsthand as a kid, and my dad would never respond with anything less than his Jerry Liu-wis smile—but deep down I know that it made him feel angry and helpless, because that's exactly how I felt.

In his first year at Queen's, my dad befriended a grad student who had come to study from India. Despite her strong English and friendly disposition, she would tell him about people moving away from her when she sat nearby, or how waitstaff would hesitate to serve her at restaurants. Once, she had arranged to view a potential rental apartment with the landlord, but when she arrived, the landlord took one look at her and immediately told her that the place had already been rented. She told my dad that she felt that Canada was straight-up, in-your-face racist. She didn't come back after her first year.

Now, don't get me wrong, I love Canada, and I believe that it is a tolerant place. I've loved the range of people and the diversity of experiences that I've come to know in my home country. But at the same time, I *have* been called a chink, and I *have* been told to go back to China. Canada is not unilaterally friendly, nor is "friendly" even something that an entire country can be. Sometimes, it feels a bit like we try to cover up our uncomfortable truths with a veneer of tolerance and inclusion.

My dad absolutely adored Mary, but he would find that her kindness was more of the exception rather than the rule.

In March of 1991, Liuchen and my dad made the three-hour drive from Kingston to Toronto to pick my mother up from the airport. My dad had settled nicely into life in Canada, and so when the paperwork for my mother's spousal visa came through, he had called her right away and booked her ticket. Since he didn't own a car, he once again conscripted his pal Liuchen to help.

Seriously, Liuchen is shaping up to be the low-key MVP of the story.

Once the three of them were reunited and began their drive east toward Kingston, my mom grew increasingly anxious as the tall buildings of Toronto faded away and were replaced with . . . well, not a whole lot. Was this the supposed land of unlimited opportunity? All she could see along Highway 401 were scattered forests and farmland.

The next morning, as she headed down the stairs for breakfast, my mother found herself face-to-face with a very excited Mary.

"Oh, my dear, I've heard so much about you! It is *so* nice to have you here," the old lady exclaimed as she took my mother's hands in her own.

At a literal loss for words, Mom could only smile and nod. It hit her in that moment, the gravity of what she'd done; she'd left behind a successful career in Beijing, during which she co-authored two books and several research papers, and come to an entirely foreign place to start from scratch.

This would be her greatest challenge yet.

My mother had not initially planned to find work in Canada—she was only supposed to study for her TOEFL exam, after which she would apply for a master's in engineering at Queen's. But money was always tight, and the promise of financial security that came with a second income was too great to pass up; she was eventually able to find some work washing dishes at a little restaurant in downtown Kingston. Her time working in the fields served her well on the job, as she established herself very quickly as an absolute workhorse. My mother was the embodiment of immigrant grit. No disrespect to any of the other dishwashers working there, but they didn't stand a chance.

During her time at the restaurant my mom was particularly fascinated with Matthew, a seventeen-year-old Canadian boy who was washing dishes to pay off a debt to his parents for wrecking their car. The concept of owing your own parents money was completely alien to her, and she struggled to understand the reasoning behind it (especially with Matthew at the critical age where he was supposed to be thinking about college). Growing up, no matter how angry she was, or how badly I messed up, she would never subject me to the same punishment. Money was always shared in our family, and could never be *owed* to each other.

Over time, my parents settled into something of a routine in Kingston. As my dad went to class each morning, my mom would pack a can of Coke and a couple of slices of bread to go to the library and study English until the library closed. Her language skills were far weaker than my dad's, and she knew she would have to close the gap if she stood a chance at pursuing higher education in Canada. If she could not get into a proper graduate program at a Canadian university, her engineering degree would be useless, and she would be relegated to unskilled labor for the rest of her life. On the weekends, she would study at home during the day and work the dinner rush at the restaurant, often washing dishes late into the night. The restaurant manager saw my mother's insane work ethic and canned the other dishwasher on the shift, because she was easily five times as productive. My mother, none the wiser, took on the additional workload without so much as a murmur of protest.

One night after a particularly tough shift, the manager saw my mother hunched over a sink, washing the last of the dirty dishes. Taking pity on her, he reached into his wallet, grabbed a twenty-dollar bill and slipped it in her back pocket.

"I was so happy I rushed back home and I showed your dad immediately!" my mom exclaimed to me proudly. As she has clearly not lost any sleep over this incident, I've given up trying to get her to realize that it was borderline sexual harassment.

To be clear, don't ever do that to someone.

At home my mother was welcomed with open arms by Mary, who had heard so much about her already from her conversations with my dad. Before my mother's arrival in Canada, my dad had tried to offer Mary more rent to account for an extra person in the house. Not only did Mary ardently refuse the extra money—she actually *lowered* the rent so that my parents would be able to save more money. In turn, Mom helped Mary around the house, cleaning and dusting and doing the shopping that Mary wasn't able to do.

To keep expenditures as low as possible, my parents had to become masters of thriftiness. They bought some veggies and a little chunk of ground meat every week and stir-fried a little bit each day. They would eagerly look forward to the end of the academic semester, when students would often throw their used furniture to the curb. They would comb the streets at night, pick up what they could and bring it back with them, giddy with the thought of having acquired such good furniture for free.

Mary's health would unfortunately take a turn for the worse in 1993—one day while attempting to carry a chair down the stairs, she tripped and fell, breaking bones in her leg and shoulder. When my parents rushed to the hospital upon hearing this, Mary was already so heavily sedated that she couldn't recognize them.

Mary was moved to an assisted living facility but passed away shortly afterward. My parents figured that this would likely mean Mary's next of kin would sell the house and evict them, but no such notice ever came. Mary's niece, who had stepped in to care for her after her accident, allowed them to stay in the house for an entire year before they'd have to find a new place.

I didn't know Mary or her niece personally, but I know that their exceptional kindness and generosity made a tremendous impression on my parents. Today, both my mom and dad are the most accommodating and gracious hosts you could ever dream of, to the point where I get endlessly frustrated over how often they allow themselves to be taken advantage of. I know that a big part of that comes from their time with Mary, their landlord with a heart of absolute gold.

Even as my mother studied tirelessly each day, it became apparent that English would not come naturally to her. In February of 1992, she would fail her first TOEFL exam.

It felt similar to when she was studying for the gāokǎo in Changping, yet at the same time totally different. She was completely out of her comfort zone and struggling to learn a language that made very little sense to her. It seemed that no matter how hard she stared at the sea of English words in her textbooks, they just weren't settling in her brain. Her score came just a few points shy of the cutoff for Canadian universities. My mother was nothing if not hyper-prepared. Knowing that she was probably going to have to retake the exam multiple times before she got a high enough mark, she'd booked three consecutive test slots, each a month apart.

The second time around, she went in knowing what awaited her and barely passed with a 573. The university cutoff was 550.

That third test wouldn't be necessary after all.

"Your dad only scored a 587, and he spent a whole year doing nothing but studying English in Nanjing!"

With the TOEFL score in hand, my mom wasted no time in getting her application to Queen's. She was accepted into the graduate program starting the following semester with full financial aid and a teaching assistant gig to boot.

She could not quit her dishwashing job fast enough.

Although she had passed the TOEFL, the language barrier would continue to be a challenge for my mom. After her first day of classes, having failed to understand a single word her profs were saying, she came home in a fit of tears.

"I don't know what I'm doing here, Zhenning!" she sobbed. And you thought *you* had impostor syndrome?

But my mother had overcome far too much hardship in her life to be undone by English, a stupid language in which *there*, *their* and *they're* were actual words that meant completely different things, and *i* always came before *e* except in the ten thousand cases in which it didn't (and do not even get me started on the phonetic clusterfuck that is the world *colonel*). She never gave up, and forced herself to keep pace with conversational English by identifying the key words in each sentence. By the end of her first year, she could have full conversations with her classmates and instructors.

This was the moment everything came together for us; with the combined scholarship money from both of my parents, their quality of life vastly improved, and they were able to make some big changes. They bought their first car, a shiny little white Dodge Colt, from a used car dealership for $4,000, which they took all the way down to Florida to see Disney World and walk along the beaches of Miami. They were also able to apply for a visitor visa for me, which was approved in the fall of 1993.

My dad booked a seat for himself flying from Toronto to Beijing in late December, then two on the way back in January for him and his four-year-old son. He would return home hailed as a success, far from the naive and broke boy he was when he left the country three years ago. That unlikely dream that he and my mom once glimpsed from afar was now very much a reality; our family would finally be together.

CHAPTER SEVEN

ZHENNING'S HOMECOMING

After nearly four years abroad, the prodigal son would finally make his triumphant return to China.

If you jumped here straight from chapter one, shame on you!

The rest of you have my sincere gratitude for letting me tell my parents' story. It was a truly incredible experience to sit down with them over many hours as they slowly opened up to me, and it made me infinitely more appreciative of all that they endured just to be able to raise me in Canada.

If possible, you should consider doing the same while you still can; you never know when it will be too late.

Before he made his trip in January of 1994, my father had the good foresight to purchase a Panasonic video recorder so that he could document the whole thing. The resulting home video, a three-hour marathon spread across two VHS tapes affectionately titled *Zhenning's Homecoming*, became my favorite "movie" to watch growing up whenever I missed my grandparents or just felt nostalgic.

Even though I can't quite catch every word of Mandarin being spoken, I've memorized this video as well as I have memorized anything in my life, and that includes the entire Star Wars trilogy, which I can recite, beginning to end, verbatim and complete with Wookiee gargles and ominous breathing.

The movie opens shortly after my dad lands in Beijing, at a table-top barbecue restaurant with my entire mom's side of the family—my lǎoyé, lǎolao, yímā (and her husband, my yífū), jiùjiu, and my two cousins Xuan and Wenyi. Ever the documentarian, Dad makes sure to get a close-up of each person as well as the sizzling meat on the grill that still makes my mouth water just picturing it. After about ten minutes, the video jumps two days to the night he arrives at our rickety apartment in Harbin. Suddenly, we're close on my four-and-a-half-year-old face as I sprawl out on my yéye's lap like a big puppy. We've all congregated in the living room, along with my gūgu, my gūfū and JingJing, while my nǎinai is busying herself in the kitchen.

This half of the family is much more low-key and much less cosmopolitan than the Beijing side; the most extravagant thing we had on the dinner table that night was a bottle of Kahlua that my dad had brought, which itself was a bit of a confusing choice seeing as nobody in the family actually drank alcohol. Maybe it was supposed to be more ceremonial than functional, a centerpiece whose Americanness blessed the very surface it rested upon, granting fortune and prosperity to all who dined with it.

"Máomao, make a scary face!" my dad says from behind the camera. I oblige, sticking my tongue out and rotating my head at an almost demonic angle like the true thespian I am. The crowd around me breaks into laughter, and then I plop down next to my yéye again. I wonder what must have been going through his mind, knowing he would have to say goodbye to me in the next few days.

There's another cut, and suddenly we're close on my nǎinai in the kitchen, who is scolding my dad for pointing the camera at her.

"Stop it, Zhenning!" she says, laughing and trying to hide her face from the camera.

We jump back to the living room, where JingJing and I are wrestling on the bed (our living room was also our spare bedroom). Seeing that she is a foot and a half taller than me at this point, it's rather one-sided. My yéye hovers intently over us like a UFC referee, warning us if we get too close to the wall or the headboard.

"HEY! Watch the head! WATCH THE HEAD!!"

I shriek as I'm taken down. Or maybe I just tripped over myself? I'm really not great at this game. Then suddenly, it's the next day, and everyone has assembled in family photo formation to record a greeting to my mother.

"Hi, Auntie!" JingJing chirps, waving and smiling brightly down the barrel.

"Hi, Auntie!" I echo.

"She's not *your* auntie, silly!"

Everyone laughs because I am adorably stupid.

Cut to later in the afternoon, when most of the family is busy prepping dinner. My dad quizzes me as I sit in the living room snacking on a bag of Chinese Funyuns:

"Máomao, who are you going to sleep with tonight?"

(I know the wording is awkward, okay? Don't make it weird.)

". . . you!"

"Are you sure? No backing out of your word now."

Apparently, I had reneged on my promise to sleep in the same bed as my dad the previous night because I was so used to being next to my grandparents. I had said the words easily enough, but when the time actually came to go to bed, I had thrown a big tantrum. Unsure of what else to do, my grandparents let me back into their bed. I knew it was wrong—my yéye had taught me the importance of keeping your word, after all—but everything about my dad was just so *foreign*, down to his smell.

"Yeah, I'm sure." As uncomfortable as it made me, I knew that I couldn't break my promise this time.

"And who am I?"

". . . Zhenning Liu!"

• • •

At some point over my dad's stay in Harbin, he wrote a letter to my mother:

Dear Zheng,

How are you? As soon as I began this letter, a wave of memories flashed through my mind—remember when we wrote each other all the time? I arrived in Beijing at around 10:30 a.m. on December 14. Aside from the flight being delayed about an hour, everything was pretty smooth. Getting luggage took another hour, roughly. Your siblings were already waiting outside. They looked healthy, and haven't changed much. They were pleased to see me, but naturally disappointed that you couldn't come along.

I arrived at Harbin yesterday morning, and finally saw my long-missed family and Máomao. Our son is tall and chubby, and in much better health than I expected. When I first met him he was a bit unfamiliar, but he still showed the courtesy and manners I expected, and he seemed to be a well-behaved child. I was very impressed. Máomao is a child who easily attracts a lot of affection. He is quiet, smart and introspective, just like we named him. I raised two arithmetic questions with him (5 + 6 and 5 + 2) and, without using his fingers, he was able to get the correct answers quickly. He also showed me how to do a jigsaw puzzle (for children nine years old and above). He took only 33 minutes, which is a record, as Grandma said it had taken over 50 minutes before.

Obviously our child is not without his shortcomings; mainly, he cannot eat properly by himself without being fed by adults. He also likes to be praised and does not take criticism well. All these will have to be corrected in the future.

First of all, how *dare* he body-shame a four-year-old; December was *obviously* bulking season. And as for his comments on my ability to handle criticism, I think it's pretty unfair for someone to make that kind of statement about a kid he just met a day ago. Maybe I was *amaz-*

ing at handling criticism. How would he know? He wasn't even there! He didn't even raise me! *HE'S NOT MY REAL DAD!!*

... On second thought, he might have a point about the criticism thing.

Regardless of who he said he was, or what toys he brought me, this man was a stranger; if I was agreeable or obedient at all, it was because Yéye had told me I needed to be that way.

The night we left for Beijing, my family conspired to come up with a plan that would result in the least amount of unnecessary emotion and/or crying. The idea was for each of them to gradually disappear, to prevent me from catching on to the fact that this was a goodbye. There would be no tearful farewells, or prolonged hugs; everyone was to play it totally cool, at least until the package was en route.

It was a cold night in Harbin, and the whole gang walked to the bus station outside our apartment with the thick weight of unsaid words hanging in the air.

"Where are we going?"

"To the bus station, kiddo," my gūgu replied.

"Okay. Are Yéye and Năinai coming?"

"... yes," she replied. "... To the bus station."

"And then after?"

"Keep walking, Máomao."

I should have known that something was fishy—the mood was more solemn than usual, and my grandparents were uncharacteristically quiet. I should have caught on when my dad asked me which of my favorite books and toys I wanted to take with me earlier that day.

Then again, how could I possibly understand the significance of what was happening? I was only four.

When we arrived at the station, everyone made a show of getting onto the bus. And then—and I cannot stress enough how seamless this felt—they just *weren't*. It was as if my yéye, my năinai and Jing Jing had suddenly vanished into the frosty air, like the steamy breath that came out of me whenever I exhaled. Yéye and Năinai were the very founda-tion of my life to this point, and I was their little idiot who stuck his finger in power sockets, drank the dirty fish tank water and threw embarrassing tantrums in the middle of Héxìnglù. But regardless of how sick I got, how loudly I fought with them or how close I came to fully electrocuting myself, we would always sleep soundly at night knowing that we were together. I know now that my grandparents both fought back tears as they snuck away that night. I know that it broke their hearts to have to give away the child they raised as their own.

I fear that in an attempt to uphold the traditional Chinese values of stoicism, my family deprived us of a human moment. I wish we had held each other for an eternity as tears streamed down our cheeks, crystallizing in the frozen air. I wish that I had kicked and screamed at my father, telling him I didn't want to go. I wish I had gotten the chance to say a proper goodbye not only for me, but for Yéye and Năinai, so that they could have known at that moment just how much I loved them.

All I can do now is hope that they knew.

After a long and sleepy ride to the train station, the remaining four of us got on board and took our seats. My gūgu and gūfū gave me candy and did their best to keep my mind off of what was happening. I dozed off, and when I awoke, I saw only my father.

"Where did Gūgu and Gūfū go?" Deep down, I already knew; even a four-year-old could figure it out by this point.

"It's just us now, Máomao."

As the train pulled out of the station, I looked out my window and watched as the life I knew vanished behind me.

By the time I arrived in Beijing in January of 1994, it was already beginning to resemble the sprawling, smoggy megacity it is today. The city was buzzing with undeniable (if environmentally unstable) energy, and there was something new to see at every turn.

Not that I cared about any of that—my first memory of Beijing was sitting in a corner by myself, rummaging through my cousin Xuan's bin of discarded toys.

"Máomao, stop playing with those toys—they're all broken!" My yímā laughed. Clearly, she had never seen *Toy Story*.

We were in my maternal grandparents' apartment in Beijing, the same little place my mother grew up in. I was feeling a bit overwhelmed by all of the new family members I had just met immediately following an eighteen-hour train ride, and was more than happy to retreat into a corner to play with banged-up toys from the reject pile.

Xuan was my yímā's daughter and five years my senior; her parents were viciously strict and never hesitated to raise their voices at her in front of the whole family at the slightest sign of disobedience. As a result, she was always overly polite and straitlaced. On the other end of the spectrum was Wenyi, my jiùjiu's daughter, born just a couple months after me—she was the spoiled, fussy princess of the family, famous for bursting into tears over practically nothing. Wenyi's catchphrase "*I WANT TO GO HOOOOOOOME*" was often said between earsplitting sobs. As comically different as they were in age and personality, Xuan and Wenyi were very close; they reminded me of the way Jing and I used to play together.

My father's entire trip up until this point had gone off without a hitch—he had flown halfway around the world and successfully brought me from Harbin to Beijing without a single tear shed, and our flight to Canada was only days away. It seemed that nothing could go wrong at this point . . . which of course meant that something was definitely about to go wrong.

Unfortunately for my old man, he had not yet spent enough time with me to know about my penchant for danger. After spending the day hanging out together, I had decided to introduce my cousins to one of my favorite pastimes with JingJing: bed-trampoline! I was hopping up and down with Wenyi on a little single bed when I suddenly fell and felt a sharp pain shooting up my wrist. All the adults thought it was just a little bump initially—I mean, who breaks their arm falling onto a padded mattress—but quickly rushed me to the hospital once they realized I couldn't move my hand.

The whole debacle may have caused my dad to shit a couple of bricks; it was literally his *first* day of actual fatherhood, and his kid had already injured himself.

I spent the next few days jet-setting around with my left arm in a sling and a thick cast. In honor of my upcoming trip to North America, the family decided to take all of the kids out to a groovy new fast-food joint that had just dipped its toes into the Chinese market—a restaurant chain called Màidāngláo, famous around the world for its tasty burgers and its iconic logo with two golden arches.

Like Kentucky Fried Chicken before it, Chinese McDonald's received a major international glow-up when it came to the Middle Kingdom—the flagship Beijing location in the Wángfǔjǐng shopping district had a seating capacity of seven hundred and even featured its own playpen and rides—including a carousel, which I rode with my cousins, atop bizarre and creepy creatures with the body of a dragon and the head of a hamburger. I guess Ronald McDonald didn't test well with Asian audiences?

A couple of days later, it was time to go. We said our goodbyes, taxied to the airport, checked our bags, and headed toward the customs gate. As he handed the officer our papers, I could see the arch in my father's tense shoulders start to relax: after all these years, all this time, all this effort, the finish line was in sight. Surely, he was in the clear now?

"Exit papers please, sir."

"Yes. Of course, it's . . . uh . . ."

It was then that my father realized that while he had acquired my visa to get into Canada, he had forgotten to get my exit approval papers signed in Beijing, where my parents and I were officially registered as residents. My grandparents couldn't do it in Harbin, and had neglected to remind my dad, and so he had assumed I had all the papers I needed. Without that approval, the customs guard told us, I wasn't allowed to leave the country.

Just then, in our most desperate hour of need, the customs official in the next booth looked up and saw my dad pleading with his colleague, and me in a sling standing pathetically next to him.

"Just let them go," he said gruffly, gesturing at me. "They're headed to Canada anyway, and the kid's got a broken arm."

I guess you could say that I saved the day with my clumsiness.

So after that, on the plane we went, to travel a distance too great for my little brain to fathom, to go to a place that had only been described to me as a perfect utopia.

Nearly a full twenty-four hours later, our tired and sleep-deprived bodies finally touched down in Toronto, where my mother was eagerly awaiting our arrival. As I scanned the crowd curiously, looking for her, I realized that I didn't even know what she looked like.

After a moment, my dad grabbed my shoulder and gestured toward a woman in a puffy gray coat standing alone near the back of the gathered crowd. Her eyes lit up as she met my gaze, and she began waving furiously.

"That's your mom, kiddo," my dad whispered to me. "Go on, say hello!"

I immediately ran down the hall, toward the woman with the puffy jacket, and toward my new life. My mother's eyes widened in shock as she saw her son waddling toward her with his arm in a sling; I guess my dad had forgotten to tell her. Nevertheless, she picked me up and held me close as he caught up to us. We walked out of Pearson International Airport together for the first time as a complete family, fulfilling the vision that my parents had once imagined in their tiny apartment in Beijing. Back then, the West was only an idea, a faraway pipe dream.

Now . . . it was home.

ACT TWO

CHAPTER EIGHT

LIFE IN THE LAND OF POUTINE

As far as happy endings went, 1994 came pretty damn close.

My parents had spent three years in Kingston building a new life from the ground up and dreaming of the day they'd be able to bring me over from China so that we would finally be together as a family. Before that, they had defied all odds to graduate in China's legendary class of '77, which immediately followed a ten-year drought of all university admissions, and then built successful careers in Beijing before risking it all to come to Canada. My arrival in January was the culmination of all that they had strived for and marked the beginning of a bright new era in their lives. If this were a movie, I could imagine the picture fading to black as the three of us walked out of the airport together, hand in hand, as the music swelled and the credits rolled—a perfect Hollywood send-off.

But hang on a minute, Spielberg; seeing as we're not even midway through this book, it's pretty obvious that my parents don't get to ride off into the sunset just yet.

After all, anyone who has had a child would tell you that there is no challenge greater than parenthood—even more so when you are effectively adopting a four-year-old and bringing him halfway around the world to a country that he is completely unfamiliar with. Mom and Dad were about to experience the myriad of new responsibilities and burdens that came with raising a child, and would learn very quickly that "parenthood" was a lot more complicated than just living together.

I, in turn, would learn that life in Canada with my new family wasn't all that it was promised to be.

To be perfectly clear, my first impressions of Canada as a whole were overwhelmingly positive. The differences between Harbin and Kingston in 1994 were quite pronounced; I went from not having regular access to running water to being able to take as many showers and hot baths as I wanted in the house that now belonged to Mary's niece. I stared in total awe as my parents drank water straight from the tap, without having to boil it first. All of the roads were paved, and all the cars driving on them were new and shiny. There were parks, trees, giant shopping centers and movie theaters, and a whole lot less dirt.

My first couple of weeks in Canada were jam-packed full of fun activities. We watched *The Jungle Book* in the theater together. We went to Pizza Hut, which at the time had an all-you-can-eat salad bar (almost three decades later, you still cannot convince my father of a better dining experience than a buffet). My parents even let me play with a computer for the first time, kicking off what was to be a *very* love-hate relationship with the internet.

There was a lot to love about Canada as a country—Tim Hortons, pond hockey, a universal health care system—and both my parents and I have only grown to appreciate it more over time. However, fully adjusting to life in this new family unit proved to be a bit more difficult for all three of us.

When I arrived in Kingston in 1994 my parents were still on their holiday break. Soon, they had to go back to class, which left me without a caretaker during the day. So, barely two weeks after arriving in a totally foreign country, I found myself staring out the window of a day care, bawling my eyes out as I watched my parents back out of the driveway. I didn't know a single person, and couldn't understand anyone; English sounded like a gibberish language to me. But I didn't want to make friends or learn the language—I just wanted my yéye and näi-nai. I cried all day until I was picked up, that day and every day for the next few weeks. Unbeknownst to me at the time, my parents had to pay for my day care entirely out of pocket, whereas Canadian citizens and permanent residents in the same income bracket would have had their childcare costs covered through government subsidies.

They were paying an arm and a leg for me to be sad.

I remember another time when, just mere days into our halting get-to-know you process, I woke up from a nap to find the house completely empty. While I was asleep, my mother had realized there wasn't any food in the fridge, and hoped to sneak out to grab some groceries and make it back before I woke up.

As per Murphy's Law, I of course woke up almost immediately after she left.

Without any indication of where my mother was, I resolved to go out and look for her in the dead of winter. I dressed myself as best I could with my one operable arm, struggling into my snow pants, jacket, scarves and toque (and not really considering the fact that I had no idea how to get around town or to speak with the locals). By the time I got my gloves and snow boots on, though, I experienced a sudden loss of confidence. It was a rare display of common sense that no doubt saved my life; I sat at the top of the stairs and cried instead. When my mother finally came through the front door a short time later, she took one look at me, bundled up and puffy eyed, and all of the color drained from her face. She knew immediately that she had messed up.

Hold up, though—before you take out your pitchforks, time-travel to the mid '90s and call child protective services, consider that my parents were woefully ill-equipped for their new jobs as full-time care-givers. They had just spent the last three years only having to look after themselves; of *course* there was going to be an adjustment period. There was no learning curve, no gradual easing-into process—I simply showed up one day young, hungry and frustratingly dependent.

A few months after I had come over, Mary's niece finally gave notice that she would be selling the house. We soon upgraded our living situation to a more spacious brick apartment in a broken-down part of town that was occupied by mostly low-income families, including eighteen other Chinese families like ours (most of whom were graduate students like my parents). As time went on, and my English became progressively better, I would befriend the other children in these families. We'd all gather at each other's houses, playing games and speaking in English as our parents would sit and gossip in Mandarin. There was a familiar comfort in this—it may not have been home, but at least it felt like community, the first time I'd felt it since I'd left Harbin.

Although it was a government-subsidized building, the rent for our new apartment was still far higher than Mary ever charged; with an extra mouth to feed, daycare costs that were through the roof and a much higher rent than they were used to, my parents found themselves once again pinching every single penny they could to survive.

It wasn't long before I stopped feeling like my parents' happily ever after, and more like their burden.

At some point between my arrival in Canada and the day I started first grade, I was introduced to something that I initially thought was quite harmless, but which would ultimately fester and grow to become a constant malignant force in my life.

In the beginning, satisfying my parents was a pretty easy thing to do. Actually, I'm not sure that I had to do anything at all; I could make my mother smile and laugh just by existing, could make my father applaud my artistic talents with the ugliest creations on Microsoft Paint. I'm sure that they were still caught up in the honeymoon period of having a son as cute as I was. However, as time went on, Mom's smiles grew smaller, her laughs became mere chuckles, and Dad stopped reaching for the camera to document every little thing I made. I effectively became a *Big Bang Theory* rerun—something once fresh and shiny and new that became progressively less funny with each repeat viewing, until every punch line and the subsequent audience laughter that followed grated on you like nails on a chalkboard.

To be clear, I still did all of the kid stuff—my parents signed me up for summer camps and swimming lessons, and let me play with my friends outdoors all the time. My mother would chase me up and down the block as I learned to ride a bike, ready to catch me if I lost my balance. I fondly recall the pure joy that I felt when they bought me my very own Thunder Megazord. After a season or so of the traditional Dinozords, Zordon upgraded the Rangers' powers, resulting in new robotic Zords that combined into the giant and majestic Thunder Megazord. Refreshing the toys every couple of years to keep the children wanting more; it was pure marketing genius! My parents, fully aware of this consumerist gouging, dug deep into their wallets anyway and bought me the toy (which was really five toys) at full price.

Later, when another kid in our enclave became the first to get Super Nintendo, I came home jealous-crying that I didn't have one. It was just about the *coolest* thing I had ever seen, and it tore me up inside that I couldn't tear through Mushroom Kingdom on my own. My parents made the snap decision to buy a Sega Genesis the following week—again, at full price. Anybody who grew up in any immigrant household will understand how big a deal that is. Despite growing up "poor," I truly never felt like I was missing anything material in my life.

What I did miss, and greatly so, was curling up between Yéye and Nǎinai and feeling completely protected from all the bad in the world.

As time went on, I felt like I ceased to be an endless burst of joy and became something that had to be molded, or groomed, for success. Around the time I was set to begin first grade, I started to feel the weight of my parents' expectations on my shoulders, something that I had never encountered before in China, where being my adorable self was enough.

It began as an innocent question, not asked of me directly but posed implicitly—*don't you want to make your parents happy?* Well . . . of course I did; happy parents meant trips to McDonald's and garage sale shopping sprees! It meant that I could play with the friends that I had made in the building. Most important, it meant receiving the affection, validation and praise that my yéye and năinai had always been so generous with back home in Harbin.

Mom and Dad were unquestionably happiest when I was reading or accumulating knowledge. We would come home from the library with stacks of books that I would pore over, ranging from Dr. Seuss to the adult novelization of *Return of the Jedi*. I often had no idea what I was even reading but was still able to absorb the structure and the syntax of the English language. So what if I thought Jabba the Hutt was actually a person, and found the idea of Leia being chained to him weird and ineffective?

Meanwhile, my parents also began to fast-track my math skills. By the time I was five, I had my times tables memorized; by the time I was six and about to enter first grade, I could do long division. One day, my father pointed the camcorder at me and quizzed me like I was on some sort of prime-time game show:

"We want to show Yéye and Năinai your progress," he said, as if my value was tied to whether or not I knew what seven times eight was. I answered gleefully, seeing that I made him happier with every correct response I gave.

Tied to this new expectation, of course, was the consequence of falling short of it. I will absolutely never forget the first time my mother yelled at me. It had been a long day spent running and jumping off of things, as a child does, and I'd felt too exhausted to do the "homework" that my parents had assigned me. After inspecting my work, which was sloppy and riddled with errors, she erupted at me:

"I asked you to memorize EIGHT WORDS. You've been sitting at your desk FOR AN HOUR. If you're going to take ALL DAY to learn EIGHT EASY WORDS, how will you do anything else??"

My mother's volume and intensity stunned me; it was a completely different side of her than the woman who had scooped me up in her arms at the airport, hugging and kissing me and refusing to let me go. Her words stung like hot lashes on my skin, punctuated by the speed and the ferocity of her voice. In shock and with absolutely no idea what to do, I closed my eyes and wept silently as she berated me.

"Do it AGAIN, and do it PROPERLY. You write these words TEN TIMES EACH, and don't even THINK about getting up. I don't care if we're here all night, you're going to SIT THERE for as LONG AS IT TAKES."

Instead of stepping in to mediate the situation, my dad secretly recorded the incident on his camcorder, thinking that it would make an amusing addition to the tape that he was preparing to send overseas. Weeks later, on the other side of the world, my yéye and năinai sat helplessly as they watched the tears streaming down my face on their TV. It was not funny to them, and it certainly wasn't to me.

That day, because of those eight words I couldn't remember, my trust in my parents shattered. I no longer felt loved unconditionally, no longer felt that they could keep me safe.

I fully realize that my mom's scolding is considered par for the course in many immigrant families—parents need to discipline their kids, and it's totally unrealistic to expect them to only ever offer praise and words of affirmation. On the other hand, I couldn't help but think back to the way that my grandfather sat me down and reasoned with me when I was throwing too many tantrums in public places. Regardless of what I did—and you will remember that I did a lot of very stupid things—there was a line that Yéye never crossed with me. There were never any lingering feelings when we went to bed each night, and he certainly never gave me any reason to fear him.

Too young to be able to recognize what was happening, I simply swallowed my feelings and hoped that they would go away.

I began my academic career at Sydenham Public School, in a 150-year-old stone building across the street from the Queen's campus that looked more like a generously sized house than a school. Around this time my mom had found a job at Bombardier, an iconic Canadian manufacturer of locomotives and airplanes, while my dad was finishing up his PhD. I didn't know it at the time, but my father had also interviewed for that job—in fact, they had prepared for it together, and even arrived at the office at the same time. After their joint appointment, though, only my mom would receive an invitation to the next round. It was a bittersweet moment for my dad, who wanted to be happy for his wife but was also faced with the reality that he was no longer the bread-winner.

What should have been a moment of jubilation ended up putting a great deal of stress on our family. For my mom, the excitement of get-ting a job offer soon turned into an overwhelming pressure to perform in the office. My dad, meanwhile, struggled to find a job in his field of study, and became stressed-out and irritable as a result.

On the other hand, barely a year and a half after landing in an en-tirely foreign country with virtually no English skills, I was dominat-ing in every major statistical category—math, language, gym, crafts and even French, which was compulsory in Canada (*malheureusement, j'ai oublié la plupart de mon français*). In our combined grade one and grade two class, I was immediately placed with the upper-year students and given the same work assignments, which I also aced. I was studious and I never talked back or misbehaved—in short, I was a walking poster child for model-minority Asian excellence. It was a testament to all of the hours my parents had invested in preparing me for school, and I was determined to make them proud.

I even made a couple of best friends—Robin, lanky and curly haired, and Max, a stockier kid with freckles and a bowl cut. The three of us were truly inseparable, spending every minute of recess together and even having sleepovers and street hockey dates on the weekends. Robin's parents were separated, and I never saw them much, but Max's family gave me my first peek into what a "Canadian" family was like—warm, affectionate and full of love for not only one another, but for me as well. I never once felt like I was the odd kid out, even though I defi-nitely was; I was a year younger than both Max and Robin, and also the only Chinese kid in the whole class.

That Halloween, my parents bought me a Super Mario costume

from the secondhand thrift store and took me trick-or-treating with my friends. At the start of winter, they took me skating for the first time at the public rink, holding my hand as I slipped and slid my way across the ice on my little yard-sale skates. On Christmas morning, I awoke to find the Sega Genesis game I wanted neatly gift wrapped under the tree with a personal greeting from Santa. My parents were neither negligent nor lethargic in my upbringing—I had birthday parties and went bowling, ate Happy Meals and rented movies from Blockbuster.

Underneath it all, though, the weight of their expectations was already beginning to tear at our foundation.

The first time I told a lie was after a class trip to the local swimming pool. When picking me up from school, my dad casually asked me who the fastest person in the class was.

"Me!" I fibbed innocently, wanting to impress him, even though I knew I definitely wasn't the strongest swimmer. How would I even know who was fastest? It's not like they were timing a bunch of six-year-olds doing lengths.

My dad was immediately skeptical, and I don't blame him; I was a pretty runty kid.

"Okay . . . who was the second fastest?"

"Um . . . Anthony!"

Anthony *was* the most athletic kid in my class.

"Máomao . . . are you sure?" my father asked sternly. "You know, honesty is very important."

My cheeks burned bright red as I felt my house of cards collapse. I had been exposed. I decided it was time to own up to my mistake.

"I . . . I made it up," I confessed. "Please don't tell Mom."

"I won't," he assured me. "You did the right thing."

I was grateful that my dad had taken my honesty into account. From what I had learned from Yéye, giving your word was binding yourself to a social contract. Thus, there was no reason to assume that my father would not uphold his end of the bargain.

Later that night at dinner, my mom asked how my day had gone at the swimming pool.

"It was fun," I had said, and expected to leave it at that.

"Actually, Máomao told a lie today," my dad said, half smiling, as if I had just taken my first steps. My heart immediately stopped. "He said he was the fastest in the class, but he admitted that he made that up."

I don't think my mother heard the last part. She sprang into action immediately. Silently and abruptly, without any warning, she took my hand, marched me out of the apartment, closed the door in front of me and locked the latch. It all happened so quickly I barely even had time to blink, or look at my father.

If I had to guess at how long I was out there, I'd put it between fifteen minutes to a half hour. To a child trapped in a hallway, it was an eternity. At one point one of the other Chinese mothers who lived on the same floor came up the stairs with a bag of groceries. She took one look at me, red faced and puffy eyed, and immediately wanted to comfort me.

"What's wrong, Máomao? What happened?!" she asked intently.

"My parents locked me out of the house." I sniffed, snot coming out of my nose.

"Oh." The tone of her voice changed immediately. Without another word she looked away, opened her apartment door and walked in.

I learned a lot about a lot of things that day.

First—the Chinese parents in our enclave were not to be trusted. The same woman who had left me out in the hallway had herself locked her son out in the weeks prior. In fact, I'm absolutely positive that that's where my mom had gotten the idea. Months later, that same woman would fracture her foot while kicking her eight-year-old son (she had missed and struck a table leg instead), darkly foreshadowing what lay in store for me down the road. This was so shockingly different from the images of Max's family that had left such a positive impression on me. I couldn't reconcile how our parents could be so cruel in comparison.

Second—my own parents were not to be trusted either. Despite my father's assurances that I had "done the right thing" in owning up to my fib, he completely failed to keep his word and watched as my mother grabbed my wrist and forced me outside. It was clear to me even at the age of six that I was not going to be governed by a consistent set of rules and principles, but rather by whatever my parents felt like doing at the time.

Finally—next time I was going to lie, I needed to commit fully. There was no room for doubt and certainly no room for honesty. I would not be rewarded for coming clean, nor would I be commended for owning up and telling the truth. Keep my parents happy at all costs or risk their wrath—that was the name of the game now.

Suddenly Canada did not seem quite so shiny.

CHAPTER NINE

SIMU THE GENIUS

I was seven when I was first identified as a "gifted" child.

No, fanboys, a bald English man in a pimped-out wheelchair did not recruit me to go to his top secret school . . . but it certainly felt that way.

After a yearlong search, my dad was finally offered a job at a major aerospace company located all the way in Toronto. Although he and my mom knew that it would complicate our living situation, he had no choice but to take it–it had been a long and grueling job-seeking process for him, and the financial stability of a dual-income family had been the endgame all along. I bade farewell to Robin and Max and headed to the big city with my dad while my mom remained in Kingston for a time, until she eventually managed to secure a job at that same company, in the same department and under the same manager as my dad. I missed my mother in the time we were apart, but the distance did give me a few months of respite from her harsh words and high expectations. She was, by her own admission, 90 percent good and 10 percent bad. What happened in that 10 percent, though, would leave deep emotional scars that couldn't be reconciled by the other 90.

My mother was tireless in her efforts to raise me, and often went above and beyond to ensure that I had everything she never did. This woman literally force-fed herself sardines every single day when she was pregnant with me, because she had heard that they would make me smarter. But there was a definite dark side to her, and when her anger flared up there was seemingly no limit to the hurtfulness of her words. I was often called *stupid* or *useless*, and sometimes even slapped for my disobedience. The following day, she would carry on as if nothing had happened, leaving me alone to grapple with what she had done. I had developed a genuine fear of her that would morph into a resentment and even a hatred in later years.

In 1997, though, I just wanted to make her happy.

At Broadacres Junior Public School in Etobicoke, I would continue my Shaq-like statistical dominance across all academic categories. I wrote a calligram poem that was selected to be published in a provincial book showcasing student work. I was a frequent "student of the week," which was kind of like "employee of the month" but with more rainbow stickers. I was so used to perfect scores on my math assignments that I remember the look of surprise on my teacher's face when I made a single careless error on a worksheet.

"Simu, I'm surprised! You never make mistakes like this."

I promptly cried and then never made an error in anything ever again.

For our family, mediocrity was simply never an option. Because most immigrants did not have cushy safety nets to catch them in times of crisis, the only things keeping my parents from being completely destitute were their biweekly paychecks. To that end, absolutely nothing mattered more than their continued job security, which they could only ensure by being absolutely *exceptional* every single day. In Kingston it was commonplace for my mother to pull overtime late into the night, coming home as I was going to bed only to be up and out the door for work before I woke up the next day. I was always first in and last out at the before- and after-school programs, often frustrating the supervisors who just wanted to go home to their families.

Despite all their hard work, both my parents would readily agree that they've had to do twice the amount of work as their white Canadian counterparts for the same amount of recognition. They were, after all, minorities in a white-dominated country—it would have been unrealistic to assume that their lives would be free of any disadvantage. From their own language deficiencies to racial biases in the workplace, the bamboo ceiling was ever present in each of my parents' careers—but they still fought as hard as they could, pushing it up inch by inch.

Twenty-five years later, my dad still refuses to complain.

"Nobody forced us to come here," he says. "We made a choice to immigrate. We knew that nothing was going to be handed to us, and we knew we were going to have to work twice as hard as everyone else."

My parents were not interested in concepts like political activism or social equality; there was only *work*, and *survival*.

If there was any time left over in their days, Mom and Dad would spend it trying to instill in me their very same work ethic and absolute commitment to being the best. They would do so by effectively trying to dump as much knowledge into my brain as possible, like I was an iCloud drive with unlimited storage; my desk at home was constantly covered in stacks of library books that were mostly biographies of famous scientists, from Copernicus and Galileo to Newton, Darwin, Edison and, of course, Einstein, the Michael Jordan of this '92 Dream Team of Science. This was the bar my parents unwittingly set for me—not to become a doctor or a lawyer, but someone who changed and shaped the world.

One day about halfway through the semester, I was asked to stay after school by my teacher, Mrs. Petrowski. By this point my parents had already made me pretty terrified of all authority figures, and I was immediately nervous. Sensing my unease, she smiled reassuringly.

"Don't worry, Simu, you're not in trouble . . . we just think that you might be very bright."

You have never seen a person's face change color quicker.

Bright, eh? I thought as I beamed with excitement. *I am soooo getting McDonald's tonight.*

After class, Mrs. Petrowski introduced me to a man I would later learn was from the Identification Placement and Review Committee in the Ministry of Education, whose job it was to determine whether I was smart enough to be placed in an enriched program. We sat in a room together and he asked me a range of general knowledge questions, and then asked me to solve some math problems and spatial puzzles that, if we're totally honest, were pretty uncomplicated compared to the work my parents were assigning me at home.

I want to be clear here—in no way did I possess a MENSA-level genius brain; there will be plenty of examples of my idiocy in later chapters that will make you facepalm so hard you'll leave a bruise. I was just a moderately intelligent kid that was raised with a bit of a head start by parents who saw good grades as the only surefire path to financial stability.

Meanwhile, all I wanted was for someone to buy me a Happy Meal.

A few weeks later, my parents were called into a meeting with the school board to discuss the results of my evaluation. Now, you could imagine a tiny, nondescript meeting room in an old office building—or, if you've seen the same types of movies I have, you might instead envision the Jedi Council chambers high above the bastion planet of Coruscant, or Harry's little room at 4 Privet Drive, or the headmaster's office at a certain professor's School for Gifted Youngsters.

You'll have to forgive the nerdy movie references—what's important is that you understand that this was a pivotal (if very movie trope-y) moment in my life, where my parents began to believe that I was some sort of child prodigy destined for greatness, just like the Boy Who Lived, or the Chosen One.

The man who had performed my assessment sat across from my parents. "I'm very happy to share that Simu is an incredibly bright boy. His aptitude scores suggest that he would do well in a more stimulating environment, like our gifted program."

This was music to my parents' ears. For two immigrants who were perpetually at the top of their class, nothing could be better than hearing that their child was diligently following in their footsteps.

"I was especially impressed by his answer to a particular question," the man continued. "When I ask children what books contained, nearly all of them would say 'words.' When I asked Simu, he said that books contained 'ideas.' He is definitely a special kid."

And there it was— "special"—the word that would set my parents' expectations of me for the rest of my childhood. The word that allowed them to believe that I could achieve anything they dreamed of for me.

"We want him to become an engineer, like us," my father offered. "Or a doctor. Definitely a scientist of some sort."

The man hesitated for a split second, as if he knew that my parents would not like his response.

"Well . . . nothing is to say that Simu couldn't become an engineer, if that was what he wanted. However, his results clearly indicate to me that his strengths lie in the language arts. He could be a great writer."

My parents smiled politely as always, but scoffed internally. *A writer? That's not a career! He might as well be flipping burgers at Wendy's!* In the absence of any Abrahamic or Taoist influences, science was their only gospel—to suggest that I could be anything other than a scientist was blasphemy.

Suffice to say, the next few years were pretty intense for me. Galvanized by my evaluation, my parents would max out my stats like I was some Dungeons and Dragons character.

There were piles upon piles of reading comprehension workbooks to boost my literacy. The Chinese term for studying is dúshū, which literally translates to "read book." The importance of academic success was firmly rooted in Confucian principles, and was predicated around the ability to read. There was a sense that as long as I was reading a book and properly absorbing its knowledge, I was bettering myself. Unfortunately for me, Confucius didn't say much about going outside, playing with friends or eating ice cream.

Then there were advanced algebra textbooks, sample Math Olympiad contests and myriad IQ diagnostic software programs to level up my math and logic. It was a never-ending rinse and repeat of taking tests, getting graded against a bell curve, learning from my mistakes and then taking more tests. It was as tedious as it sounds—although I actually did have fond memories of learning geometry from an anthropomorphic painting named Pablo, whose face was made of triangles, in Math Blaster Mystery.

Finally, there were science books that children had absolutely no business reading, like Robert Zubrin's *A Case for Mars* and Richard Dawkins's *The Selfish Gene*, to build my scientific knowledge. I was obsessed with *Star Wars* and anything to do with space exploration, which my dad was more than happy to cultivate by buying me books about astrophysics and, like, *literal* rocket science.

Although my academic performance was my parents' main priority for me, they also wanted me to be the best at everything else—especially compared to the children of their peers. The Chinese immigrants in their office formed a new little friend group that, just as with the enclave in Kingston, *loved* to brag about their kids. Not ones to be outdone by anyone, my folks never let me fall behind:

When they caught wind that Amy—the daughter of another husband-and-wife employee duo—had been put into Chinese school, I too was immediately signed up. Every Saturday for two years I had to sit in a classroom with a bunch of other Chinese kids who would rather have been watching *Looney Tunes*. Instead, we stared at calligraphy books, learned pinyin, and traded Pokémon cards when the teacher wasn't looking.

When they heard that another coworker's daughter, Cheryl, was taking piano lessons, I was signed up for those as well. I started out with Karen, an exceedingly kind and patient teacher who ran a school out of her house just down the street from us—but my parents soon grew impatient at my rate of progress. Apparently, I wasn't supposed to actually *enjoy* piano; my only job was to surpass Cheryl and be the best. So, instead of continuing to learn at a perfectly normal rate with Karen, my parents transferred me to Judy, who was much older and much more . . . Chinese. Judy treated piano players the way she did in the Old Country, which meant that she was fixated on results and completely uninterested in concepts like "self-expression" and "fun." I jumped six piano grades in the span of a year, during which Judy made me cry nearly every week for not practicing two hours per day. This, my parents were convinced, was much better than taking it easy with Karen and playing fun Disney songs every week.

My parents had faced harsh realities in their upbringing that molded them into incredibly hardworking individuals. Each of their triumphs, from leaving the country to graduating from Queen's, finding a stable job and buying a house, reinforced the notion that success only came as the result of grinding tirelessly and never taking their foot off the gas. When it came to me, a kid who had been seemingly given everything, no amount of work I did was ever enough. I mean, sure, they would express an appropriate level of satisfaction whenever I brought home a straight-A report card or won the runner-up prize in a municipal short story competition—but they were just as quick to show their disdain whenever I didn't meet their standards. I was often made to feel bad for wanting to have things that regular human children did, like hobbies, or friends.

For starters, I was guilted for nearly everything I liked, even though it was totally commonplace for most boys my age—things like video games, Pokémon cards or anything Star Wars, Power Rangers or Ninja Turtles. My parents would indulge me with a pack of cards or a movie every so often when I performed especially well at school, but I could tell that they hated seeing me doing anything that didn't involve studying.

"Good kids like Amy and Cheryl don't waste their time like you do," they would constantly say to me. "Why aren't any of your school friends like Amy or Cheryl?"

On more than one occasion, I wondered if they were just allergic to joy.

One loophole I could always exploit was my parents' soft spot for books of any sort. I went deep into the Animorphs, a middle-grade book series about a group of shape-shifting teenagers and their telepathic alien friend Ax, which was allowed because it kept me in the house and reading. I inhaled each book from cover to cover, totally enthralled by the world that K. A. Applegate had created.

What can I say, I was a straightforward kid—if you showed me anything with space travel, aliens or superheroes, I would want it. Bonus points if the protagonist was a normal kid who yearned for adventure but was trapped in his uneventful life, who discovers that he has a destiny far greater than he could ever comprehend . . .

My parents were more or less cool with comic books too, but that quickly changed on one of my birthdays when my dad ventured into a comic store to buy some stuff for me. Evidently, he had gotten pretty spooked by the tattoos and antiestablishment vibes that the staff were giving off—he bought a few comics, practically tossed them at me and declared that he would never buy comic books for me ever again.

I don't want you to get the wrong idea; I was by no means kicking and screaming every step of the way through the daily IQ tests, the Wednesday-night piano lessons and the Saturday-morning Mandarin classes. I loved making my parents proud, and I was a willing participant in all of it (at least for a time). When I was chastised by my parents for a bad test score, I pushed myself to be better. I mean, think about it: I was constantly being fed a narrative that I was special, that I was smart, and that I could be a top performer in everything I put my mind to. Who wouldn't want to be all of those things? Who wouldn't want to be *great*?

Equipped with what were basically the cheat codes for education, I tore through the rest of primary school and left a trail of accolades in my wake. The peak of my achievement came when I made the town paper in fifth grade for placing nationally in the Pythagoras Contest, a math competition for—gasp—*sixth graders*.

For my parents, everything must have seemed so perfect; we were the model Chinese family in every way, inspiring envy from all the other families we knew, with two working professional parents and a kid who was seemingly destined for success. What could possibly derail a family built on such upright, Confucian values?

Apparently . . . puberty.

My priorities shifted as my voice deepened and my equipment dropped. More than I wanted to be a genius, or even to make my parents proud,

I now wanted to be *cool*. I never really had a problem making friends when I was younger, but when I got to the fifth grade, where social hierarchies began to form, I realized that I was the nerdy kid at the bottom of the pile with little to no social skills. Plus, since I had moved schools so much, I was the perpetual new kid who always had to start from scratch. I was frequently the butt of my classmates' jokes—the dork, the keener, the awkward Chinese kid who didn't understand anyone's pop-culture references. I made the kind of friends that didn't really stick up for me when it mattered, but I always laughed along because I wanted to be a part of the group. I pretended like their jokes didn't bother me, but deep down, I always dreamed of being popular—like a class comedian or a star athlete who was universally admired.

My desire for popularity stemmed from that one major development in early preteen life, one that my parents had no interest in educating me on. Yup—my 'nads dropped just in time for sixth grade, my sexual emergence manifesting into a gigantic crush on Jackie D, the coolest and prettiest girl in class. Jackie had brown hair, listened to *NSYNC, and spent many a recess hanging out with Thomas MacDonald, a twelve-year-old Aaron Carter lookalike complete with frosted tips and a silver chain around his neck. Most of the girls in our class had crushes on Thomas, so I guess he was something of a cool guy himself. Am I still bitter about this? Of course not—I am writing about this memory in my book two decades later because I am totally over it and definitely not at all bitter.

Predictably, my parents didn't have much to offer on the subject of coolness or puberty, other than that it was a totally meaningless diversion from the true purpose of childhood: getting into Harvard. The only thing they said that was even remotely close was "If you are not the best, you will be poor and nobody will love you," which wasn't terribly helpful. I was left with no choice but to navigate the complexities of the opposite sex all by my highly insecure self.

Jackie and I were on opposite sides of the same friend group—she was the It Girl, and I was the punching bag. Despite the social discrepancy, though, she was always super nice to me; we talked all the time in class and on MSN Messenger, but I never really knew how to act other than to be super into everything she was into. I forced my parents to buy every *NSYNC album, memorized all the songs, and tried to become as close to a prepubescent JC Chasez as humanly possible (she wanted no part of that JT shit).

In order to spend more time with Jackie, I had signed up for a choir performance of "Colors of the Wind" from Disney's *Pocahontas*, in our school's annual recital. Jackie (our best singer) was the title character, and I was one of her less-talented background vocalists. I'm not being modest; let's just say that I definitely did *not* sing with all the voices of the mountain.

My parents actually ended up coming to this recital, during which I spent the entirety of the musical number in the corner looking at my feet. On the drive home afterward, they proceeded to skewer my on-stage debut:

"You didn't even look like you wanted to be there," my mom said.

"Yeah, you should probably just . . . stick to math," my dad agreed.

In the end, although she was genuinely moved by my effort, Jackie just could not bring herself to like me back. I came out of the whole experience with a lot of anger—not at Jackie, who had been nothing but great, but at myself for being completely ill-equipped to deal with my feelings, and at my parents, who I felt had trapped me into a life I no longer wanted. They had given me neither the emotional maturity nor the social wherewithal to have any shot with girls.

And then, of course, there was the total mindfuck that came with growing up Asian and male, in a society that saw us as nothing more than a bunch of derogatory stereotypes. Asian men were frequently depicted in Western media as awkward, nerdy and completely undatable—pretty much exactly what my parents were trying to make me into. I know this is a lot of really heavy stuff to put into the psyche of a twelve-year-old, but it definitely affected me, and it definitely affected every Asian boy that grew up in a Western country. The double whammy of being teased on the playground with *ching-chong* noises and then seeing ourselves ridiculed on the screen robbed us of our natural confidence. Without proper guidance from our parents, who were not terribly concerned with our self-confidence, most of us grew up feeling like we weren't worthy to be loved or desired; like whatever we were was not enough.

Disillusioned and embittered, I began to pull away from my parents, my upbringing and my heritage. I started acting out, talking back and refusing to do homework. I didn't want to be a math genius, or a scientist, or a sidekick—I wanted to be Thomas MacDonald, the mediocre-yet-charming leading man who got B-minuses and called his parents by their first names. I didn't want to be Jackie Chan or Jet Li—I wanted to be hot stuff like Justin Timberlake, the kind of guy that dated Britney Spears and had bras thrown at him onstage.

Obviously, my parents were not down with my newfound rebelliousness.

"Look at everything we've invested in you," they spat. "You're a spoiled brat who's squandering all of our effort and money, and wasting time on useless things. You're nothing but a loser!"

"Fuck you! I don't want any of it!"

WHAP!

I can't pinpoint exactly when my parents graduated from spanking to full-on hitting, but I remember that this one particular argument ended with a slap to the face. My cheek stung from where it had been struck, and I felt my eyes well up immediately.

Honestly—they weren't wrong. Compared to the circumstances my parents grew up in, I was already spoiled simply by virtue of having access to running water. But I couldn't help that I grew up in Canada, or that my problems were different from theirs. I didn't come to Canada by choice, and I would have been just as happy growing up in Harbin with my grandparents. Because I *was* in Canada, though, I was constantly surrounded by images of what a family *ought* to be; and mine wasn't it.

I caught glimpses of a picture-perfect family through the friends I made and through TV and movies. I felt a pang of sadness whenever I'd visit a a friend's house; they always seemed so close to their parents, who in turn showered them with love and affection. My parents always seemed happy and exuberant on the rare occasion I was allowed to invite friends over, but they'd often drop the façade as soon as the last car pulled out of our driveway.

The image of a picture-perfect family was reinforced whenever I watched shows like *Full House* or *The Fresh Prince of Bel-Air*, where the parent characters were always so patient and kind. Uncle Phil wasn't even Will's real dad, and he was already doing a better job than mine. Even Catherine O'Hara's character in *Home Alone*–a movie centered around an act of parental negligence–moved heaven and earth to fight her way back to her son, and then held on to him so tightly that I thought she would suffocate him.

I, on the other hand, had grown physically distant from both my parents in the past few years. Even as I struggled to make them proud, I felt myself pulling away from them emotionally. I stopped wanting to rush into their arms, stopped wanting to be held by them and stopped confiding in them. I'd felt so happy being embraced by my mother when she picked me up from the airport. It felt like a lie now, a promise of a better life that went unfulfilled.

My parents worked hard to ensure that I was given every possible opportunity available to me–I never questioned that. But they had failed emphatically at creating a home environment that was safe for me–a place filled with warmth, physical affection and unconditional support. Whereas I was once a goofy and cheerful kid who loved giving hugs, I grew to be quiet and despondent; angry, even. I became convinced that my parents did not love me; they loved having a child that was "gifted."

Beneath all the test scores and all the accolades, there was a twelve-year-old boy who just wanted to be normal.

CHAPTER TEN

SIMU THE REBEL

With both my parents working full-time as professional engineers by the turn of the millennium, we found ourselves suddenly catapulted into the upper-middle class. That meant no more trawling around the discount aisles of supermarkets and buying groceries on the verge of going bad. It also meant upgrading from a little two-bedroom apartment to an actual house in Mississauga, a suburb half an hour to the west of the city.

Even in their splurging, my parents never spent frivolously. Our house was the smallest on the block, and most of our living space lay empty and unfurnished for years because none of us knew what to do with all the additional space (my attempts to get us a puppy were quickly and swiftly shut down).

When it came to education, however, no expense was to be spared, as long as it gave me the best possible chance at getting into Harvard, or another of the Ivy schools at the very least (Dartmouth if we were *really* desperate). And so, at the end of my sixth grade, my parents presented me with the intriguing proposition of attending what was basically the closest real-life equivalent to Hogwarts that you could find in Canada.

The not-so-magical institution in question was UTS, short for the University of Toronto Schools—an inner-city private school spanning grades seven through twelve that was also affiliated with the University of Toronto, which was widely considered to be Canada's top college. It was colloquially known as a "doctor factory" for its reputation for producing high-achieving graduates that included Olympic medalists, politicians, Rhodes scholars and yes—doctors.

Lots of doctors. *SO many doctors.* Seriously, at our ten-year high school reunion, MD degrees were like Birkenstocks on college campuses.

My parents learned of this mythical place through the Chinese immigrant grapevine and were immediately intrigued, because of *course* they were—UTS was the kind of place they dreamed of for themselves, a utopian paradise of academic achievement and constant grading. In essence, it was the next step in the natural progression of a "special" kid like me.

We attended an info session at the school together, during which we learned about its storied history since its opening in 1910. Personally, I was more impressed that, just like Hogwarts, the school had a house system that was named after its founding headmasters and had a bunch of sports teams you could try out for. You could even compete for a House Cup! I didn't care that Quidditch wasn't a sport, or that magic wasn't real, or even that J. K. Rowling named her only Chinese character *Cho Chang* and stuck her in Ravenclaw—I was in!

(Just so we're clear, *Cho* and *Chang* are both last names ... in Korean.)

Over a thousand hopeful students from across the country took the UTS entrance exam, with a format that mimicked the many IQ tests I had done at home. I made the first cut of about 250 and, after an extensive interview process, was offered a spot at the school in the fall. I picked up the acceptance letter in the mail after school, and remember thinking how funny it would be to prank my parents and tell them I didn't get in.

"Hey, it's me," I said to my mother over the phone. "I just got a letter from UTS. I didn't get in ..."

"Oh. Uh. ... okay. We'll talk about it later when I get home."

"... nah I'm just kidding. I got in. Goodbye."

Call me sadistic, but it felt good to wrestle the power out of my parents' hands, if even for just a moment, and take away that dream they had been incessantly pushing me toward. Hearing my mother's crestfallen and utterly disappointed voice confirmed what I had suspected all along—that neither she nor my dad actually cared about me. There were no words of reassurance, no "we're still so proud of you," no "this doesn't change anything," and certainly no "I love you." All she cared about was that I had failed.

So why go to UTS at all, you might ask? Why continue to play into their expectations when I had already become so disillusioned with all of it?

Well . . . it all came down to freedom.

UTS was located in the city, which was a twenty-five-minute train ride and then a half-hour subway away from Mississauga. That meant that from the moment my parents dropped me off at the train station, I was on my own. I could do whatever the hell I wanted, so long as I made the last train home at 7:15. It also meant that I needed pocket money on me at all times to buy train tickets and the occasional lunch. The alternative was staying in Mississauga, being penniless, taking a school bus every day and coming home just in time to practice piano and study for more shit I didn't care about. Where was the fun in that? I yearned to be out in the world, learning all of the things that you couldn't find in textbooks. Going to UTS was the clear and obvious choice. I figured it also wouldn't be the worst thing in the world if I somehow wound up a doctor while I was there.

At this new school, I promised myself I would finally break free of the chains of my parents' oppressive regime. I wanted to redefine myself from the nerdy kid who was shy and socially awkward (and romantically inept) to become the cool kid on campus. It was going to be life changing. It was going to be a new and exciting chapter. It was high school, which meant that it was peak incredible for like two or three people who just happened to be cool and hot and smart and rich . . . and fucking awful for the rest of us.

In the beginning, UTS was every bit as magical as its fictional Harry Potter counterpart. Before the start of the school year, we all went on a weekend retreat where I was sorted into the Lewis Vikings, which going by Hogwarts house colors was the equivalent of Slytherin. I was not a huge fan of this initially, but after a weekend of activities and house rallies I was a Viking through and through, screaming our cheer at the top of my lungs:

L, L, Give 'Em Hell
E, E, You Will See
W, W, We're Gonna Trouble You
I, I Tell You Why, 'Cause
S, S, We're the Best!
GooooOOOO LEWIS!

(I am actually, per the supreme authority of Pottermore.com, a Gryffindor.)

The UTS school building was big and ancient, a three-story brick castle almost as old as Canada itself. You could smell its age the moment you walked through its doors and could hear the floors groan and creak with each step you took. It was a school known not so much for its athletic prowess as for its total dominance of intercollegiate trivia competitions and science fairs. And then there was the Classics Conference, an annual four-day Greco-Roman extravaganza in which students from across Ontario would dress up in togas and compete in their knowledge of the Ancient Greek and Latin languages and histories, and also in athletic challenges like the discus throw and chariot race. I regret to say that I never participated in one, but my peers definitely held it down in my absence. As of the year 2020, UTS had taken the top prize twenty-three years in a row.

It was all so exciting; my parents got me my first cell phone, an old Nokia 3360 that typed text in T9 and had *Snake* as its only game. I was given my own money with which I had to buy monthly train and subway tickets but could pocket the few extra dollars to buy a beef patty or a samosa at the deli next door. It was a whole new level of freedom for me, and I promised myself that I would use this opportunity to finally break out of my shell and become that popular, extroverted, life-of-the-party guy I'd always dreamed of.

On my first day of classes, I was surprised to see that I was no longer a member of a visible minority. My grade was over 70 percent Asian, full of kids like me whose parents had pushed them their whole lives to excel academically. There were kids whose genius level far surpassed mine, like Kent Nguyen, who was taking advanced-placement calculus at age thirteen. His mom waited for him every day to finish school and take him straight home, so he could continue his studies. Socially awkward but absolutely brilliant, students like Kent were a reminder of everything I wanted to turn away from. I saw so much of my own upbringing in Kent's that I forcibly distanced myself from him. I had come to UTS with one primary goal: to be popular. Someone like Kent would only drag me down.

(By the way, Kent went on to graduate from MIT with a dual degree in math and computer science; meanwhile, I dress in tights and pretend to beat people up for a living.)

In my efforts to rebrand myself as a cool kid, I started gelling my hair, wearing baggy pants, and talkin' like I was one of the New Kids on the Block, *ya dig?!* While I didn't completely give up on my studies, they took a definite backseat to my hippity-cool makeover. I even bought this gross blond-colored hair paste that simulated frosted tips—because like I said, I was definitely not still harboring any sort of jealousy toward Thomas MacDonald.

My attempts to be popular were only moderately successful—I was coming out of my shell and becoming more outgoing, but it mostly just resulted in eye rolls from everyone around me, including the girls whose attention and adulation I craved so desperately. Lacking any sort of real skills with the ladies, I resorted to attention-seeking behavior including (but not limited to) acting loud and obnoxious whenever they were around, referring to myself as "hot" and "sexy" in what I suppose was an attempt to corner the market on those words, and doing anything I could to "elevate" myself to a sort of "celebrity" status within the school.

This brings me to—and I'm so beyond embarrassed to write about it—the story of LX4, UTS's very own (and incredibly short-lived) pop sensation.

You see, so *not* fixated was I on the idea of being in a boy band and retroactively winning Jackie's heart . . . that I actually started one. At a classmate's birthday party early on in the year, someone had made the comment that myself and three other Asian boys should totally start a boy band together.

"You guys should totally start a boy band together!"

Nobody needed to tell me twice; I thought this was the greatest idea ever in the history of great ideas. What could possibly be cooler than being in a pretend boy band? I guess being in an actual boy band, but given our lack of real talent, that was obviously not going to happen. Thus, after an intense brainstorming session, LX4 was born—named after the initials of our last names . . . times four. There was Jason L (not the Jason at the beginning of this book), the guitar-playing boy next door who wore plaid shirts and, occasionally, a fedora. There was Michael L, the goofball comedian with wild hair who was also our rapper—because duh, every boy band needs a rapper. There was Adrian L, the tall and sensitive soul who probably cried during *The Notebook* (and probably still does). Finally, there was me—Simu L, the self-proclaimed heartthrob (even though the title most definitely belonged to Jason) and also the one who took this whole boy band thing way too seriously.

No, really—WAY too seriously.

I was the guy who sent constant emails to the rest of the group brainstorming song ideas and "performances" that included shuffling awkwardly at school dances to songs like *NSYNC's "Girlfriend" Remix (ft. Nelly) or B2K's "Bump Bump Bump," and a lip sync of *NSYNC's "Gone" at a school assembly. While I'm sure the other guys went along with it ironically, because they were much smarter and more self-aware, I was living out my dreams in earnest. At the peak of my delusions I sketched out an entire album—complete with songs in Mandarin and Cantonese because we were of course going international—and suggested that we ask our music teacher to manage us.

Just planning ahead, I wrote, *not cuz I'm bossy but because I really like planning ahead! =P*

Just a heads-up—I was totally being bossy. I *hate* planning ahead, almost as much as I hate the fact that Adrian still has a record of this email somehow.

Before internal conflicts probably related to my narcissism eventually broke us up, we did actually manage to release a song in the *Twig Tape,* the school's annual album featuring original student music, called "For You." Since UTS recently digitized all of their *Twig Tapes,* you can probably find it online if you look hard enough—but I implore you . . . *please* don't.

Although our little group met an untimely demise, Asian boy bands today have become something of a global phenomenon. When I see K-pop groups like BTS and EXO tearing up the charts now, I can't help but think of LX4 and our deep, heart-wrenching lyrics:

Passing by you in the rain
Hope to see you smile (just maybe)
You turn away from me again
Tell me can't you feel this way?

If that's not the absolute epitome of awkward teenage angst, I don't know what is.

My parents, meanwhile, had both ascended within their company to positions that were as prestigious as they were demanding. They had both hoped that sending me to such a distinguished private school would alleviate the pressure on them to be as hands-on with me as they had been. But as they saw me trying my absolute darnedest to become a UTS pop star, they grew increasingly anxious. We argued whenever I stayed out late or wanted to go to a party—which was often—and our relationship deteriorated significantly. I can't say I blame them; my parents were paying nearly $10,000 a year in tuition and transportation fees under the pretense that I would be benefiting from a world-class education—aside from the house, they had never made a larger purchase in their entire lives. Meanwhile, I was more interested in being educated in all of the ways that I could make my hair look nice so that I could maybe get a girlfriend.

"What did I do to deserve a no-good son like you?"

"What did *I* do to deserve shitty parents like you?!"

Oh yeah—another interesting side effect of puberty was that I had developed a bit of a knack for talking back. I no longer saw my parents as perfect people with infallible judgment and I was quick to let them know how I felt. I'm sure you can imagine how much they enjoyed that.

If my parents were anxious about my shenanigans at the start of the year, my first report card would send them into a red-hot fury. My lackadaisical efforts in class culminated in an 82.6 average—an A-minus buoyed by a high grade in gym (94) but low ones in French (73) and history (72). Even my math grade—which up until that point was as reliable as a Steph Curry corner three—was neither here nor there (84).

My teachers' comments all generally echoed the same sentiment—that I delivered occasional bursts of good work that were often undermined by inconsistent focus and effort. Also, apparently I never handed anything in on time. Eek!

Most damning of all, UTS printed the median grade for each class next to the individual one, and I was below average in everything except for gym. Suffice it to say that my parents were *furious*. For a couple of immigrants who had never been anything other than the top of the class, having an underachieving kid was probably their worst nightmare. What was worse than working yourself halfway to death to give your child a future that they were just going to throw away?

To be honest, even I was a little flabbergasted by my performance. I had never been a bad student before; in fact, I distinctly remember using the term "Shaq-like statistical dominance" in the previous chapter.

How could I have fallen so far from grace so quickly? How did I go from prime Lakers Shaq to sluggish, meandering Celtics Shaq in the span of a single year?!

First—as hard as it is to admit, I was already a little out of my depth at a school like UTS, where there were zero academic scrubs. It was no longer possible just to coast on being smarter than everyone else; every student at UTS was hyper-intelligent and high-functioning, and the pace of the classes was designed to reflect that. I mean, the guy that sat beside me in English class ended up graduating from Harvard Law, then went on to work for the Chief Justice of the Supreme Court of Canada. What the fuck, right?! Even if I kept up with my workload and didn't let myself get distracted, cracking the top quartile of the class would have been damn near impossible. While I wasn't intentionally tanking my grades, I wasn't winning any awards for my work ethic either—my days as the prodigal boy genius were numbered.

Second—I was clearly too caught up in trying to be the second coming of Nick Lachey (Gen Z readers can replace this reference with "Harry Styles") to put up a serious effort in my studies. I remember having a crush on nearly every girl in my class at some point or another, like a lost puppy trying to latch on to anyone who would give him scratches and treats. One week I was head over heels for Francesca (another future Harvard Law alum, ugh), and another I was totally smitten by Zoe from the grade above. By the end of that week, though, I had already moved on to Ashley, the rebellious girl with a belly button piercing. These crushes didn't just *materialize* out of nowhere—they were cultivated over hours spent talking on MSN Messenger, when I probably should have been finishing my school assignments on time.

Looking back, it's easy to see that I was just looking for the love and intimacy I wasn't getting at home.

I can only describe my relationship with my parents during this time as . . . robotic. If I got a good mark, they would hardly react; it was *expected* that I do well, after all. If I got a bad mark, I was berated for being either stupid or some variation of a failure, a useless person or a waste of money. If I talked back, they would smack me around a little bit, just so I would know that they meant business. If I was reading a textbook when they came into my room to check on me, they would say nothing. If I was playing a video game or chatting on MSN . . . well, you can probably imagine.

Eventually, I grew hypersensitive to the sound of my parents coming up the stairs so that I could tab out quickly; it was practically a superpower. But, just like the Borg, they adapted to my tactics; my dad would slink up the stairs silently and peek through my open door, then explode at me if I wasn't working. I responded by maneuvering my computer setup so that the screen faced away from them (remember, kids, I come from a primitive era that predates smartphones and Mac-Books). Outsmarting them became something of a game—at least, until they would go nuclear and snap my computer game discs in half, rip up the Magic: The Gathering cards I had collected or just shut off the telephone line that our DSL modem needed to connect to the internet.

Never did they really sit down and ask me how I was doing. Never did they make me feel I was respected as an individual; not as a thing they were merely obligated to feed and clothe, but as a person with his own lens of the world. Never did they just tell me they loved me, or that they were proud of me. In my parents' mind, they had already gone far beyond what any parent was expected to do for their child. Perhaps they felt no additional obligation to be compassionate, or patient. They were like a couple of Pavlovian machines to me, hardwired to respond only to basic information inputs:

IS SIMU DOING WORK

IF "Yes," THEN DO NOTHING

IF "No," THEN GET ANGRY

DID SIMU PRACTICE PIANO TODAY

IF "Yes," THEN DO NOTHING

IF "No," THEN BERATE SIMU UNTIL PRACTICE PIANO = "Yes"

WHAT "MARK" DID SIMU RECEIVE ON <RECENT ASSIGNMENT>

IF "MARK" > "85," THEN DO NOTHING

ELSE: BERATE SIMU

SHOULD SIMU BE ASHAMED OF HIMSELF

IF AVERAGE > "90," PRACTICE PIANO = "Yes," UNIVERSITY = "Harvard"

OCCUPATION = "Doctor" OR "Lawyer" OR "Engineer" THEN SIMU IS OK

ELSE: CONTINUE TO BERATE SIMU BECAUSE SIMU = "FAILURE"

And then there were the parent-teacher interviews.

Few things in life will ever give me as much anxiety as waiting for my parents to come home from parent-teacher nights. If I got anything less than a glowing review from any of my teachers, they would just come home and unload on me. I could see the meeting playing out in my mind so clearly:

Teacher: Thanks so much for joining me, Mr. and Mrs. Liu, I'm—

Dad: Yeah, yeah. Just tell me; should I yell at my son tonight?

Teacher: Uh . . . no, that's not what I want, I—

Mom: But he scored below average.

Teacher: I mean—yes, but I think we should be looking at specific strategies to—

Dad: We have a strategy. Yelling at him.

Mom: It doesn't really help, but it makes us feel like we're doing something!

Teacher (shifting uncomfortably): Erm . . . but don't you think that you should try something else if that's not working?

Mom: What's the use? He is a garbage kid. He is useless, and stupid.

Teacher: Actually, I think Simu is a bright kid; he just shows inconsistent discipline and—

Dad: So he's throwing away his natural talents. That's even more reason to yell at him!

Teacher: No, please—

Mom: Thank you for your time. Simu will be harshly disciplined.

(This conversation was entirely fictionalized, yet somehow also completely real.)

It was only years after I graduated from high school that I realized that parent-teacher night wasn't just about throwing kids under the bus, and that parents could not only discuss specific learning strategies but also be their child's advocate when they felt the teacher was being unfair or overly harsh. My parents could have fostered a collaborative environment where we all worked together to make sure I put my best effort forward; instead, they treated me like a punching bag.

I really, honestly started feeling like I had the worst parents of all time.

About midway through my first year at UTS, the unthinkable happened—I *finally* got a girlfriend! Although my options were quite limited within the class pool due to my general buffoonery, I was ultimately successful when I expanded my search radius.

The lady in question was Jackie Chang—not to be confused with international martial arts superstar Jackie Chan, whom I most definitely did *not* date. Jackie didn't go to UTS but had several friends who were in my year. When she came to one of our school dances, she made a comment that I was "kinda hot"—and I was pretty much in from there. We proceeded to engage in a steamy teen romance that included handholding, cheek kissing and holding each other at arm's length as we slow-danced to KC & JoJo's "All My Life." It was everything a thirteen-year-old's romance ought to be, and I was so happy. In February, I took Jackie to our annual semiformal, which was kind of like a miniature prom complete with snacks and nonalcoholic beverages.

My dad came to pick me up when the dance ended at midnight. On the way home, he started on a casual line of questioning that quickly took a turn for the worse.

"So, did a lot of your friends go to the dance tonight?"

"Yeah, our whole group was there."

"Did you . . . dance with anyone?"

I shifted uncomfortably, not liking where this was going.

My dad and his sister (my gūgu), circa 1961. Not that it's a competition... but I think I was cuter.

My mom, her two siblings (my jiùjiu and yímā), and her mother (my lǎolao), circa 1964.

Mom's cohorts work in the fields of Changping during the summer of 1977.

1980–Mom and Dad pose in front of Tiananmen Square with their classmate Liuchen.

1984–My parents honeymooning in the Yellow Mountains. Something has clearly attached itself to Dad's head.

Mom and Dad on the day I was conceived. TMI? Probably.

My mom and my grandma (my nǎinai) had to manually boil water on the stove in order to give twenty-day-old Simu a warm bath.

I call this one the Joe and Hunter Biden.

Dad sitting in his shared bedroom in Tempe, where he studied at Arizona State University for a semester in 1990.

My grandpa (my yéye) giving me his best Steve Buscemi impression.

1992—My parents introduce their landlord Mary and her friend Dorothy to the wonders of mapo tofu.

Three-year-old me throwing gender norms out the window and wearing the shit out of this gorgeous dress. Sorry Harry Styles; Simu did it first!

My dad and I visit Tiananmen Square with my cousins and my yímā. I'd be on a plane to Canada the very next day.

Baby's first (Canadian) birthday!

Moments before my mother's thesis defense in 1994.

Foreshadowing my work ethic as a first-year accounting associate at Deloitte.

Mother and son, circa 1996; still one of her favorite photos of us.

Happy 2000! Bundled up at Ontario Place watching
the first fireworks of the millennium.

1999—Reunited with my Harbin
family for the first time since
I immigrated in 1994. I cried
on our last day and begged
my parents to let me stay.

Little league soccer
championships, 2000—
scored the winning goal in
sudden death overtime. Pretty
sure my life peaked here.

Mike L, Simu L, and Adrian L—three out of four members of the legendary boyband Lx4 (the legends were greatly exaggerated).

Spent the 2004 summer break with my mother's family in Beijing.

"Um . . . yeah. Kinda."

"What's her rank in the class? Is she smart?"

"I don't know actually."

"What do you mean, 'you don't know'?"

Ah, fuck.

"Well . . . she doesn't go to UTS."

As expected, my dad did not like this. His face dropped instantly into a scowl.

"You brought a girl that doesn't even go to your school?"

"She's Katrina's friend, it's not like she was just a random girl . . ."

I trailed off because I already knew he wasn't listening anymore. He had already made up his mind that he was going to be angry.

"You're such a shame to this fucking family," he muttered, as he stared forward in disgust. "Goddamn piece of . . ."

And then he hit me.

"WHO THE HELL ARE YOU? ARE YOU EVEN MY SON ANY-MORE?!" he screamed, as he struck me repeatedly in the head with his free hand. I didn't know what to do; I cowered as far away from him as I could on the passenger side and put my hands up to protect my face until he stopped.

We rode the rest of the way in silence.

I wept silently in my bed that night, grieving for the last vestiges of the little carefree child that once looked upon his parents with wonderment and admiration. Although our time in Canada had not been perfect, I still held on to the many happy memories of my early years with them. They'd planned birthday parties for me, accompanied me onto roller coasters they could barely stomach riding, and watched me wolf down Happy Meals while they themselves pretended not to be hungry. Despite all of the bumps and bruises that we had been through since, a part of me had always held on to the hope that we would find our way—that my parents would one day sweep me into a deep, powerful embrace that would mend the holes in my heart and melt away all of my doubts and anxieties. But that fantasy was gone now, burnt to ash and replaced with the kind of darkness and rage that My Chemical Romance wrote songs about.

From that night onward, my parents ceased to be my guardians and protectors—and became my enemy. Home was not a place to go to feel comfortable and safe—it was a war zone where violence could break out at any second. In order to survive, I'd have to pick myself up out of my own self-pity and man the hell up. I steeled myself to this new reality by developing a new set of rules to live by. I would not let the enemy into my life—it would just give them an opportunity to exploit my vulnerabilities. I would not show weakness—my tears would just make them think that they had power over me. I would not fear pain—if I got beaten, I would hold my head high to show them that they could not break me.

Most important, if I had to hurt them back in order to protect myself, so be it; if that was the cost of staying alive, it was a price I was willing to pay.

CHAPTER ELEVEN

EYE FOR AN EYE

Over the next few years, my parents would become the primary antagonists of my life. Our interactions at home were overwhelmingly negative, resulting in either raised voices, slammed doors or slaps to the face. It was always two against one; as an only child, I didn't have an ally in the house to stick up for me or to calm my parents down.

For the most part, my performance at school continued to be mediocre, which only fueled our conflict more. I was a perennial underachiever, scoring consistently below the class average in every subject except for gym, which I always just crushed. All of the feedback given by my teachers reflected more or less the same thing:

> *"He needs to continue to work on his test preparation skills."*
> —Ms. Straker, 7th grade science

> *". . . has yet to acquire the patience to do the necessary practice to improve his drillwork and basic skills. Until he does this, he will continue to make needless and careless mistakes."*
> —Mr. Weiss, 9th grade math

> *". . . capable of excellent work, but his efforts appear inconsistent, with occasional weaker work or late assignment."*
> —Ms. Straszynski, 9th grade science

*"Simu lacked the discipline for making a consistent effort
in this course. Consequently, his progress was limited."*
—Mme. Collier, 9th grade French

*"Simu shows talent as a performer. His sense
of presence is a strong foundation to develop
skills as an orator, presenter, and actor."*
—Dr. Gamble, 9th grade English teacher and, apparently, wizard

The picture that these comments paint . . . is 100 percent accurate. Without the proper discipline or the mindset to excel at school, my marks went straight to shit. In courses like physics and chemistry, which required a ton of home study in order to properly grasp the concepts, I got the lowest marks in the entire class. For my parents, two decorated engineers, it was a slap in their face (figurative, unlike the actual slaps in the face that I got).

Meanwhile, not only was I not doing my homework, I was also barely going to class—I was leaning heavily into my identity as the sporty kid and was constantly cutting out of classes early to go to our football, basketball and volleyball team games. I had shed my runty, scrawny frame as I sprouted to a solid 5'11" with broad shoulders, fast twitch muscles and a six-pack, which I didn't really deserve but was happy to take credit for. It wasn't like I was some sort of sports phenom, though—every team I was ever a part of was mediocre at best, and absolutely cringeworthy at worst (our basketball team once got beat 72-11 by Central Tech, a nearby school). UTS was a doctor factory, after all, not an athletics juggernaut; I was merely playing in a small pond.

My parents would always deflect any compliments I received from their colleagues about my appearance. They loved to quote the Chinese proverb sìzhīfādá, tóunǎojiǎndān—roughly, "developing in all areas of the body except the brain."

Ouch.

For what it's worth, I always managed to keep my average above 80 percent, despite very lackluster marks in the sciences. True to the diagnosis of the man who evaluated me nearly a decade prior, I was a natural when it came to English and history. My math grades were mediocre, but I did always have flashes of brilliance when we participated in provincial math competitions; I guess you could call it muscle memory or something. It was enough for my parents to continue paying for my tuition year after year, in the hopes that I would finally turn things around. Despite all of the fights that we had, they were still committed to the idea of giving their child what they themselves never had growing up. While it was an admirable decision on their part, it also meant that they had something with which they could lord over me constantly.

"We're not rich like your friends' families. Do you think it's easy for us to send you to this school? Do you even *know* how much money you are costing us? Have you never ever thought about how much you let us down?!"

I always hated how much they cared about money—it was easily the one thing they would bring up the most in our arguments. It became almost insufferable to be at home with them, so much so that I would lie and miss trains on purpose just to get home later.

This was an incredibly bleak time for the three of us—one that was particularly difficult to revisit in the process of writing this book. My parents certainly weren't keen on potentially being portrayed as sadistic monsters who took pleasure in constantly arguing with their only son, nor was I champing at the bit to air out all of our dirty laundry. Still, I also couldn't shy away from the realities of what happened. My parents were not monsters—they were frustrated at their inability to connect with their son, tired and overworked from the constant grind of their jobs, and resentful of how much money I was costing them.

As sympathetic as I am to all of this now, though, I also know that it doesn't change how deeply and profoundly I have been affected by their abuse. My parents have come a long way since the events of this chapter, and we all look back on this time with complicated feelings of guilt and remorse. Our hope is that families like ours will read our story and understand where we went wrong, so that they can make a different choice—a choice to listen, and to be kinder to one another.

• • •

There is a line from *Good Will Hunting*, one of my favorite movies, that resonates deeply with me. In one of his therapy sessions, Matt Damon's character talks about the abuse he suffered at the hands of his foster dad, who made him choose between a stick, a belt or a wrench to be beaten by.

"I chose the wrench."

"Why?" Robin Williams's character asks, confused.

"Because fuck him, that's why."

Sometimes, red-faced and ears ringing after getting slapped hard across the cheek, I'd stick my neck out toward them, asking for more. At least then, I was the one in control; at least then, they would understand that no matter how hard they hit me, they would never bend me to their will.

This probably resulted in me taking way more beatings than I needed to. It was scorched-earth warfare; you hurt me, I hurt you right back.

My mother was a constant instigator, as stubborn and unwilling to back down as I was, and ever so quick with her venomous words:

"Cheryl's mother called last night," she would say with an air of nonchalance. "She won a school-wide award for having the highest average in her grade—a 96.8. Isn't that just incredible?"

"You should stop comparing me to other people," I'd mutter back.

"Compare?!" she would say incredulously. "Don't flatter yourself; you're nothing like Cheryl, and you never will be."

My fate was sealed from that point, because there was no way that I was going to take that from my mother without a fight.

"Fuck you," I spat. It was basically my way of saying "just fucking hit me." And she would.

One time, I thought I would get the last word in by provoking her and then barricading myself against the door in my room. My mom came upstairs, forced her foot through the door, pried it open and delivered an MMA-style beatdown as I curled up into the fetal position to protect my head.

My father was no doormat, either. Over time, his docile, harmless personality had twisted into a sort of Jekyll and Hyde–like dynamic—he was gentle and even-tempered most of the time, but would redline in the blink of an eye. He didn't lose control often, but when he did, it always hurt. He would hit with his feet and his closed fists, all the while stringing together curses in Mandarin that would make a sailor blush.

Although he definitely hit harder than my mom, my father's physical violence paled in comparison to his skill in psychological warfare. He excelled at invading my privacy and thereby eliminating any shred of safety and security I still felt at home. He would frequently barge into my room to yell at me, sometimes six or seven times a night, as if to let me know that there was no hiding from him.

I also quickly learned that keeping my thoughts and ideas in a physical journal was out of the question, as he would rifle through all of them when I wasn't around. Amid my LX4 delusion, he came across a song I wrote in a notebook called "Celebrity," about a guy gloating at the girl who rejected him because he had become famous.

"I read the little 'songs' you wrote," he sneered at me. "'*Oooh, look at me, I'm a celebrity*'? It's the saddest thing I've ever read."

Admittedly my "song" was an absolute turd sandwich, but sue me; I was fourteen and I wanted people to notice me. I tore up my pages and never wrote another line of music. It seemed like there was no line my parents weren't willing to cross; to this day, I still struggle deeply with setting boundaries for myself and for others.

After I stopped leaving any physical traces of my life that could potentially be discovered and exploited, my dad went digital. He discovered my MSN Messenger chat logs, which were auto-generated, and read every online conversation I ever had—including, unfortunately, my sorry-ass attempts at flirting with girls. Again, this was all used against me in one way or another. My dad would always find a way to slip something into conversation that let me know what he knew, as if to tell me that there was no way to hide from him.

To teach my father a lesson, I would fabricate conversations between me and my friends and save them in the chat log folder, knowing he would read them:

Simu: btw be careful what you write here, my dad reads my chatlogs lol

Stan: wtf that's so messed up

Simu: right?!

Stan: seriously my parents would never do that. they are so great, and definitely don't beat me

Simu: wish i could say the same man . . . unfortunately i can't. cuz they totally beat me

Stan: damn dood. that's child abuse!

Simu: yes. yes it is.

Stan: invading your privacy is, like, really uncool too. your dad should b ashamed of himself

Simu: i agree. he should totes b ashamed of himself.

Stan: kk . . . well i gtg. hang in there you handsome fox!!!

Although I'm certain he read them, my writing didn't end up changing much. As you can clearly tell, it wasn't exactly riveting stuff.

The next step in my counteroffensive was to destroy my parents' spotless reputation. My mom and dad had risen quickly through the ranks at their workplace, and had become something of a power couple. They were admired for their work ethic and for raising a UTS-worthy child. They were walking embodiments of the immigrant dream fulfilled, and I resolved to put a black smudge on their perfect legacy.

I started spilling our family drama to anyone who would listen, including my parents' colleagues and their children. I spun a narrative that painted them as the aggressors and myself as the victim who just wanted to make his parents happy, knowing that the juicy gossip would find its way to their workplace. I'd even confide in my aunts and uncles in China when we would visit during the summers, hoping that they would somehow talk sense into my parents.

It never happened.

I'm not proud of lashing out like this, but I also stand by my reasons. A part of me really hoped that if I just made enough of a fuss, someone would step in and fix what was wrong with us. I was alone and desperate for help, while the two people I was supposed to count on were actually the cause of my suffering.

The single incident with my dad that lingers the most in my memory was actually not violent at all. It happened in tenth grade, after multiple consecutive days of verbal and physical arguments. I was particularly beaten down, drained and dispirited. In a rare instance where I showed weakness to my enemy, I lay in bed and just cried. When my father came through the door, he paused, took one look at me . . . and ridiculed me:

"You're such a phony. Who are you acting all dramatic for?" he said angrily, as he approached me. "Were you expecting us to feel sooooo guilty seeing you crying? *'Oh, my poor wittle child, my poor, poor baby!'* " As he mocked me in his crying voice, he pretended to hug me reassuringly, patting my back like he was consoling an infant.

I have never felt more betrayed than in that moment. The truth was that, deep down, there was actually nothing I wanted more than a true moment of reconciliation with him. But my father saw me showing a sliver of vulnerability, and then twisted the knife in the wound.

I know that my father was not evil, and I know that he didn't deliberately intend to inflict deep emotional scars. It must have been difficult empathizing with a child who he wholeheartedly believed had a far easier life than he did. I didn't really know what it was like to grow up constantly hungry because there wasn't enough food, or to have to uproot your entire life to travel halfway around the world to start from the bottom all over again; my biggest concern was figuring out why I wasn't more popular at school. Our respective teenage problems were not even *remotely* similar, and it's not hard to come to the conclusion that I was spoiled when you compare them side by side. My father couldn't see his son crying out for connection when he burst through the door; he saw only a petulant, self-indulgent child who refused to listen. Try telling that to sixteen-year-old me, though.

The next day, utterly alone and tired of fighting a losing battle, I decided not to come home from school. I hadn't planned to run away or anything, but when my last class ended, I just couldn't stand the thought of being back under the same roof as either of my parents. I stayed at my friend Peter's house that night, and just went to school with the same clothes the next day—yes, including underwear. My phone had long since run out of battery at this point, but I didn't care to check in with my parents. I stayed at my friend Andi's that second night, and my other friend Adam's the night after that. Being a good Asian kid, I never missed a class the whole time. The longer time went on, the better I felt; I am not exaggerating when I say that I wasn't homesick in the slightest.

(Disclaimer to all of the kids reading this—if you insist on running away from home to spite your parents, be safe, keep up with your homework and for the love of God have the foresight to pack extra underwear!)

On my fifth night away from home, my parents grew panicked and began to call my friends' houses to try to figure out where I was. Of course, if they had known anything about their extremely ostentatious son, they'd have known that it was a school dance night—and I *never* missed dance nights. A call was made to my LX4 bandmate Mike L's cell, and then finally patched through to me.

"Hey," I said flatly.

After a long pause, my dad spoke:

"*Hi, Máomao. Are you all right? We were worried about you.*" His voice was somber and apologetic, which kind of made me feel bad for ghosting him until I remembered that both he and my mom waited a whole five days before bothering to look for me.

"Uh-huh."

Another long pause.

"I know things haven't been perfect, son. I know it hasn't been easy with us. But just . . . just come back home, and we'll work it out. I promise."

I didn't believe him, but I was also fresh out of food, money, and clean underwear; I had no choice but to relent. My parents drove downtown and picked me up after the dance ended.

As I stared out my backseat window on the ride home, I came to terms with the fact that I was losing this war. Even as I scored small victories, they never amounted to anything that even remotely benefited me. I was spending most of my energy fighting when I should have been studying or planning my future. In fact, I'd allowed this conflict to define my entire life. Meanwhile, I was still fully reliant on my parents, and would stay that way so long as I was stuck in their house and not making any money of my own. In order to truly win, in order to be truly *happy* . . . I needed to be free of their control. In the short term, that meant being as self-sufficient as I possibly could. Long term, it meant landing a good enough job that would get me as far away from them as possible.

It was time to put my anger and resentment aside and start actually giving a shit about my life.

CHAPTER TWELVE

THE ASTRONAUT

When I was a little boy in Kingston, I would devour any book I could find about the wonders of space. I would read about astronauts like Neil Armstrong and Buzz Aldrin, and would watch shows about spaceships boldly going where no one had gone before.

(Although I have to say, I never much cared for *Deep Space Nine*, which wasn't so much about an exploratory vessel and more about a stationary facility.)

I'd imagine myself floating in a vast and infinite expanse of nothing, far beyond the reach of Earth's gravity—weightless, unburdened . . . and totally free.

In an eleventh-grade playwriting unit for English class, I wrote a short piece about my relationship with my parents called *The Astronaut*. In it, a teenager dreams about playing with his father as a young child:

"What do you want to be?" the Father asks.

"I wanna be an astronaut!" the Boy exclaims, pointing upward at the ceiling.

"You can be an astronaut, soaring in the sky and going to space!" The Father picks his son up and twirls him around in the air, the two of them giggling the whole way. "You can be anything in the world!"

It's a beautiful (and totally cliché) moment between parent and child, until we go LIGHTS OUT.

"Wake the *hell* up!"

LIGHTS ON to reveal the present day, as the teenager is woken up violently by Father, who has since become mean and abusive. Father rips the sheets off the bed to wake his son up, berating him for being worthless the whole time.

"What are you doing with your life? What do you even want?"

"To be an astronaut," the Boy replies simply, leaving his father to grapple with the happy memory they once shared.

The week I turned sixteen, I got my learner's permit and got a job making coffee at Country Style, a Tim Hortons knockoff that in my opinion had equal if not superior coffee compared to its name-brand competitor. My friend's mother had bought the franchise, and it just so happened to be down the street from where I lived—it was a perfect situation for a first job. I started out doing a couple of shifts on the weekends, and gradually got more hours as I got better.

I wish I could say that I was working out of some altruistic desire to repay my parents for everything they had done for me, but it couldn't be further from the truth; I only ever wanted to be free from them. Having money and the ability to drive would further diminish any power and authority that they had over me.

My desire for independence was so great that I would take the car out for joyrides around the block illegally when my parents weren't home. In Canada, the learner's permit only allowed you to drive with a parent or guardian in the passenger seat, but I obviously didn't care, being the kind of edgy rebel that runs away from home only to still attend all of his classes.

One day, after doing a couple of laps around the street, I pulled back into my driveway . . . and accelerated straight into my garage.

Yup.

I never fully figured out how I managed to confuse the gas pedal and the brake in my brain, but I did, sending all two hundred horses of V6 engine power straight through the door and the brick beam in the middle. I sat in my car for almost ten minutes, utterly shocked and mortified, knowing that my parents would kill me when they got home. And oh, boy, did they ever.

You'd think I'd have learned an important lesson that day about taking things without asking, but I found myself feeling strangely ambivalent that night, as my parents yelled and screamed at me. It just felt so . . . predictable. I knew that there was nothing I could say or do that would change their behavior; so why try at all? I had run out of empathy for my parents many beatings ago and had long since made up my mind that I wasn't going to let them stand in the way of what I wanted.

If anything, it solidified the opposite—that in a world where the yelling and hitting would come anyway, asking for permission was just stupid.

Going into my senior year, with graduation looming just over the horizon, I finally began taking the reins of my life, rather than just allowing myself to be dragged along. I gave up on being an engineer or a doctor (I think we all knew that was coming) and dropped all of the science courses that were weighing me down. I built my course load around English, art and math instead, which were my strong suits. My average skyrocketed to a 91.5 after the first term, which opened me up to my pick of the litter when it came to college programs (as long as it didn't have anything to do with chemistry). When I triangulated the convergence of all of my talents, it led me to . . . business and economics?!

It all made sense as far as I could tell; economics was the study of money, and I wanted to make lots of money to move far away from my parentals. I also didn't hate the idea of driving a nice car to work every day with a fancy suit—so business it was!

After a few hard years, senior year was when it began to turn around for me, and it was due in no small part to the friends I made. My parents used to tell me all the time that blood would always be thicker than water. In essence—nobody will *ever* truly love you as much as your own kin. It may have been true for them, but having gone through what I had, I wasn't prepared to accept the reality that their version of "love" was the only one out there.

My athletic rival in every sport was Jason (not to be confused with Jason L, the fedora-wearing heartthrob from LX4), a spiky-haired Asian kid with as much of a chip on his shoulder as I had. From basketball to volleyball to break dancing, we both always gravitated to the same hobbies and interests.

Jason and I each shared a desire to be noticed and popular but were similarly relegated to the B-tier of the social hierarchy. The *real* kings of UTS were Raman, Ricky and Robin, who represented the trifecta of athleticism, academic prowess and sheer coolness. We all fancied our-selves to be good dancers, but whereas the R's were always encouraged by cheers and applause, Jason and I were often met with laughter and eye rolls. This of course instantly bonded us, and we set about trying to prove to the world that we, too, belonged with the cool kids. Years later, I don't think we've stopped.

My big brother and my rock was Peter, a tall and lanky white kid who was more fascinated by how cars worked than how to execute the perfect body wave. Peter was the introvert to my extrovert, the scientist to my free-spirited artist. Our friendship first began on subway rides home together, where we connected over our mutual love of video games and Star Wars, and evolved to sleepovers and weekend cottage trips with his family. To me, the Goshulaks were the perfect example of what a family ought to be—unconditionally loving, always patient and unflinchingly supportive. They graciously took me in when things with my own parents were turbulent, dubbing me the sixth Goshulak after Peter and his two sisters, and even nicknaming the basement "Simu's room."

I know you're probably thinking that the Goshulaks white-saviored me, and you may not be *entirely* wrong—but it really just came down to them seeing a child in need, and making the decision to help. Peter's family didn't solve all of my problems by being white—he and his par-ents, Deb and John, taught me how to be a part of a functional family, including the responsibility that came with it, so I could create one of my own one day. They never once made me feel like my Asianness was the problem, or something to be ashamed of. The Goshulaks taught me how to love, and I was in turn able to teach my own parents years later. For that, I will never love them any less than my own flesh and blood—even if some of them still can't use chopsticks properly.

Despite my renewed motivation to do well in school, I obviously never outgrew my attention-seeking ways. By senior year I had developed into a pretty good singer and hip-hop dancer, becoming a permanent fixture at the school's various dances and coffeehouse nights. My favorite part of the year was the night of the culture show (affectionately dubbed "the Show"), a massive school-wide production filled with crazy outfits and dance numbers in salsa, wushu, Bollywood and more. It was an opportunity to strut my stuff in front of a captive audience, and I relished in it. Years removed from the anxiety of that *Pocahontas* performance in the sixth grade, I had grown to love the spotlight. It felt unlike anything I had ever experienced before, even back in Harbin—it felt like I was truly home.

A few months before Show night, out in the grass parkette beside my school where we often played pickup soccer after class, my mind was blown when I saw Ricky (of the UTS "kings" I mentioned earlier) launching his friend into a massive backflip.

"DUDE, THAT WAS SO COOL!"

Ricky was a provincial dance champion, who wound up being in the final round of cuts on the first season of *So You Think You Can Dance: Canada*. He could do it all, from ballet and jazz to hip-hop and acro—and although I'm sure you've stopped caring at this point, he also ended up going to Harvard. Naturally, I thought he was the coolest fucking human being I had ever seen, and I absolutely *had* to learn a backflip from him in time to do it onstage for the Show. I begged him to teach me his awesome ways, and he most generously accepted.

"Sure, bro, come on over and put your right leg up on my hands!"

I went over to face Ricky and put my hands on his shoulders to balance as I propped my right leg up as I was told. Ricky braced his hands against his knee for support and gave me a reassuring nod.

"Okay, bro; we're gonna go on a 'five, six, seven, eight' countdown. Throw your hands up on '*seven*,' swing 'em down on '*eight*,' then jump and lean back and let me do the rest. Vlad and Jeff are gonna be right there to catch you if anything happens. Got it?"

"I think I'm gonna throw up, but let's do it!!" I felt my heart beating out of my chest in anxiety, but I was too committed to back out now.

"Let's do it, brother! Five, six, seven, eight, GO!"

With that, I leaned back and felt my stomach turn inside out and upside down as I hurtled through the air. After what seemed simultaneously like an eternity and a split second, I felt my toes touch the ground. A few disorienting seconds later, my brain finally caught up with what had just happened. Adrenaline surged through my veins as I looked at Ricky with my mouth agape.

"HOLY SHIT! HOLY SHIT! YESSSSS!!!"

"FUCK YES, BRO, YOU DID IT!"

"TEACH ME HOW TO DO IT FROM STANDING!"

"THAT'S GONNA TAKE A WHILE BUT YOU WILL TOTALLY GET THERE!!!"

True to his word, Ricky would meet with me almost every day to teach me the standing backflip, counting down with me and keeping a hand on my back for safety until I got it. It's no wonder he was so universally loved at school; the man was a legend through and through.

If I could describe the feeling of doing a backflip to you in a single word . . . it'd be *free*. Free, like the feeling of driving a car alone, cruising down an empty street with the windows down. Or the feeling of making $7.50 an hour pouring coffee on the weekends.

Or the feeling of floating weightlessly across the sky, as the world below watched in awe.

Upside down in the air, I was everything I had ever wanted to be: ostentatious *and* awe-inspiring, showboating *and* charismatic. I hounded Ricky to learn other tricks, like an aerial (kind of like a cartwheel with no hands), a round-off back tuck (a cartwheel where the legs come together and punch into a backflip) and a 540 (a flying spin kick derived from wushu), and pulled all of it out onstage for the Show.

Beyond just the adoration of the crowd—which, believe me, I loved—I became addicted to the rush of doing the seemingly impossible. Outside of school I joined the "tricking" community, a movement-based art form that borrowed from martial arts, gymnastics, breakdancing and parkour. Tricking was a countercultural art form, and most of its people were not unlike me—a little socially awkward, and often coming from difficult family situations. They all saw what they did as an escape, and I was no different.

Needless to say, my parents thought that this was a colossal waste of time. But what could they do? I was pulling an A-plus average in senior year and was on track to attend a top business school in the country—not to mention I was making my own money, too. Like I said before, I had lost interest in winning my parents' approval a long time ago.

The extra cool factor with tricking was that its most prominent members were stuntmen in TV and film. Even in Toronto, I'd either met or heard rumors of people who had worked with Jackie Chan when he came to town to shoot *The Tuxedo*. I remember how excited I was just to know a guy who knew a guy in the biz—my only other encounter with Hollywood up until that point was in the ninth grade, when UTS was chosen as a location for the ballroom dancing movie *Take the Lead* starring Antonio Banderas.

Did it cross my mind then to give acting a try? Absolutely. *All* the time. Movies were a form of escapism for me, and—given my situation at home—I needed a *lot* of escaping. My parents would drop me off at the theater on a Saturday morning if they'd have to work overtime, and I'd hop from movie to movie with my refillable popcorn and soda until sundown. I'd watch whatever was out (I think I saw *X2: X-Men United* three times in a row), imagining myself as the hero of the story while millions of people watched from their seats. I longed to entertain them, and to bask in their admiration and praise . . . but it was never more than just a fantasy. I may have been a gutsy kid, but even I was scared to give myself permission to pursue a career as an actor. As far as I knew, people didn't just *become* actors—they were chosen or anointed, either due to nepotism or their transcendentally good looks. I, having neither one of the two going for me, figured it was just a fun thing to daydream about as I pursued a successful career in business.

When college acceptance letters came out in the spring, I was two for two between business schools at the University of Toronto and Western University, the latter of which was the highest-ranked business school in the country *and* was farther away from home—both massive ticks in the "pro" column. So just like that, after five years of mediocrity from seventh to eleventh grade, I wrestled victory from the jaws of defeat and landed myself in a very respectable program . . . while still playing on sports teams, going to dances, working at Country Style and, of course, learning to backflip.

This time, there would be no pranks; I laid out the acceptance letter on our dining table at home the day I got it and waited to show my parents when they came home. It might have been the first time the three of us smiled together in years.

Would this be the moment that my mother and father would finally come to terms with their mistakes? Would we shed tears of joy as we embraced each other, finally reconciling as a family?

Come on, now; we're barely halfway through the book . . . that's way too early to resolve the central conflict.

Just when I thought that we had maybe gotten to a good place, my parents left me hanging high and dry during my own graduation ceremony. It was supposed to be a time of celebration, with all of the proud mothers and fathers watching from their seats as their children crossed the stage and received their high school diplomas. I guess for my folks, it was a time to get mad at all of the amazing scholarships that everyone *else* had.

"Raman Srivastava, attending Western University—Nesbitt Gold Medal, Dr. T. M. Porter Award and Beverley Matthews Awards for School Captain, Western's Continuing Scholarship, Wendy's Classic Achiever Scholarship Award, Canada Millennium Scholarship, Apple National Scholars Award."

"Peter Wills, attending Mount Allison University—University of Toronto Schools Spirit Award, Literary Pin for Extracurricular Contribution."

And then, there was me:

"Simu Liu, attending Western University—Entrance Scholarship."

I guess that my lack of multiple scholarships must have really offended my parents, because at the post-ceremony reception where the students in my graduating class were all laughing and taking pictures with their families, they were nowhere to be found. I searched around, worried they might have gotten lost, and found them in the school's front foyer about to leave.

"Hey . . . there's a reception in the gym after the ceremony. All my friends are there with their parents."

"We're going to go home," my dad responded curtly. As I searched each of them for answers, their faces told me everything I needed to know; they were too ashamed to stay.

"Okay," I said, as simply and flatly as I could. "I'm gonna go to the after-party and then stay over at Peter's. I'll see you tomorrow."

"Sure."

I had a great time with my friends and slept perfectly fine that night. I'm pretty sure I even did a drunken backflip in someone's yard. I mean, why would I lose any sleep? Of *course* they would still be ashamed of me; I was their utter failure of a kid who never practiced enough piano, wasted time playing basketball and flipping around, and graduated with but *one* lousy scholarship to the best business school in the country. If I had learned anything throughout my senior year, it was that I didn't need my parents in order to feel happy, or listened to, or loved; I had my friends for that. I had already spent far too much of my life crying over the way they treated me; I wasn't going to give them the power to hurt me anymore.

When I say that high school was the worst fucking time of my life, I'm not being hyperbolic. I was a troubled child plagued by insecurity and self-doubt, with a massive hole in his heart that he was always trying to fill with the love of other people. Some people were nice to me, some rolled their eyes, and some straight up bullied me. Hey, I get it; high school was a dog-eat-dog world, and I was an easy target. *Someone* had to be the punching bag.

But although I may not have been the kind of jock-y, super-popular stud that I saw on TV, or the captains of the school like my friends Raman and Ricky, at least I had *tried*; between playing on sports teams, dating girls, losing my virginity and even starting a band, I had somehow managed to piece together a pretty comprehensive high school experience for myself. If it were up to my folks, none of that would have happened; I'd be letting my teenage years pass me by, doing dumb shit like vectors and advanced calculus and definitely *not* having sexual relations of any sort. And while some of my classmates may have been feeling anxious about leaving home for college, I could not have been more excited. Homesickness was for people who actually *had* homes; I was an astronaut, after all, whose only home was the eternal vastness of space through which I floated, untethered and unencumbered by any familial attachments.

High school was over, and I was finally on my own; I was finally free.

CHAPTER THIRTEEN

SIMU THE SUPERFROSH

There were no tears the day my parents dropped me off at Western University.

After we had moved my last piece of shitty plastic furniture into my shared room, I walked my parents back to their car for our final farewell. It was the late afternoon of a beautiful fall day, and despite being located in the otherwise gray and dull city of London, Ontario, the Western campus was absolutely picturesque—its mix of old-style gothic and newer brutalist buildings stretched across over 1,000 acres of land, which itself was beautifully landscaped and full of hills and lush greenery. The ground was covered in maple leaves in autumn colors, lest we forget that this was the *Canadian* London, not the English one.

"Well . . . I guess this is it," I said, quoting every college send-off scene in cinematic history.

"Be good," my dad replied. Unsure of what else to do, he whacked my shoulder and laughed.

I nodded. "Sure."

"Phone us if you need anything, all right?" my mom said as she got in the car.

I nodded again. "Mm-hmm."

Even though none of us said it out loud, I knew that we were all feeling the same thing—not sadness but *relief;* relief that after six years of disappointments, unmet expectations, arguments and even physical violence, there would finally be peace. I knew that they wanted to leave the past behind every bit as much as I did—and believe me, I *really* did—but something stopped me just short of wrapping them both in a hug and acting as if everything was just fine. Things *weren't* fine, as none of us had actually addressed anything that happened over the past six years. Still, a bit of distance meant we at least wouldn't be within striking distance of each other. Given that talking about feelings was exceedingly rare in our household, a cordial relationship was the best we could collectively muster.

As I watched my parents drive off into the horizon, I felt a weight begin to lift from my shoulders. I was finally untethered, finally *free*—I could stay out late with friends, play video games in my room without constantly looking over my shoulder, and eat dirty-ass junk food for breakfast, lunch and dinner. I could be whoever I wanted.

My college experience would differ pretty significantly from Beijing Jiaotong University circa 1977—for starters, I'm pretty sure my parents never got to experience the total shitfuckery of a 9 a.m. pancake kegger. Unbeknownst to them, Western University had a reputation for being a bit of a party school—so much, in fact, that *Playboy* magazine once ranked it the fourth-best school for student life in *all of North America*. That should tell you everything you need to know about the culture at the school in the pre-woke era of 2007—it was the place to be if you wanted a *gooooood* time. I have to admit that while that wasn't the primary reason I chose Western, the idea of getting absolutely *schmammered* with thousands of female freshmen every night certainly didn't repulse the younger and dumber version of me.

According to legend there was no place "wilder" or "sexier" than Saugeen-Maitland Hall, a two-building residence that housed a third of the entire freshman population in its 700-plus shared rooms. Nicknamed "the Zoo" for the outrageous parties and shameless fornicating that occurred in its halls, Saugeen had a reputation that extended far beyond the walls of Western's campus and across all of Canada, mixing truth and fiction along the way. Yes, the stories of the Saugeen stripper of 2005 are completely true, but no, Saugeen was *NOT* on a David Letterman Top 10 List of Places to Get Laid. My roommate-to-be Derek and I ranked Saugeen dead last on our residence applications, which of course meant that was exactly where we got assigned. Into the Zoo we went.

If only I had used my newfound freedom to think critically about what I actually wanted to do with my life, and about the person I wanted to become...

Oh well—time for shots!

I would have my very first run-in with fame during freshman orientation week...sort of.

It was during one of our student rallies, where upper-year student leaders called *sophs* would organize us by our faculty or our residence and hold large events designed to break the ice and get us out of our shells.

Imagine, if you will, 1,200 students wearing the same Gildan T-shirt chanting:

"DEEP IN THE HEART OF THE WESTERN JUNGLE, YOU CAN HEAR THE SAUGEEN RUMBLE—OOH. AAH. OOH-AAH!"

During a social science faculty rally, we were separated by gender and made to do this absolute gem of a cheer:

"SOCIAL, SOCIAL, SOCIAL..." the boys would scream/grunt as they thrust their hips forward three times.

"Siiiiigh!" the women, enamored by this show of manliness, would swoon.

That's it. That was the cheer. And we'd repeat it, like, sixteen times.

Aside from promoting groupthink and heteronormativity, the sophs also organized a talent competition called the Superfrosh. It was an annual tradition for Western's three science departments (social sci, med sci, and health sci—together, the "tri-sci") to put together a variety show during O-Week, where crowd reaction and a panel of sophs judging first years' talents decide who would be crowned that year's Superfrosh. In the first round, each faculty would have to choose their individual champion, after which each champion would compete against each other for the ultimate title.

It was just like the Tri-Wizard Cup from Harry Potter, except with less magic and more mediocrity.

In a crowded gymnasium, the social science sophs invited anyone to just walk out onto the floor to show off a talent if they thought they were worthy of the Superfrosh title. Some people screamed really loudly. A bunch of white guys danced off-rhythm. A guy threw a chair, like . . . not that far. I swear to God, that was the talent level that we were dealing with.

I sat there watching this clusterfuck of mediocrity from the bleachers, wanting to claim my stage but also feeling absolutely terrified of doing so. Maybe this was my opportunity to taste a bit of that thing I had fantasized about so often. Who was I to deny myself of that? I got up, walked down the bleacher stairs and out onto the floor, found an open runway among the bad dancers and chair throwers, and ripped a roundoff that punched into a backflip. I heard the crowd grow suddenly quiet as I sailed through the air . . . and then explode as I landed on my feet. Just like that, I was quickly ushered over to the sophs and crowned the champion of social science!

Later that night, with the entire freshman body assembled at an on-campus park, I was brought out onto a larger stage in front of a larger crowd of over 4,000 new students. As the other champions were brought onto the stage, I quickly realized that we had done something wrong; both med sci and health sci had selected *two* representatives, whereas I had to carry the mantle of our faculty all by myself by pulling double duty!

In round one, I faced off against a rhythmic gymnast from health sci and a singer with a smooth voice and an acoustic guitar from med sci. When it was my turn to take to the stage, Timbaland's "The Way I Are" blasted from the speakers and I twisted, flipped and bodywaved my way across the stage to the delight of the crowd, using everything I had taught myself in high school when I probably should have been studying. In this super low-stakes competition where absolutely nothing was on the line, I was experiencing the biggest rush of my life.

Round one ended with three strong performances and no clear winner. In order to take the title and win the fame that I had so desired, I knew I was going to have to step up!

Round two began with yet another singer from health sci and a juggler from med sci. As my turn approached, I knew that the right strategy would be to show a different part of myself rather than more dancing and flipping. And so, I told the sophs to kill my music, walked out onto the platform, and launched into an a cappella rendition of "This I Promise You" by *NSYNC, a song that I had dreamed of serenading someone with one day. Now I was doing it to an audience of 4,000.

"When the visions around you . . ."

The crowd was dead quiet, but I could feel their energy in the air, pointed toward me. I closed my eyes and sang softly.

". . . bring tears to your eyes . . ."

Then, murmurs of people beginning to join in.

By the time I reached the chorus, thousands of voices all sang in unison:

"THIS I PROMISE YOU!"

Maybe I had chosen the perfect song to connect with the audience. Maybe it was the fact that I got to show two completely different talents while the other champions only showed one. Either way . . . I WON!

(Objectively, I'd say that Nathalie, the rhythmic gymnast, was definitely more talented.)

It was honestly like playing out a weird childhood fantasy; I was the big man on campus for a few months, which was not a common thing for an Asian guy at a Canadian university in 2007. I was inundated with offers for high fives, drinks and yes . . . *phone numbers.* People screamed "It's the Superfrosh!" to me on the street. I was even in the homecoming parade on the social sci float—sporting a purple crown and a lei per the official school color. I sang Backstreet Boys songs into a microphone as the parade wound its way through the streets of London and as my floatmates yelled and screamed in front of me.

I basked in my Superfrosh "fame" the way that any awkward eighteen-year-old would—completely shamelessly. Many of my high school classmates had judged me for being a bit of a tryhard and a show-off, leading me to constantly question myself. Now, my weird skills and talents were not only being judged, but *celebrated* by the entire school?!

Sorry, Mom and Dad, the universe hath spoken.

Although I had undoubtedly made a big splash in my first week at university, I *was* going to have to actually go to class at some point.

The HBA program at the Ivey School of Business was a two-year program that accepted students from both high school and sophomore year in university. Students that were pre-accepted from high school like me were called AEO (Academic Excellence Opportunity) applicants. As long as we took a full course load and maintained an 80 average, we could enroll in any major we wanted for our freshman and sophomore years of college. I chose Business Management and Organizational Studies (B-MOS) to give me a solid foundation in the field that I was deeply passionate ab— Nah, just kidding; it had an easy course load, which would leave plenty of time for the student life that Western was so famous for.

The enriched curriculum offered by UTS prepared me extremely well for freshman-year classes; if I'm honest, it probably made me even lazier. I stopped going to calc after a few classes because they were just reviewing what I had learned in senior year. I showed up to my sociology classes to take the quiz for participation marks, and then left during the first break. I never met my statistics prof but finished the course with a 91 percent (I always had a knack for probabilities and permutations).

By no means was I the sort of boy genius that my parents had hoped for . . . but I certainly acted like it. More so than ever before, I committed myself to doing the absolute minimum amount of work possible to ensure that I kept my average. Why try any harder than I had to? Besides, who had time to study when there were so many enriching, thought-provoking clubs to be a part of?

First, there was CAISA, a club for all of the "cool" Asians on campus. You'd think that with a name like the Canadian Asian International Students' Association, we'd spend a lot of time talking about racial issues to achieve a better understanding of our cultural identities ... but no; it was more or less a glorified excuse to throw house parties, wear Abercrombie and go clubbing on Richmond Street, London's student nightlife hot spot—you know, traditional Chinese stuff. A sophomore girl I met at a CAISA party and briefly dated would get me my first fake ID—I was briefly twenty-seven-year-old My Van Nguyen of Windsor, Ontario! She even gave me a matching credit card with his name on it.

Come to think of it, I never did ask her how she got those ...

Then, there was the CSA (the Chinese Students' Association)—a far cry from the Chinese Students' Association that had picked my father up from the airport in Arizona eighteen years ago—which for all intents and purposes was the same as CAISA, except some of their socials were held at Chinese restaurants and bubble-tea joints. CSA ran a singing competition called the "Asian Idol," which I gleefully auditioned for and subsequently got into with my smooth rendition of Edwin McCain's "I'll Be," only to lose to a Korean freshman with the voice of an angel.

Damn you, Peter Lee, you magnificent human ...

There was also the VSA (Vietnamese Students' Association), whose pho socials and clubbing nights I also participated in with great enthusiasm—and no, you did not have to be Vietnamese to join the club.

Fortunately for me at the time, my roommate, Derek, was in a long-term relationship with someone who lived on campus in a suite-style residence, meaning that I could have the room to myself most nights.

I didn't deliberately set out to be a part of all the Asian cultural clubs on campus—since all of my friends were in the same clubs, I never really gave it much thought. Looking back, I feel like there was some level of comfort in being around people who had very similar lived experiences as I did. We all had our different friend groups from class, or intramural sports, or otherwise; in our Asian bubble, though, we didn't have to worry about being judged, or discriminated against—we could simply exist.

That isn't to say, by the way, that I didn't join other clubs or activities; I went to meetups for the rock-climbing club and participated heavily in intramural sports. Derek and I even got ourselves cast in the Saugeen musical, in a little production of Andrew Lloyd Webber's *Joseph and the Amazing Technicolor Dreamcoat*. While I had a lot of fun doing all of those, though, I never quite felt the sense of community that I did with the cultural clubs.

But then . . . there was Hip Hop Western.

In the mid-2000s, the world was caught up in a particularly bad case of dance fever; *So You Think You Can Dance* was the highest-rated show on TV, movies like *Stomp the Yard* and *Step Up* dominated the box office and the Jabbawockeez had just been crowned on *America's Best Dance Crew* (although I was always more of a Kaba Modern fan). I swear, one summer I even overheard my parents raving to each other about Katee and Joshua's beautiful hip-hop duet to "No Air," choreographed by the legendary Tabitha and Napoleon.

If you don't know what I'm talking about, you need to drop this book and YouTube it. Now.

I myself had always loved to dance, harkening back to my perfect school dance attendance record at UTS and the school-wide culture shows I had participated in. When I heard that Western had a hip-hop team that performed at school shows and traveled to compete against other universities, I just about lost my mind. Even though I had never taken an actual hip-hop dance class in my entire life, I knew in my bones that I had to try. After all, I had just won the Superfrosh by free-styling onstage in front of thousands of people—this was another opportunity for me to spread my wings and dance in front of a crowd!

I signed up for the hip-hop club, registered to audition and promptly found myself in a small-town Canadian version of *You Got Served*. The team was led by a girl fittingly named Flo, who coincidentally graduated from UTS two years ahead of me. Flo was every bit as smart and capable as anybody who'd walked UTS's halls, but she was also a mold breaker who wore baggy cargo pants with one leg rolled up—and not to mention, a *dope* dancer. I was equal parts inspired and smitten, which was unfortunate, seeing as she had a very cool, very talented boyfriend who was also *very* thirty.

Flo's passion for dance gave me permission to also deviate from my prescribed path. There was no long-term plan, other than to just continue doing things that made me happy.

It wasn't all fun and games, though; I had made a commitment to be a part of a competitive team, and we needed to train.

It was the UTS culture show on a whole other level; the crew practiced almost seven nights a week leading up to OUCH, the Ontario Universities' Competition for Hip-Hop, which was held at the nearby MacMaster University in Hamilton. It was like a full-time job—when we weren't learning and drilling choreography, we were attending drop-in classes or dissecting dance moves on YouTube. I'd quickly learn that dance wasn't just about expressing oneself, but about being a team player—and that meant understanding the importance of staying in formation and syncing your movements to everyone else's.

The concept of the performance was fun and campy, like most dance numbers were—we were mannequins in a department store that came to life and threw down when the lights turned off. We moved seamlessly from song to song, showing off our different styles; the precision and rhythm of step, the rawness of krump, the body control of pop n' lock. My friend Jon and I brought an array of tricks and flips to the table, which helped punctuate our performance even more. At the end of our three-and-a-half-minute set, we returned to our mannequin forms, sliding back into our positions as the store opened again and the crowd exploded into applause.

We ended up placing fourth out of eleven schools, which we could not have been happier about. Most of Flo's teammates had graduated the year before, so we were virtually an entirely new team that had surpassed all of our individual expectations. The competition committee had brought in Luther Brown, an industry vet and choreographer for artists like Nelly Furtado and Shawn Desman, to judge the crews. I didn't have a clue who he was before, but based on the resume alone, Luther was immediately elevated to hero status in my books.

After the competition, we waited as Flo went over to retrieve our official score sheet from the judge's table. When she emerged from the crowd with the sheet in hand, we all anxiously scanned it for Luther's comments.

My heart stopped as I got to the bottom of the page:

Those flips were SICK!

Holy. Fucking. Shit. There it was.

Getting props from the audiences, the judges and my teammates was validation on a level that I had never experienced before. Growing up, I had always been scolded and held back. Now, for the first time, I was being told to *go for it.*

That night, as we celebrated, I began to wonder for the first time if there was a world where I could be doing something like this for a living. *What if I could be in a music video? Or go on tour with a famous singer?* I pushed the thought away almost as soon as it entered my mind. I was definitely NOT ready to throw away everything my parents had invested in me. I loved performing, being onstage and expressing myself through movement . . . but I couldn't throw away my entire education for a pipe dream.

At least, that's what I was trying to tell myself.

In reality, my mindset had already grown dangerously self-destructive; by the time freshman year ended, my care level for what I was learning in class was at an all-time low. I was dragging myself through the motions while most of my friends were doing everything they could to prepare for Ivey. Meanwhile, all of my time and effort was spent either on Hip Hop Western or trying to look cool in front of girls.

It's amazing how your mind can play tricks on you sometimes. While I was consciously rejecting the notion of pursuing my dreams and my passions, there was no denying that a fundamental change had occurred inside of me. Like a sleeper agent oblivious to his own programming, I continued to play the part of an engaged student in front of my friends and family.

"How are classes, Máomao?" my parents would ask without fail every time they called.

"*Really* good! I'm learning so much about how businesses are run," I'd answer. "I definitely think I picked the right major for me. I think I'd do well at a job where I can work with numbers."

I don't know which thought is scarier—that I was capable of lying to my parents and myself so convincingly . . . or that under different circumstances, I might have actually gotten away with it.

CHAPTER FOURTEEN

ABERCROWANNABE

Over the summer, my AEO friends racked their brains looking for sum-mer jobs that would bolster their resumes—internships at financial in-stitutions, data-entry clerkships, even bank teller positions—you know, building blocks for an actual future in the business field. I, on the other hand, had set my sights on something that would bolster, shall we say, a resume of a very *different* kind:

I wanted to be an Abercrombie model.

Maybe it was because my parents never raised me to be "cool," or because the media always portrayed Asian men as nerdy, asexual sidekicks—either way, I had grown sick and tired of having that social status withheld from me. I wanted to be HOT, goddamnit!

In pre-recession 2008, Abercrombie and Fitch had a monopoly on the "hot guy summer" look; blond windswept hair, fair sun-kissed skin, broad shoulders and abs that could scrub the stains off of your dirtiest clothes—an Aryan wet dream. I both resented and admired this white bastion of male beauty and wanted nothing more than to be ogled and pined for the way that these minimum-wage employees were. Everyone remembers what it felt like to pass by an Abercrombie or Hollister store at the mall—to smell the pungent fragrance that the entire store was drenched in, and to peek in at the "models" that were hanging out in ripped jeans and flip-flops practically ignoring the customers. It was so painfully obnoxious, yet you couldn't help but want to be a part of it, even just a little.

Word on the street was that store managers would "scout" you to be a "model" if they deemed you to be Hollister or Abercrombie "material." As I clearly did not fit their ideal mold, my trips to their stores were always peaceful and very much uninterrupted.

Damn. If I was going to get my foot in the door, I was going to have to get their attention another way.

One of the few things I picked up in my first year in a business program was how to convey professionalism and speak eloquently. I knew that if I could just get an interview with the store, I'd most likely beat out the competition. So, dressed in a crisp shirt and tie and with a manila envelope of resumes in my hand, I walked into a Hollister and asked to speak to a manager. Hollister was Abercrombie's slightly more accessible subsidiary, so I figured it was my best shot.

"He'll be out in a sec!"

The employee I spoke to was a Filipino girl with a gorgeous smile. It wasn't a particularly busy day, so I tried to make conversation while I waited.

"So . . . do you like working here?"

"Oh yeah, everyone's pretty chill, so it's a good time!"

That is the coolest answer to any question ever, I thought.

When the manager came out from the back, I shook his hand firmly and introduced myself. He was an older guy who looked like he could be in a topless firemen's calendar or something. I could feel him looking me up and down, trying to figure out if I was worthy. I knew I wasn't an easy yes; I never was, and I never will be. However, after some deliberation, the manager—probably named Hunter, or Brody, or . . . Riley but spelled *Ryleigh*—gave me a nod and asked me to come back for a group interview.

A week later, as expected, I crushed the group interview and became a Hollister model. A few weeks later, I befriended some folks at Abercrombie and was able to parlay a transfer. Just like that, a kid who was never going to get scouted to model anything achieved his very important and *very* meaningful goal of being the guy wearing a tight polo greeting customers with a smirk and a tagline (*Hey, how's it goin'?*) at the front of the store.

I continued to work for Abercrombie for the rest of the summer and again during Christmas break, dropping it into conversation at every opportunity because of *course* I would. Judge me if you want, but I had a point to prove: that Asian guys came in all shapes, sizes and types—including smokin' hot.

(In retrospect, I was like a 7 in the body and a 6 in the face on a good day; I'm quite sure that I was just a diversity hire.)

Like the Abercrombie brand, I'd like to think that I've matured significantly since then. I've learned that there is so much more to life than looks, and that I had so much more to offer than just wide shoulders and a six-pack. Although, to be perfectly fair, I had those too.

Whether you like it or not, you're getting better at something every day. I know that sounds like some esoteric TikTok life coach bullshit, but bear with me.

No matter what you choose to do with your day, you are either helping to create a new habit or solidifying old ones. When you are making an active decision—say, learning French, or picking up the bassoon—you are teaching your body to pick up a new skill. When you are engaged at work, you are becoming more knowledgeable and more efficient at the tasks that comprise your job. Have I just been paraphrasing Malcolm Gladwell's 10,000 hours theory? Maybe.

The thing is, though, Gladwell's theory applies to more than just music lessons or learning a new language—it includes the bad stuff too. Did you put off an important task today? Congratulations, you just got better at procrastinating. Were you late for a meeting? Awesome, you're becoming a master of tardiness! Did you stay quiet about something you should have spoken up about? Cool, just keep chipping away at that backbone and it'll be gone in no time!

By the time freshman year ended I had grown quite proficient at skipping class, scrambling to catch up, and then somehow pulling off a respectable grade in the final (thank goodness for lazy profs that recycle questions from past exams and don't even bother to change the numbers). That trend continued into second year, where the curriculum had definitely advanced to the point where it required more of my attention; we were delving deep into financial modeling and economic theory, neither of which I knew the faintest thing about. Unfortunately for my grades and for my future, I had gotten really good at not caring.

So what *did* I care about?

When I look back on my years in university, I see an anxious and insecure young boy who was constantly made to feel like he wasn't enough. Whether it was wooing an audience on a stage with my singing voice, dazzling them with dance moves or impressing them with my Abercrombie job, I really just wanted people to like me. Even the decision to go to Ivey had much more to do with the optics of attending a top business school than with any real interest in economics and capital markets. I wanted to be seen, to be admired, and—most important of all—to be loved.

It probably doesn't surprise you that I had some pretty major attachment issues during this time.

I had cobbled together some twisted idea of attraction and romance through AskMen.com and *Cosmo* magazine (you had to know what the other side was reading!) and through movies like *How to Lose a Guy in 10 Days* and *Hitch*. I'd throw my heart at any girl who gave me even the slightest sliver of attention, while convincing myself that I was in love with her. Maybe you've been this guy, or dated him at some point—a walking rom-com caricature, full of sweet words and grand romantic gestures but short on substance or any modicum of self-respect. While it may sound sweet and cute on the surface, especially to some of the younger readers, imposing your view of love onto others is probably one of the most selfish things you can do.

I could tell you countless embarrassing stories of the lengths I went to in order to win a girl over—the "perfect" dates I tried to engineer, the disgusting hypermasculine bravado I adopted—but there is one that

I'm particularly ashamed of. Naturally, that's the one I have to tell. For science.

There was a freshman at Western—let's call her May—who exuded a bright and vivacious energy to all those around her. She was as beautiful as she was smart, as athletic as she was beautiful ... and criminally flirtatious to top it all off. I fell hard for this girl, and I was absolutely ecstatic to learn that my feelings were reciprocated ... sort of. May liked me, but perhaps not enough to make me her boyfriend; per millennial dating etiquette, we were in a casual fling. Of course, being me, I wanted to be with her forever.

Talk about coming on strong.

May was understandably a little put off by my enthusiasm, and maybe a little embarrassed that she even liked me. She was very adamant that we keep things under wraps, and so I became something of a guilty secret. It was kind of like an affair, except I was literally competing with no one—and losing. I knew that May was a bit of a volleyball nut, so I went with her to the student rec center almost every day in an effort to impress her. In public, she would barely acknowledge me—in private we snuggled and kissed and talked for hours on end. I kept on diligently, hoping that I would eventually win her over with my persistence and be able to hold her hand in public.

What else was I gonna do ... study? *HA!*

May and I were making out in her dorm room one day when a few of her male friends texted that they were coming over to drop off some class notes. Naturally, May freaked out.

"I can't be seen with you," she said, looking frantically around for a possible solution. When her eyes settled on the bathroom door, I knew immediately what she would ask of me.

"I need you to hide in the bathroom."

Now, anybody with even a modicum of self-respect would have told May to go to hell and then walked right on out of there. Unfortunately, I was still a few years away from figuring that part out; I obliged and stood in the darkness for fifteen minutes as she greeted and chatted with her guests. In my naive mind I thought that this could be my grand romantic gesture that could finally win May over. All it really did, of course, was cement my status as a complete loser in her eyes.

I continued to pine for May much longer than I'd like to admit, but we eventually did break things off—not that there was much to break off in the first place. She was fickle and probably enjoyed love and attention as much as I did, but it was nothing to hold against her; we were both young and stupid in our own ways. It took a long time of us sorting through our own insecurities, but May and I eventually became really close friends—as a bonus, I'm also still pretty great at volleyball.

I reached out to May when I was deep into writing this book to help me go through our early days and to provide some insight into what the hell was wrong with me. She, like me, had matured into a steadier and more self-assured version of herself.

"Little Simu tried really hard," she wrote me. "He craved attention and praise but didn't actually have the experiences or confidence to back it up. It was almost too easy to bully him because he always made such a big scene about himself."

It hurt, but it was a fair assessment. But May wasn't done:

"You worked really hard to make every interaction movie-magic—picnics, hand holding, nose snuggling when we were cold at night. I felt it! Expectation. You always wanted a fairy tale. You were constantly proving yourself: to me, to your family, to your friends, to yourself. Everything had to be a statement, a loud one. You couldn't quite relax, and that meant I couldn't, either."

All right, May, getting a little real now—

"I felt like you wanted us to be perfect—already. There, then. Ten years ago. The cutest. So complete you wanted to scream it to the world. You already lived so obnoxiously in your own spotlight. There was no room for failure; it was too suffocating before it even started."

Wait—

"Your words were manipulative, mean, and designed to hurt—a skill we both inherited from our parents and upbringing. I'm admittedly still a tiny bit careful now. In the breakup, you wanted to tarnish my reputation . . . you wanted everyone to know how I messed up and how

I wronged you. We met up a few times, and you towered over me to recite my sins to my face while I cried."

Oof.

"By the way . . . can you make it clear in your book that we never had sex?"

May was absolutely right; I was miserable every day and thought that I could only be happy once I found the love of my life. Sure, she definitely should not have asked me to go into that bathroom—but my love-life issues were mine alone, the result of a total absence of intimacy in my home life. I made myself into a victim and blamed everything on May, using her to justify my anger just as I had used her to justify my love earlier. In trying to undo what my parents had done, I had become just like them—vindictive, hurtful and cruel.

Meanwhile, as I was dancing and playing volleyball and pining for May, I almost failed out of school. Another year spent half-assing my classes had sent my average plummeting below the threshold to get into Ivey; my end-of-year average came out to 78.5 percent (that's abysmal by Asian standards), missing the floor by a mere 1.5 percent. I tried to focus and push through to get where I needed to be, like I did at the end of high school, but there just wasn't enough time to reverse the damage that being lazy had done. By the end of my sophomore year, I was staring at an average that was too low to get into the prestigious program I had been fast-tracked into.

But I wasn't willing to give up that easily. Despite being a pretty undermotivated guy, I did possess some talents—I was scrappy and resourceful when I needed to be. Surely, I could figure out a way around this. I scoured the school's website for options and found what was to be my saving grace—students that fell short of the AEO cutoff could explain any extenuating circumstances and ask to be granted leniency.

Bingo.

As luck would have it, I rolled my ankle playing pickup basketball and ended up not going to classes for almost two weeks. So, I wrote a heart-wrenching essay that painted the picture of a diligent student who fell behind in class because of a terrible injury and was never quite able to catch back up, and submitted it to the admissions office.

Between you and me, I probably wouldn't have gone to most of those classes anyway—but Ivey certainly didn't need to know that. If they ever saw the true extent of my laziness, there'd be no chance in hell that I would be admitted, and my life would have played out very, very differently. Thankfully, the admissions office took pity on me and let me in.

I had averted disaster.

I wish I could tell you that this close call was a moment of clarity for me, after which I really locked in and focused on my studies—unfortunately, what actually happened was pretty much the exact opposite. I had become an expert at not doing any work; the more I got away with it, the more my behavior was enabled.

The Ivey School of Business modeled itself after Harvard's case study method—every day, in classes of about seventy-five, we would tackle a real-life business scenario that had been adapted for the classroom. Our classes covered a wide range of topics, from Sales and Marketing to Leadership and Public Speaking. It was a highly effective method of teaching that was directly applicable to the real world, provided that students prepared adequately for each class—which, of course, I didn't.

On my first day of classes I could immediately tell that I was dealing with a vastly different breed of student. Incumbent Ivey kids were not at all like the dumb, borderline illiterate eighteen-year-olds that I'd wiped the floor with during my freshman year—these guys read the *Wall Street Journal* every morning and monitored the stock market religiously. They were alphas, who strode around campus with the absolute conviction that they were the literal white knights at the vanguard of a capitalist society just ready to be exploited for all it was worth, and they were ready to make it go their way. Most of them came from considerable wealth—some were scions of multibillion-dollar corporations.

You could mock their *American Psycho*-level douchery and harp on their arrogance, but there was no denying that these were men and women with *goals*. Unfortunately, the same could not be said about me.

And so, instead of preparing the next day's casework and reading *The Economist*, I continued to invest heavily in extracurricular activities like volleyball, *Halo 3* and *Guitar Hero* with my new roommate, Mark, a lanky and shaggy-haired white dude with whom I instantly bonded over our mutual love of Xbox. I'd show up to classes underprepared, sometimes without having even read the case.

You may be wondering how I managed to even pass a single class at this point.

Actually—I almost didn't.

One semester in, I opened my grade report and nearly had a heart attack upon seeing that I had scored a 55 in Finance. *This is insane,* I thought. I knew I wasn't the perfect student by any means, but no way did I deserve a 55! I immediately scheduled a meeting with my prof, to see what was going on. Perhaps she had a vendetta against me because I had fallen asleep in her class one too many times?

"Actually," she said to me sympathetically, "I tried to boost your mark as much as I could."

Wait . . . what?

"Your effort level just wasn't there, Simu. It's like you don't even want to be here. The best I could do was to not force you to repeat the course; I'm not going to adjust your mark any more."

Damn. I showed up to the meeting ready to proverbially throw down, but wound up getting my proverbial ass handed to me.

That 55 cast a black mark on my career prospects coming out of school. You see, the name of the game at Ivey was landing the best possible job out of graduation—and in order to land a good job offer out of graduation, you needed to secure a strong summer internship after your junior year.

There was a definite hierarchy to the types of jobs we could get—the most coveted and well-paying jobs were investment banking and management consulting, which went to the top 10 to 15 percentile of the entire class. Following that top tier was a variety of other jobs in corporate finance—analysts for banks, corporate finance for businesses and marketing analysts for consumer packaged goods. At the very bottom of the pecking order was accounting—infamously unsexy and painfully dry, accountants enjoyed an incredibly low starting salary but relatively high job security.

I was self-aware enough to know that I would never land a top-tier offer with my marks, but I had always felt that an accounting job was within my reach. My lower starting salary would grow over time, provided that I became a chartered professional accountant, but the work would be easy enough that I could continue doing what I loved—playing Xbox with Mark.

Perhaps most important, a career path in accounting gave me the means to finally get my parents off my back. Raised in simple, working-class families, my parents knew nothing of the financial markets or corporate structures—to them, there was no difference between an investment banker and an accountant. In fact, they might have preferred the latter, as one of their close friends from China led a highly successful career in the field and was now an accounting prof at a nearby university.

"*Accounting is a very safe career*," they said over the phone, regurgitating exactly what their friend had told them. "*And if you don't want to be an accountant forever, you can still be safe and find a place to teach.*"

Ugh. Between piano lessons and accounting, I was beginning to wonder if my parents had any original thoughts when it came to raising children. Still, without any direction of my own, I could only acquiesce to their wishes. If it meant appeasing them with minimal effort, then so be it—at least that meant more *Halo 3* with Mark.

As our second semester began, so too did Ivey's infamous recruiting season. Each night, a different group would come to our school to give a presentation on their firm and why we should be clamoring to work for them—afterward, the recruiters would hold a networking session in our school atrium with hors d'oeuvres and refreshments (which I always made sure to help myself to), where eager students would try to make an impression before sending in their applications.

It was like the worst kind of speed dating; for every recruiter there were anywhere from ten to thirty keener kids dressed up in suits hovering around them like creepers at a bar, clutching their uniform business cards and searching for some space to slide into the conversation.

Now, despite what you may have inferred from my work ethic, this was actually right in my wheelhouse.

You see, as shitty as I was at the technical courses like Finance that required tons of prep work, I was actually very good at the ones that focused on developing soft skills, like leadership and public speaking. I was a strong, articulate speaker, which helped me in interviewing and networking scenarios. I'm not entirely sure where this came from, but I always just had a knack for making things *sound* good. I was often the designated copywriter for group projects, having parlayed my writing prowess so that I could be spared from any of the technical work.

When the recruiters from the major accounting firms came around, I turned on the charm, asking all of the right questions. *"I was wondering how deeply your firm was impacted by the switch from IFRS to US GAAP?" "Can you tell me how Deloitte best supports its employees through the UFE process?" "What are some of the challenges of auditing a financial services firm, where most of the assets are tied to the market and therefore constantly in flux?"*

It was some of the best acting work I had ever done.

I did well in all of the networking sessions I attended, and even got a personalized gift basket from the folks at Deloitte (one of the "big four" accounting firms) to let me know that I was on their radar. But of course, nothing was guaranteed, as I hadn't yet shown my grades to anybody. I knew that my 55 would make me a hard sell despite my excellent in-person skills—I would need to pull out all the stops to even remotely have a chance.

Summoning all of my writing talents, I penned the following cover letter to Deloitte's recruiting executive:

I first wanted to say thank you for taking the time to present at the Ivey Information Session this past Monday; I had a great time speaking with you and I hope your presentations at the Universities of Laurier and Waterloo the next day were similarly successful! I wanted to take this opportunity for you to get to know a little bit more about me, and why I would be a great addition to Deloitte as a Summer Associate.

My first semester of HBA1 did not go as well as I had planned academically; I earned a very low mark in Finance, a course which would ultimately be a part of my ICAO average. I was unwilling at first to make the drastic lifestyle adjustment that Ivey required. This decision cost me dearly, and I regret that I stand before you with an academic record that is anything short of what Deloitte deserves from a candidate.

I cannot erase mistakes I have made in the past, but I can show you what I have learned from them and what I have done to come out stronger. Today, I stand before you as a well-rounded candidate with relevant work experience, strong leadership and interpersonal skills, and competitive academic marks

I am tremendously excited to have the chance to work for Deloitte, and I hope we can meet again soon to discuss how I can be an asset for your firm.

This letter had everything—accountability for my shortcomings, a promise to do better, and then tangible proof that I was taking the steps to better myself. Sorkin himself would be proud! I sent off my masterpiece and waited with bated breath the rest of the day, and then the next. Finally, the partner responded:

"Hi Simu, thanks for letting me know. It was very honest and mature of you."

Nice! What a save—

". . . Unfortunately, the mark puts you below our minimum cutoff for summer associates. I encourage you to continue focusing on improving your studies, and I look forward to your application next year."

Shit.

As the rest of recruiting season wrapped up, my higher-performing classmates were inundated with offers—most of them had to choose between two or three. One by one, they matched with their internships, until only a few candidates remained. I did end up making a real effort to improve my marks, but it was too little too late—I was among the bottom of the barrel.

Out of options, I swallowed my pride, called my old Abercrombie manager, and asked to have my job back for the summer.

CHAPTER FIFTEEN

SIMU THE FRAUD

I went into the summer of my junior year with no job prospects and my tail between my legs. I knew I was either going to have to figure something out or suffer the humiliation of coming back to school in September with nothing to brag about in front of my alpha Wall Street classmates, who I was sure would be regaling each other with stories of their summers spent with Merrill Lynch or Goldman Sachs. I needed to put my slacker ways aside–if only temporarily–to get myself out of this hole.

Over the summer my buddy Steve, a student of the Rotman School of Business at the University of Toronto, let slip the date and location of UofT's summer job fair. Now, UofT had a great business school–definitely one of the best in the country–but it was just a tier below Ivey in 2010. I knew that if I could get myself into the fair somehow, I could probably make a good enough impression to secure a job that wouldn't cause me to lose too much face in front of my parents or my classmates.

Steve procured for me his friend's ID, and I ended up getting into the venue without a hitch–probably because the guy at the door was white and couldn't tell the difference anyway. It was your typical run-of-the-mill career fair, held in a massive space with each prospective employer set up at a booth like a trade show. I immediately filtered out any minimum-wage jobs and multilevel marketing (does anyone remember those knives with Vector Marketing?!), which immediately slashed my options. I also wasn't a programmer, which whittled down my choices even further. After a few minutes of looking around, I somehow found myself talking to a recruiter from Weston Bakeries, the manufacturer of Wonder Bread in Canada, about a summer internship opportunity in their marketing department. *Jackpot.*

Now, the idea of working for a consumer packaged goods manufacturer may not seem that sexy or appealing on the surface, but it was actually an incredible opportunity to learn the fundamentals of how a brand was created. Weston Bakeries didn't just make Wonder Bread, which was their kid-oriented line; they also made Country Harvest, a female-focused line of healthy breads, and D'Italiano, which was a more male-centric bread you'd most likely see at a backyard barbecue. Everything you see on the shelf of a grocery store, from Corn Flakes and Lucky Charms to Dunkaroos and Lunchables, has its own brand team, which is constantly monitoring sales data and then coming up with ways to capture market share. Consumer packaged goods (CPG) marketing was a highly competitive environment, with heavy hitters like Procter & Gamble and Johnson & Johnson at the very top. Definitely not too shabby as far as internships went.

"So how do you like your classes at Rotman so far?" the recruiter asked.

"Ha—actually, funny story . . . I don't go here."

The recruiter actually loved the fact that I had snuck into the career fair, took my resume and called me for an interview the next day. From that point on, it was pretty much a done deal. You see, interviews were my bread-and-butter, my ultra-clutch turnaround jump shot that always swished right through the net. If I had an interview, chances were I was getting hired.

For those of you looking to brush up on your in-person interview skills, I'm gonna give away my secret sauce right here in this chapter, free of charge.

Are you ready for this?

It's all about CARBs.

Let me explain—say your potential employer asks you to describe a time when you were suddenly thrust into a position of leadership. These types of "describe a time when . . ." questions are *incredibly common* in nontechnical interviews and are designed to gauge not only your actual answers, but the way in which you give them.

For argument's sake, let's say you did a short internship at a small tax-consulting firm in the summer of your sophomore year like me, and your boss had to quickly leave the country halfway through to tend to a family issue.

You might be tempted to just answer like this:

Well, I did a short internship at a small tax-consulting firm in the summer of my sophomore year, and my boss had to quickly leave the country halfway through to tend to a family issue. So I pretty much had to be my own boss, which was pretty crazy.

I mean—sure, that technically answers the question, but it doesn't give the employer anything to go off of. What does "being your own boss" mean? What is the "crazy" you are referring to? Why do you sound like a sixteen-year-old kid trying to get a job at a Foot Locker?

So, most business schools will tell you to use the CAR technique to formulate a proper answer—Context, Action, and Result. First, provide a clear context:

Well, I was an *analyst* at a *midsize* tax-consulting firm in the summer of my sophomore year, and my boss had to quickly leave the country halfway through to tend to a family issue. *The two of us were in the middle of a massive client audit at the time, so his absence meant that I had to really take the reins of the entire project.*

Then, action—what *exactly* did you do to persevere in this scenario? Be as specific as possible:

While he was gone, I had to become the de facto point person between the company and the client, liaising directly with their accounting team to maximize the amount of money we would recover for them. I also had to increase my work output, which I managed to do by compartmentalizing my time, working through my lunches and in some instances taking work home. There were some hard weeks for sure, but I knew that my boss needed me to really step up, and I was ready for the opportunity to prove myself.

Finally, give a tangible, concrete result:

As a result, we were able to still finish the audit on time and saved our client over $150,000 in recovered taxes from the government. My boss was extremely satisfied when he returned from his trip, and it felt very rewarding to be able to take ownership and challenge myself to do more than my job description.

Much better, right? Instead of being vague and wishy-washy, I clearly identified the challenge and how I overcame it. But wait—there's more! Whereas most business school kids would stop at the R, my secret was the subsequent B: Bringing it back to the present, so that we can tie up this answer perfectly. Allow me to demonstrate:

I think it's really important for you to hire a candidate who is able to self-motivate and rise to challenges, because you never know when unforeseen circumstances are going to throw a wrench into your best-laid plans. You might think you are just hiring an entry-level employee, but that employee may find themselves in a situation where they suddenly have to take on more responsibilities. At that time, you need someone reliable who can jump into a leadership role with confidence and enthusiasm.

Although it's been over a decade since my last real job interview, it worked back then; Weston Bakeries ended up hiring me a few days later, and I very happily called my Abercrombie manager to hang up my flip-flops and distressed denim jeans for good.

Of all of the classes I had taken in business school, marketing was probably the only one I had any sort of knack for, probably because it was the only one that required any sort of creativity. So, it was actually really interesting working at Weston Bakeries during the summer of 2010. I loved the idea that something as commonplace as bread could be packaged and marketed to different types of consumers. While selling bread may not have been my ultimate calling in life, I felt engaged every day and genuinely enjoyed what I was doing. Plus, it was infinitely preferable to being the one guy at Ivey who couldn't get a job.

My most memorable day, though, was when I was invited onto the set of a commercial shoot for D'Italiano. It was an early morning start at a beautiful mansion by the lake in Port Credit, an affluent suburb just outside Toronto. I knew I should have been observing what my brand manager was doing, but I couldn't take my eyes off of the actress that we had hired—not because of how she looked (although she was very pretty), but because she was the first "working class" actress I had ever met. I was endlessly curious about the life she had.

Throughout the day, I kept asking her questions. *How did you get into this? Is it glamorous? Do you have an agent? Can I have an agent? Which agencies are best in Toronto?!* She was a phenomenal sport and entertained all of my inquiries. I had only ever been exposed to the straight-and-narrow way: go to school, get a degree, graduate, get a job, make money, buy a house and then die. For me, this woman was my first exposure to a completely different career path—one in the arts. This day on set would stir something up in me, a curiosity that is still burning bright over a decade later.

When I finished my internship at the end of that summer, I was thanked warmly and told that there unfortunately weren't any full-time positions available for the coming year. That was fine by me, because it was still my intention to get that job at Deloitte. Even though

I clearly enjoyed marketing more, I was still very much a victim of my programming—I wanted the status that came with putting a suit on every day and working in a slick office in a skyscraper on Bay Street (our Wall Street equivalent).

Despite everything we had been through, I could not help but want to please my parents. And I was about to get my chance.

Full-time recruiting season at Ivey began right at the start of our senior year in September. I prepped my resume, business cards and a collection of interview scenarios, and zeroed in on Deloitte like a hawk on its prey.

True to his word, the managing partner from the previous year offered me an interview immediately after I submitted my application and grade transcript. I met with him and a recruiter in one of Ivey's designated interview rooms (yeah, it's an intense school), and proceeded to CARB the shit out of their questions. It was masterful—I was articulate, I injected humor when it was appropriate and of course, I *always* remembered to bring it back home.

Everything was going according to plan . . . until:

"Tell me about the low mark that you got last year."

I paused for a second. It's not that I wasn't expecting the question, but I felt instantly vulnerable. I knew that this was probably the most important question for me to answer. I took a deep breath, and gave in to the power of CARBs:

C—CONTEXT: *"Frankly, I have no excuse. I came into Ivey very unprepared for the level of commitment that was demanded of me. I lived a comfortable lifestyle in my first couple of years, during which I got by with minimal effort, and I thought that I could do the same in Ivey."*

A—ACTION: *"What I can tell you is that I took that mark as a wake-up call to turn myself around. I cut out a lot of extracurricular activities that were dividing my time, and I prioritized my studies. I spoke with my profs more and participated actively in student study groups so that I would be better prepared for each class. In that way, I'm grateful that I was given that kick in the butt."*

R—RESULT: *"As a direct result of the action I took, my average shot up by 5 percent in my second semester and I have much healthier work habits today. I was able to secure a marketing internship over the summer, which I did enjoy, but in the end my heart has always been set on Deloitte."*

B—BRING IT BACK HOME: *"I sincerely regret that I wasn't able to stand before you with a spotless academic record, but at the same time I'm not ashamed of it. When I think about an ideal candidate at Deloitte, it's not necessarily someone who has never made a mistake. I personally think that it's just as valuable to hire someone who has faced that mistake and recognized how he could use it as a learning moment and change for the better. I promise I will continue to do that if I am given the privilege of working for you."*

Looking back on these few months, I see what I believe was a flash of momentary brilliance, a hint that I did possess something inside of me that resembled a fighting spirit. It may have been misguided and bordering on pathological dishonesty, but I had done it; I had set a goal, really worked for it, and was finally rewarded with success.

Was I being totally, 100 percent truthful? *Nope.*

Was I way more suited for a job in just about *anything* else? *Yup.*

Did any of that matter when they called the next day to offer me the job? *Not even a little.*

CHAPTER SIXTEEN

EVERYTHING IS LOST

My college graduation ceremony was uneventful in the best possible way; the weather was nice, we took lots of pictures . . . and neither of my parents walked out on me.

Mom and Dad beamed with pride as they posed next to me, envisioning me as a handsome young suit in the big city working for a brand-name company and making a lot of money (accountants actually have some of the lowest starting salaries among all jobs in the financial sector, but no need to tell them that).

Meanwhile, I felt like I had just pulled off the heist of the century.

It was nothing short of a divine miracle to have graduated despite all the classes I missed, all the exams I tanked, and all the school projects I totally phoned in. I mean, how many people can say that they scored a 55 in their corporate finance class, yet somehow managed to snag a job at one of the largest financial services firm in the world?! That'd be like getting accepted into med school without knowing what a uterus looked like!

Not only did I not give any fucks about what I was studying, I was proud of it, too. I laughed at all of the kids that had worked so hard, slaving away night after night, so they could end up in just about the same position as me.

I thought it made me smarter than them, but it couldn't be further from the truth.

My classmates possessed something that was beyond my comprehension at the time—a true sense of direction. Whether it was a genuine passion for their field of study or simply complying with their parents' wishes, most of my peers actually *wanted* to learn—while I was playing video games and falling in love with anybody that batted an eyelash at me, they were building toward a real future. I, on the other hand, had stretched my lie as far as it could go; it was only a matter of time before everything blew up in my face.

When it came to choosing a profession, I literally do not think I could have picked a worse fit for myself.

Accountants were generally incredibly detail-oriented and meticulous, as their job requires them to analyze financial statements line by line; I, a staunch ENFP, was free-spirited and relied on emotion and instinct. Accountants relied heavily on historical precedent in order to maintain consistency from year to year; I loved creating things that were new, fresh and innovative. Accountants were structured and regimented, functioning with a machinelike efficiency; I was free-flowing and open, preferring to spend large amounts of time pondering abstract concepts such as the meaning of life, or which flavor of Ben and Jerry's ice cream I liked the best.

Finally, accountants *definitely* didn't aspire to be the center of attention, whereas I constantly craved the validation of others, performing in talent shows, dance battles and singing competitions just so I could be seen.

I showed up to my first day of work in the brand-new Hugo Boss suit I had bought for myself as my own signing bonus, ready to embody that GQ working-professional lifestyle that my parents had imagined for me. By three in the afternoon, I was already bored out of my skull, like I had been in every single one of my accounting classes in college.

My eyelids grew heavy as I conducted my first bank reconciliation—basically a less-fun version of Concentration—where you compared the client company's cash balance with the bank's cash statement to verify that the numbers matched. It was exactly like the homework I didn't do in college, except there was no more skipping class, no more gaming the system.

Surprisingly, I didn't have an immediate existential breakdown. The best way I can put this in perspective is that you can't necessarily tell that a relationship is not right for you if it's your first one. Deloitte was the first real job that I had, so there was really no reference point for what other people were going through; I just assumed that everyone kind of hated their jobs.

I promised myself that once I made enough money I'd graduate from Hugo to Gucci, from Timex to Rolex, from public transportation to a Ferrari. I told myself that this *stuff* was going to make me happy, even if going to work didn't. As a reality dating show contestant in China once said, "it is better to cry in a BMW than laugh on a bicycle!"

If I were a little more self-aware, I might have thought twice about my parents' offer to help me put down money for a condo downtown, across the street from my office. I might have felt uncomfortable with the idea of taking their hard-earned money to live out a life I didn't want. Instead, I enthusiastically accepted; having my own place brought me one step closer to the baller lifestyle that I wanted.

I moved into my new home in October, just over a month after I started my new job. I was supposed to gradually take over the mortgage with my growing accounting salary; instead, I'd be unemployed within a year.

Be forewarned—the following might bore the shit out of you.

I worked in Deloitte's audit practice, which meant that we would be hired by a company's shareholders to examine and verify the accuracy of that company's financial reporting—basically, our clients were owners who wanted to make sure their companies weren't lying about how much money they were making. Audit teams would go to the company site and inspect its day-to-day operations, matching and double-checking for discrepancies between what was reported and what was actually there. We'd pore through papers to plug into spreadsheets, stuffed into windowless rooms in clients' offices, and monotonously check one set of numbers against another set of numbers. If we were lucky, we got to compile a spreadsheet of *even more* numbers.

Yikes; I think I fell asleep three times just trying to write that paragraph.

On my best days at the office, I felt like an outsider; on my worst, I felt like a total fucking idiot, whose error report made it clear that I was incapable of completing even basic tasks. My spreadsheets were always full of mistakes, as I inevitably would have missed a number, left out a zero, or formatted something incorrectly. My brain just wasn't built for detail.

All of the difficulties I had on the job were exacerbated during the infamous accounting busy season, which followed the fiscal year-ends of our client companies. We were on-site at the clients' offices nearly twelve hours a day and six or seven days each week, poring through documentation and interviewing employees when necessary. I had a particularly rough time on my audit because I was the only first-year on my team, and didn't have the faintest clue how to do anything on my own. When I received close guidance, I got the work done—however, most of the time my seniors were preoccupied with their own assignments, and expected me to figure it out myself.

As you've no doubt deduced by now, that never happened.

I constantly felt my seniors' frustrations towards me, which only made me more anxious. I'm not exaggerating in the least when I say that going to work felt like marching into the depths of hell.

I scoured my Gmail inbox for any evidence of work I performed during my busy season (there honestly wasn't a lot), and came upon this literary gem I wrote to one of the employees of an insurance company we were auditing:

The uncashed cheques account does not match the leadsheets. When we double-checked it was what was provided initially, though the total of the difference on the leadsheet remains. This is immaterial by CTT standards, but since this is a cash account we recommend investigating as the reported value on the Uncashed Cheque Report is higher than what is on the lead-sheet. Again, this is an immaterial difference but one we believe is worth pursuing.

I now exclusively write sassy emails with lots of exclamation points and encouraging emojis ☺. It's just so much more fun this way.

Auditing aside, I was just a bad employee all around. I was always forgetting to enter my billable hours, and even when I did it was an educated guess at best, and a complete fabrication at worst. It was a stark contrast to my coworkers—I'll never forget Andrew Golobic, a walking encyclopedia of accounting knowledge who, loudly over the cubicles, would crow about his talent for time management. "I have tracked every fifteen minutes of my life over the last six years," he said to me once, as if it was his finest achievement.

Hearing that just made me want to throw up. See, my timesheets would be something closer to this:

0900 TO 0907—STOOD IN LINE AT STARBUCKS TO AVOID GOING TO WORK.

0907 TO 0937—OPENED OUTLOOK BUT THOUGHT ABOUT BUYING A BREAKFAST BURRITO.

0937 TO 1030—WENT DOWNSTAIRS TO PICK UP (AND SLOWLY EAT) BREAKFAST BURRITO.

1030 TO 1100—WORKED ON CLIENT SPREADSHEET. CHECKED FACEBOOK WHEN NOBODY WAS LOOKING.

1100 TO 1330—LUNCH.

1330 TO 1430—POST-LUNCH COMA; ALMOST FELL ASLEEP AT THE KEYBOARD.

1430 TO 1515—HAD A COFFEE BREAK FROM ALL OF THE HARD WORK THAT I WAS NOT DOING.

1515 TO 1600—WORKED ON CLIENT SPREADSHEET. MESSAGED WITH A CUTE COWORKER.

1600 TO 1620—WENT TO THE BATHROOM. PLAYED *CANDY CRUSH* IN THE STALL.

1620 TO 1645—REPEATEDLY GLANCED AT CLOCK.

1645 TO 1655—SLOWLY AND DELIBERATELY PACKED MY BAG.

1656 TO 1700—WENT HOME AS EARLY AS WAS ACCEPTABLE.

I'd arrive as late as possible without getting in trouble, because every minute of nonwork felt like some kind of salvation. When I was at work, I'd constantly look at the clock to see how much time was left before my first break, then before lunch, then before my second break, then before I could leave. I was a real workhorse, a bona fide go-getter!

As if my physical job were not bad enough, I wasn't even technically done with school; once a week, for three hours, I had to take classes to prepare for the first of three exams I'd have to do to become a fully chartered accountant—the Core Knowledge Exam (CKE). The CKE was eventually followed by the School of Accounting (SoA), and then finally a three-day exam called the Uniform Evaluation (UFE, now the CFE). The whole process would take *three* years, after which I would become a chartered professional accountant and my salary would skyrocket.

All I had in this stressful time was my blind-faith cocksure approach to life and my complete refusal to do any more than the absolute bare-bones minimum quantity of work. As I had done throughout my four years in university, I either skipped or slept through my classes. Then, I treated our three-week study leave leading up to the exam like a vacation. I was fine pulling stunts like this in school, so I had no reason to believe that this would be any different. Besides, the pass rate for the CKE was 90 percent. What were the odds that I *wasn't* smarter than the worst 10 percent of people who took the test?

Huge surprise—I failed.

Per the Deloitte company policy, failing the CKE did not necessarily result in a termination of employment—we were given a second chance to take the test a few months later, this time with an unpaid study leave. If we failed *again* . . . well, then we'd have to look for a new job. I still had faith that I would pull through, despite my dislike for just about everything to do with accounting. With a mortgage and my parents' respect on the line, I didn't have any other choice.

By March of 2012, seven months into my job, I was already spiraling head-first into depression. I'd lie awake in bed every morning praying to be sick so I could take the day off. Sometimes—like on March 6, the day that *Mass Effect 3* came out for the Xbox 360—I just faked it. I didn't just hate the menial work that I had to do every day, either; I was beginning to question the entire industry. I was constantly asking myself what the point of anything was. We were hired by wealthy shareholders to make sure their companies were up to standard in their financial reporting, so that they could have another yacht, another cottage in the Hamptons, another private jet. In my opinion, we weren't adding any sort of value to the world or making it a better place—we just counted money for rich people. For me, that just wasn't enough.

While I was caught in the midst of my downward spiral, I'd occasionally see a post or two from my acquaintances in the tricking community and almost die of envy. Many of the people who trained in the same sprung-floor gyms as me years ago were now professional stuntmen, having worked in the film industry for years. I'd pore through their demo footage in my spare time, imagining myself working on a real-life Hollywood film set. If you had asked me then, I'd have told you dead-ass to your face that my dream was to be that one Asian guy that says one line and then gets shot. Those guys were living out their best lives, while I was watching the seconds of my life tick away as I was confined to a job I despised.

More than anyone else, I idolized Chris Mark, a prodigious young martial artist and gymnast who had lent his talents to films like *The Hunger Games, Suicide Squad, Scott Pilgrim vs. The World*, and pretty much any action movie or TV show that ever shot in Toronto. This guy could do everything from superfast fight choreography to weapons to acrobatics and wirework. To me, he was an absolute god, whose career was so far out of the reach of mortals like me that I need not even try. I fantasized about getting punched in the face on-screen, or thrown down a flight of stairs, or blown up in a massive explosion.

Desperate for even a small taste of what show business was like while lacking even the slightest clue as to how I'd navigate there, I started browsing the ads section of Craigslist.

Now, I know what you're thinking and yes, there were a *lot* of sketchy postings on "talent." I wouldn't recommend touching Craigslist with a twenty-foot pole today, *especially* if you're a woman—I was just impatient and highly, highly stupid. I really didn't know what I was looking for until I found it one day, wedged between casting calls for a busty adult film actress and (I'm not joking) a model for a seminude mud-wrestling photo shoot:

ASIAN EXTRAS NEEDED FOR HOLLYWOOD FILM

Holy shit, I thought. *That's me! I'm Asian!!*

What did I have to lose? I replied with a shirtless pic (just trying to put my best foot forward, guys) and received a response from a woman at Extras Casting Toronto almost immediately; I had been cast in the movie codenamed *Still Seas*.

The rush that I felt from opening this email was more profound than anything I had experienced in my entire academic and professional life. I couldn't believe it; *I was going to be in a movie!* I had cross-referenced the casting agency's name and email online, and everything appeared to be legit. Just to be safe, I convinced Jason to come along as well—it's fitting that seven years later he would be the first one I'd call after finding out I booked the role of Shang-Chi.

"There's just one thing," the agent said to me over the phone. *"Your shoot dates are during the week; if you have a regular job, you're going to have to make arrangements. Is that okay?"*

"Thank you for the opportunity, but I'm going to have to decline," I responded. "I have a full-time job in a field I am deeply passionate about, and I wouldn't want to jeopardize that for the chance to be on a real movie set."

Ha. Just kidding. I told her no problem, and that I'd fake an illness.

When Jason and I arrived on set for our first day of shooting, bleary-eyed at four in the morning, we quickly realized that *Still Seas* was actually *Pacific Rim,* a massive Guillermo del Toro blockbuster where gigantic human-piloted robots called jaegers fought equally massive monsters known as kaiju. In our scene, a kaiju had just exploded over Hong Kong and covered the area in its blue blood; thus, we needed to be spray painted head to toe with layers of blue and black for dirt.

Toronto was freezing in March—I distinctly remember the feeling of the ice-cold paint being sprayed across my nipples as I shivered in our holding tent, thinking that this was the single coolest thing I'd ever done.

The crew of the film had built an entire façade of a Hong Kong street that had been decimated by a monster attack, and fit it inside a hangar-size soundstage. I took my spot among the two hundred other Asian smurfs who had answered the call of Craig, my eyes drinking in every little detail of the scenery. The level of detail was astonishing, from the authentic HK storefronts to the drops of blood on the individual pieces of rubble on the ground. As I looked around me, I saw people I'd later learn were grips, gaffers, camera assistants, assistant directors and sound engineers, all full of vibrant energy and purpose. Everybody was so engaged in what they were doing, like they actually *wanted* to be there. Take after take, no matter where the camera was, Jason and I would do our best to try to sneak into the shot and make it into the movie.

Before that day, I had never understood what "do work that you love and you'll never work a day in your life" meant. We were paid minimum wage for our work, less than half of my hourly rate at Deloitte. Of course, that didn't matter—hell, I would have paid for the opportunity. After a grueling fourteen-hour day, still covered in spray paint, Jason and I got on the bus and waited eagerly for our next shoot day, as if we hadn't worked a single second.

Unfortunately for me, it would never come.

You see, some of my superiors at Deloitte had caught on to my somewhat lackluster work ethic. When I took the day off to work on set, I neglected to fill out my time sheet and so was still technically available for work. Some managers had tried to reach me to get some work done, but nobody could get ahold of me. I had to very apologetically show up to work the next day and put out the fire I had started, while Jason headed off to set alone.

If you go near the exact midpoint of the movie, you will actually see Jason in an isolated close-up in which he is carrying a little gooey blue alien across the screen. *That* was the day I missed.

I, on the other hand, was still doing everything I could to maintain the status quo. Despite how much I loved the experience of being on set, I would still never have had the courage in a million years to quit my professional job to keep doing it.

Thankfully, it wouldn't be up to me.

• • •

The circumstances leading to my firing unfolded as follows:

On Sunday, April 8, 2012, I brought Barkley home for the first time, a beautiful four-year-old husky-malamute cross whose previous owner had briefly adopted him from the Ontario SPCA but quickly decided that he pulled too hard on his leash and subsequently put him up on—where else—Craigslist. I had wanted a pupper ever since I was little and felt like I needed a companion more than ever to help me cope with the depression I was falling into. I was supposed to be off of work on study leave starting the following week—it was the perfect time to pick up a pet.

On Monday, April 9, 2012, I received a notification for a meeting on Thursday with our firm's managing partner in my Outlook calendar. I was supposed to go on study leave at the end of the week and it was the Good Friday weekend, so I figured it was just him wishing me well on my exam prep. I actually appreciated the gesture, knowing that it was my second attempt while virtually all of my peers had passed back in January. It would have been a rare show of compassion for a large company that measured employees by billable hours and little else.

At lunch I went home and took Barkley on a nice walk in the park. We shared a hot dog together. It was a good day.

On Wednesday, April 11, 2012, I had a meeting with Kim, a senior accountant who was my designated career coach. We went through my last few months with the firm, and I was able to share some of my frustrating experiences with my busy-season client. She gave me some words of encouragement, told me that it was perfectly normal to have a bad experience once in a while and told me to study hard and just keep going. Again, it was actually one of my better days on the job. I even let Barkley sleep on the bed with me.

On Thursday, April 12, 2012, at 3:00 p.m. I strolled upstairs to the boss's meeting room . . . and came face-to-face with the managing partner (we'll call him Paul Gibbon, because that's his name), flanked by a woman from HR and a building security guard.

"Hey, Simu. Have a seat." Paul emitted a tone of perfect professionalism no doubt honed over decades of delivering this kind of news. "How are you?"

I managed the biggest smile I could, hoping against hope that somehow my infectious and totally forced enthusiasm would change his mind at the eleventh hour.

"Really good! I'm so excited to start my study leave so I can focus on killing that exam!"

Everything is going to be fine, I repeated to myself over and over. I had seen this plotline play out a million times on teen soaps like *The O.C.*, or *One Tree Hill*—someone would be on the verge of breaking up with their boyfriend or girlfriend, but would stare into their loving eyes and be unable to go through with it in the end.

"*So,*" the oblivious one would say. "*What was it you wanted to tell me again?*"

"*Oh ... uh ...*" Looking into the eyes of their mate, the breakerupper would lose all willpower.

"*Nothing, baby. Let's go to Denny's.*"

Deloitte and I were no different than Ryan and Marissa from *The O.C.*, Chuck and Blair on *Gossip Girl*, or Peyton and whoever Chad Michael Murray played in *One Tree Hill*; we may have had our bad days, but it couldn't end like this, could it? We would work through it, right?

"Simu, the reason why we've called you in here today is because we are terminating your employment."

I practically felt my heart stop beating. My head started to spin, and I swear I floated out of my own body. I saw the life I had been working toward for twenty-two years shatter in front of me.

"Why ... ?" I asked, even though I already knew the answer. All of my actions—from my constant tardiness to my lack of focus on my studies to my unexplained absences—painted the picture of a really shitty employee. There was not a single manager who wouldn't have been able to sense that right away.

"We've just had to make some cuts," Paul said simply—probably so I would not waste his time trying to argue with him. Not that I would have.

As the lady from Human Resources began to speak about severance payments and career counseling services, I replayed my day on set and wondered if that had been the nail in the coffin for me. Had I thrown away my entire future for a chance to play make-believe for a day?

I absolutely hated myself. I wished I hadn't been so goddamn lazy in school and on the job. I wished I hadn't done just well enough to keep my parents' hopes alive; maybe if I had just disappointed them earlier on, they wouldn't have any expectation of me now. Instead, I had kept that flame alive for twenty-two years, with lies, false promises and last-minute theatrics that allowed me to get by.

But there would be no moment of brilliance now; I had been barely hanging on each day at work, and there simply wasn't any fight left in me.

I was the worst kind of con artist—I had convinced my parents that I belonged at a private school that cost tens of thousands of dollars each year for six years, fooled them into believing that I was worth the exorbitantly expensive business degree, and then somehow duped them into thinking that I should have a condo all to myself in the city. Perhaps worst of all . . . I made them believe that I was worthy of their sacrifice. Every step of the way, I gave them just the faintest glimmer of hope that I could turn things around and truly make something of myself; in turn, they wanted so badly to believe in my potential that they kept throwing more money into my education like suckers in a pyramid scheme. Now, I would finally be exposed as a fraud.

On April 12, 2012, everything my parents had envisioned for me when they first arrived in Canada more than two decades ago—everything they had saved up for and worked toward—was destroyed. Their once-prodigal son, the boy genius they were so immensely proud of, had grown into a complete loser who had flamed out spectacularly. *I had broken us.*

What an ending this would have been, to the story of a family of dreamers that overcame impossible odds and bitter hardships to settle in Canada . . . only to be undone by an ungrateful, indolent child.

Unbeknownst to me, this would be the defining moment of my life after which everything changed.

I didn't know it at the time, but as I crumbled and broke from the weight of my parents' expectations—to be the star child, the studious academic, the obedient son—something inside me would awaken. It was like a fire that I didn't know I possessed, hidden away and dimmed after years of living an inauthentic life. Now that I had nothing left to lose, I could finally start making choices for *me*, and *owning* them.

From the rubble of my parents' broken dream, a new one would be built—one that was not fueled by their definition of success, but by mine.

Life had finally begun.

ACT THREE

CHAPTER SEVENTEEN

DARK NIGHT OF THE SOUL

We all have memories that have been seared so deeply into our brains that we feel them viscerally for years—even decades—after they've happened.

There are the good memories, like my first kiss in middle school. Francesca Crawford was the cutest girl in seventh grade, and my heart jumped with excitement when the bottle that I spun passed by all the other girls and landed squarely on her. She smiled an effortlessly cool smile, leaned forward over the bottle, and gave me a gentle peck on the lips. I felt like I had just grabbed a power line with my bare hands.

Then, there are the bad ones—like being locked outside my apartment by my parents at age five, and never again being able to feel safe at home. I can still remember how hot my face felt the first time my father struck me after I had talked back to him in an argument. I can still hear resentment and the vitriol behind my mother's voice as she cursed the day I was born, blaming me for ruining her life.

All of these, however, paled in comparison with being laid off.

I was utterly humiliated as I went to my cubicle to collect my things in plain view of the entire office. My cheeks flushed red with embarrassment as everyone continued working in dead silence, pretending not to notice what was happening. Nobody made an effort to console me, or even offer a look of sympathy. Instead, they continued working, transfixed to their screens as if they would somehow suffer my fate if we made incidental eye contact.

That night, I stood on the balcony of my forty-sixth-floor condo that I could no longer pay for, a tally of numbers running endlessly through my head:

Two hundred fifty thousand—a low-end estimate of the amount of money my parents had invested in my education to date, wasted on an ungrateful and unmotivated son.

Four hundred ten thousand—the cost of the one-plus-den apartment in downtown Toronto that I had bought "*with my parents.*" In reality, they had fronted the entire down payment.

Five hundred—the amount of money I had been sending my parents each month to help pay for the mortgage on our condo. It was *stupidly* little, an insignificant and largely symbolic contribution that could barely cover the maintenance fee. Now, I couldn't even pay it.

Twenty-two—my age, usually a time of unlimited possibility for bright young adults entering the workforce. Definitely not the time to lose your job.

Finally, eight—the number of months I had managed to last before being let go, *eight months* for the nearly two decades spent in a classroom preparing for the "real world."

By the numbers, I was an abject failure, and a spectacularly expensive one at that. I could already imagine the look on my parents' faces, could already hear their words echoing in my head endlessly: *Stupid. Failure. Waste.* I had fought ardently against this voice before, because I had always believed in my heart of hearts that I would prove them wrong one day.

As I stared at the ground hundreds of feet below me that night, I finally believed them.

To be perfectly clear, I didn't have one foot over the ledge or anything—I did, however, wonder how quickly I would lose consciousness after I hit the pavement; would I smash into a pulp instantly, or would I lie there in horrible pain for an eternity as I died slowly? What would people say about me at my funeral?

I slept in late the next day, and upon realizing that I didn't have to go in to work, felt an immediate weight lifted. Although guilt and shame of losing my job remained, I had been liberated from the chains that bound me to my former life I had come to loathe. At least I wouldn't have to go another day pretending I was someone else; I was free, now, to choose what to do with my days.

As it turns out, what I wanted to do was *act*. Still fresh off my first on-set experience, the memory of my time on *Pacific Rim* was all I could think about. Something inside me just felt compelled to find my way back onto a film set. By noon, I was back scouring the internet for gigs.

It wasn't as if I had made the decision then and there to quit my life and become an actor—I still had every intention of going back into the business field at some point, after I had scratched my showbiz itch. It was just meant to be a fun side project, a little self-care to treat the burnout I had experienced at Deloitte. All I wanted in the beginning was to see myself on-screen for a split second, just to say that I had done it—at least, that's what I told myself.

After sending out a bunch of emails with a very shitty headshot, I received a response back from a director (let's call him Jeff) asking me to audition for an independent short film called *Bike Cop Begins*.

Wait—*Begins*? Did I miss the original *Bike Cop*? Why did Bike Cop need an origin story?

I didn't care either way; I wanted in. This was going to be a litmus test for my potential as an actor, a reality check to see if I truly had what it took.

As ridiculous as it sounds—and it *was* ridiculous given that the character I played was inexcusably racist—I was absolutely exhilarated the whole way through.

The audition was at Jeff's place, a small unit in a creaky old house in an industrial corner of northwest Toronto. This was a far cry from a Hollywood blockbuster—this was a film school graduate shooting a thing on his Canon DSLR in the hopes of scoring a big break. Jeff earnestly planned to use *Bike Cop Begins* to launch a Bike Cop franchise

(*Bike Cop: Tokyo Drift? Bike Cop Episode IV: A New Spoke? Bike Cop 2: Electric Bike-aloo?*).

My character was Yakusa Koto, the leader of a trio of Japanese mob-sters, and one of Bike Cop's enemies. I understood right away what Jeff wanted from me: a self-skewering parody of Ken Watanabe, complete with that thick, guttural accent that children use to imitate Japanese men. It was maybe just a hair more acceptable than Mickey Rooney's bucktoothed I. Y. Yunioshi in *Breakfast at Tiffany's,* but roughly on par with Matthew Moy's Han Lee in the despairingly recent *2 Broke Girls,* if only because I was actually Asian.

I should also mention that Jeff chose not to dignify this charac-ter with speaking in his actual mother tongue; he wanted *gibberish* Japanese—because comedy, I guess—and I, ever so young and desperate to validate my dreams, chose to give the man exactly what he wanted. I chewed with actorly intensity and brooded with all my might, as I bellowed:

"The Buhr-eeding Dragons wirr not-a stand for your insorence!"

Jeff loved the take, letting out a huge guffaw as he cut, and I felt like a million fucking bucks. I feel idiotic saying it now, but I was *so* god-damn proud of myself; it was the affirmation I badly wanted, some sort of validation that I could be a good actor. For what it's worth, Jeff was a consummate professional. Sure, his sense of humor was more than a little misguided, but I genuinely don't think he meant any ill will; he was just a white guy who thought accents were funny.

Needless to say, I booked the role.

We shot most of our scenes on a farm in Cambridge, Ontario, over the course of a twelve-hour day—my "Japanese" subordinates and I are in the middle of a drug deal with a "Mexican" drug cartel (who also spoke gibberish Spanish, so at least Jeff was dishing it out evenly) when everything goes sour and we all start shooting each other. It was then that the eponymous Bike Cop shows up and saves the day by killing all of us.

There was also a scene where—oh man, this is bad—the three Bleeding Dragons gang members turn to bow to one another repeatedly as a gong went off, ringing each time we dipped our heads.

As much as I want to go back in time and slap the shit out of my younger self, I think it's worth mentioning that, back then, nobody was having conversations about Asian representation in mainstream media—not even Asian people. As far as I was concerned, playing into stereotypes was an occupational necessity.

Over the next month or so, I continued to check Craigslist every day and wound up being an extra on a variety of sets, including, randomly, a French-Canadian ice cream commercial (I may or may not have fibbed about my fluency in French). I said yes to everything, so long as there was a camera being pointed in my general direction. I even got into some modeling, although not the high fashion stuff that people really brag about—no, I answered an ad to be a stock photo model that paid $100 for a full day's work.

Little did I know, the shoot would be *wildly* successful, and the images would end up being used for everything from pamphlets and brochures to corporate ads and billboards. I even saw myself on the cover of an accounting textbook, an irony so palpable I swear I could taste it.

You might be thinking that all of this usage would net a pretty sweet royalty fee for me, but no—all stock photo models sign away their rights up front, after which the photographer owns them *in perpetuity*. Someone could buy those photos to sell anal wart or hemorrhoid medication and there's absolutely nothing I could do to stop it.

One day, I was in the middle of my routine online sweep when I stumbled upon an ad for an agency in Toronto that was looking for new actors and models to add to their roster.

I was having an absolute ball saying yes to everything I could find and making every mistake in the book, but this was an opportunity to take my talents to the next level—or get scammed out of a lot of money. Skepticism aside, I knew deep down that I wouldn't be content starring in people's passion-project short films. I answered the ad with cautious optimism and received an email from someone named Breann asking me to come to their office in the city.

There were two people in the entire shoebox-size office: Jessica, the agency owner, a dead ringer for Nelly Furtado as she looked up at me from her laptop—and Breann, a millennial like me who wore a beanie and sipped a Frappuccino. It was a small operation, but there was no doubt that it was legitimate.

"So, you didn't go to school for acting and you don't have training of any kind?" Jessica pressed.

I had expected this question and prepared an answer. I took a deep breath, summoning my business school training:

"No. But these past few months I've been learning on set every single day whether it's as an extra or as someone with a speaking role. I'm treating this as a business; as soon as I make any money—and I promise you I will—I'm going to reinvest it in myself and my training. I promise to be professional, to always be on time, and to always represent you guys well."

It felt just like giving one of my patented interviews at Ivey, except that my answers were completely genuine. Actually, I surprised myself a little; it was maybe the first time I had truly been honest with myself about what I wanted, and it felt good.

Breann and Jessica looked at each other and nodded.

"Awesome—we can't wait to get started. By the way, can we suggest a photographer to take your new headshots?"

I'd later learn that it was commonplace for some smaller agencies to recommend a photographer and then get a referral fee, or "kickback." And so, $800 later, I was an actor with representation; I could now audition for bigger, more legitimate roles in commercials, TV shows and even movies! I didn't even care that I just got completely fleeced on the headshots.

"Holy shit, it's just like *Entourage*," Jason said when I told him. We used to idolize the HBO show that followed fictional A-lister Vincent

Chase and all of the Hollywood exploits and shenanigans he got into with his friends and his agent, the iconic Ari Gold.

"Fuck yeah," I said, completely oblivious to the show's rampantly misogynistic themes. "Just like *Entourage*."

Looking back, it was easy to see the value that I provided to Jess and Breann. As a boutique agency that didn't rely on star power, their business model relied on volume—if each of their hundred-or-so clients booked just a couple of jobs each year, that was still a couple hundred pieces of commissionable income in their pockets. I was Chinese, approachably attractive and in shape, which made me a perfectly nondescript token Asian in a friend group. Ad agencies loved that kind of pseudo-diversity. I don't know whether Jessica or Breann had any expectations of me beyond just being a two-to-three-gig-per-year guy, but I was determined to be their superstar, their Vincent Chase.

The first audition the agency sent me on was for a Gillette commercial. You've seen this a million times, where the handsome guy checks himself out in a mirror as he strokes his freshly shaven face—easy, right? I felt so nervous walking in that, when the cameras were rolling, I walked over to the wall at the far end of the room—where the camera was most definitely *not* pointed—and went through my action. The camera guy cut immediately as the room looked at each other in confusion.

"Um . . . let's try that again, Simu, but could you do your action *toward* the camera this time?"

I didn't get the role.

A few days later, I was asked to do a dramatic monologue for a casting director. I had never done a monologue of any sort, let alone a *dramatic* one . . . and so I picked a clip from the basketball movie *Coach Carter*—you know the one where the troubled student stands in front of the class and recites the "our greatest fear is not that we are inadequate" quote by Marianne Williamson—and memorized it in an English accent, because I guess I thought that was what real actors did, or whatever.

It was, and still is, the worst audition I have ever given. Let that be a lesson to anyone out there who thinks that they can just *wing* an English accent—you *cahn't*.

Though these were certainly very embarrassing failures for me, I refused to give up. To Breann and Jessica's credit, they kept sending me out. At the end of that first month, I had accumulated just as many success stories as humiliations.

On a commercial audition for a telecommunications company, I expertly fake-ran a small business from my makeshift desk, tucking a phone between my ear and my neck as I frantically jotted down notes. The agency loved my convincing portrayal of a young entrepreneur and booked me!

Within that same week I was sent on an audition for the CW spy show *Nikita*, to play a desk cop in Hong Kong delivering news to his superior. My scene was as follows:

HK Desk Cop: Inspector, you have a call from Headquarters . . .
Inspector: Where??
HK Desk Cop: Headquarters . . . Beijing.

I did my version of the scene, with Chinese accent and all, in front of casting director Tina Gerussi.

"Perfect, Simu. Just perfect." I'll remember those words forever.

The next day, I got the call that I booked that job *as well as* a print modeling gig for a major bank that would pay over $3,000. Between the three gigs, I had made over ten grand in the span of about a week and a half.

A week later I was on the set of *Nikita,* getting a mic put on me so I could act in a scene with Shane-freaking-West from *A Walk to Remember.*

My legs were quivering as I opened the door to the interrogation room on the director's action, to deliver my two lines.

"And CUT! Great! Moving on to the close-up on Simu!"

I could have died happy in that moment. In the span of six weeks, I had gone from disgraced accountant to shaking Shane West's hand. I was a *real actor,* with my own close-ups! As I contemplated what lay before me, any thought of potentially picking my accounting career back up faded away. I had been telling myself that I was only dipping my toes in the water, that I would be over the moon to simply have the opportunity to say a line on TV.

I was lying to myself.

What I genuinely wanted was some sign from the universe that would allow me to take that leap of faith—some form of external validation so I knew that I wasn't completely bonkers. My *Nikita* role and my telecom commercial were irrefutable proof that I was worthy of this crazy dream that I had concocted in my brain. Jessica and Breann echoed my enthusiasm; they will always have a special place in my heart because they truly believed in me, the kid that showed up at their door without any idea of what he was doing.

I leveled with myself—maybe I would never progress past a television journeyman who did bit parts for whatever productions came into town . . . but I'd be damned if that didn't sound like a total dream in and of itself. The repeating thought that *I could really do this* sent an electricity through my body that was a thousand times more exhilarating than anything I had ever felt in a classroom.

After years of aimlessly chasing the wind, I was finally finding myself.

Amid this month of profound excitement and self-discovery, I got a call from my dad:

"Máomao, I was just taking a look at your account and it looks like there was just a large sum of money deposited by Deloitte. Is everything all right?"

Shit.

That large sum of money was my severance package. For whatever reason, my bank account had always been linked to my parents'; it made transferring money between us very easy, but made keeping secrets nearly impossible. I knew that the day would soon come when I would have to come clean to my parents . . . but I just wasn't ready yet; I needed more time.

So, like I had done a thousand times before, I lied.

"Yeah, it was a lump-sum payment to cover my study leave. Don't worry, everything's fine."

It was a fragile one that wouldn't last very long—but then again, it didn't have to. I just needed to buy some time until I was ready to tell the whole truth.

"Oh . . ." my father said suspiciously. *"Okay. I was worried you had gotten laid off or something."*

"Haha . . . no, I'm still working."

Another suspicious pause.

"All right then. You're sure you're okay?"

It was a loaded question. Just last month I was looking over my balcony feeling like I had lost everything. But in the last twenty days, I had done more soul-searching than I had in the past twenty years. Maybe I still had no clue what I was doing, or where I was going with all the auditions and Craigslist gigs—but it didn't matter. For the first time in a long time, I actually liked who I was becoming.

"Don't worry, Dad. I've never been better."

CHAPTER EIGHTEEN

PROFESSIONAL CRAIGSLIST ACTOR

Those who know me at all know that I am not great at moderation. I read the seventh Harry Potter book in one sitting. I saw *The Force Awakens* three times in twenty-four hours when it first premiered in theaters. When *Mass Effect 3* came out, I took the day off work and played it for sixteen hours straight, pausing only to order pizza and to pee out the horrifying amount of Diet Coke that I had consumed. My approach to my new career was no different; I knew I was starting later in life, so I had to work ten times as hard as my peers in order to catch up to them.

I had come out of the gate in 2012 guns blazing with a commercial, a print ad and a speaking role on a TV show, and for some reason I was convinced I was destined for ultimate success. My agents seemed to agree; I started being sent out on larger auditions, and the prospective roles got meatier. On my own end I had expanded my purview beyond just Craigslist and was committed to being on set as much as I physically could. Using nothing but that blind determination to power me, I charged forward, doing anything and everything I could get myself cast in, including:

- $100 to play an office worker in Avicii and Nicky Romero's music video for "I Could Be the One." You can still spot me if you search for it on YouTube.

- Meals and transportation to play the main villain in an amateur movie about cops that know kung fu that I pray to sweet Jesus you never see the footage of.
- $400 to play a police officer in an AlarmForce commercial.
- $50 to play a "murder victim" in a weird and perverted situation involving a guy who was the spitting image of Harvey Weinstein in a hotel room gleefully filming me getting fake murdered as he screamed at the "killer" to "enjoy it more"; from a website called ActorsAccess.com, which was otherwise pretty legitimate. I'm not gonna lie, this one really sketched me out. In retrospect, I feel like I was in some sort of softcore murder fetish video.

Every day, I sprang out of bed motivated and hungrier than ever. I checked all of my websites and Facebook groups like clockwork, applying for any role that even remotely fit my description. There was no method to this madness—just a raw force of will. Sometimes I ended up on sets that were incredible learning experiences, and others—like that sexy murder movie—I would get home and wonder what the fuck I was doing.

One of the latter cases had me taking a train forty-five minutes out of the city to audition in an office that was suspiciously littered with headshots. The "casting director" called himself Mike Hertz and had a very typical show business swagger, sporting slicked-back hair and a crisp white shirt unbuttoned a bit too low, exposing his silver chain and his hairy chest. I read a short scene with Mike, after which he acted as if he had just witnessed the second coming of Brando.

"Wow, man, just . . . wow. Okay. I'm going to make some calls. Can you come in again tomorrow?"

Against my better judgment, I took the train back the next morning and showed up outside Mike's office, equal parts skeptical and excited. A mother and her son were waiting there as well. They casually struck up a conversation with me and talked about how long they had been in business with Mike and how much they loved him. They were very vague with his job title—apparently he was a casting director but he also represented and managed actors. They were essentially making him out to be a miracle worker. I joked, "If I didn't know any better, I'd say you must be working for him!" They laughed, maybe a little too hard.

Before I had time to process, Mike strode in. I nearly gagged on his cologne.

"Sorry I'm late. Hey, Simu, is it okay if I just meet with these guys first? Real quick, I promise."

I said sure and sat in the waiting area. Meanwhile, behind closed doors, Mike and the mother-son team were talking *very* loudly about a recent job that the son had just booked. It was just so ridiculous—NOBODY spoke that loudly, and especially not about deal specifics. I started to look more closely at the literal hundreds of headshots strewn out across the coffee table, my Spidey-sense now practically punching me repeatedly in the back of my head. A few moments later, Mike called me in, and like clockwork:

"I got good news, Simu. We have a HUGE offer for you for a new show that shoots in New York. Fifteen thousand dollars for a week of shooting."

I played along and asked for more details. The show was called *Universal Bible* and didn't have a network attached yet but was going to find a home very shortly. I would be playing a police officer. It was all going to be done under Screen Actors Guild (SAG) contracts, an—oh wait, I was SAG . . . right?

"You're not SAG?!" He feigned a horrified look, as if it was totally normal for a Canadian kid with no credits to his name to be a part of the *American* actors' union. "One second."

He pretended to dial a number.

"Hey, it's me. I got news about Simu . . . he's NOT SAG! I know, it's crazy . . . We can still get him on the show, right? He just needs a permit, right? Okay, great. I'll let him know."

And there it was; in order to "work" on this "production" I would have to write a check addressed to the Screen Actors Guild for about $2,500. I asked to have some time to think about it and promptly left the premises.

Years later I would see a police ad on Craigslist requesting information from anybody who had ever been conned by this man; they had caught him and were building their case. I don't blame anyone for having fallen for this trick; I nearly did. Despite all of my misgivings, I really truly wanted to believe him. If Mike had only asked me for $500, I would probably have gone to the bank right then and there. We all want to believe so badly that we have what it takes to make it, and when someone shows up offering a shortcut we can't help but consider, "What if it's true?" I don't know what terrifies me more, the con artists like Mike Hertz who act like showbiz hotshots in order to scam unsuspecting victims out of a few thousand dollars, or the actual powerhouses of Hollywood who abuse their very real power and influence to prey on young actors. If given the choice, I'd rather just be out a few bucks.

I would never encourage anybody to be as reckless as I was ... but with a little bit of the street smarts I clearly did not possess, I do believe that the full-court press is the way to go. I was a person of color in a pre-*Black Panther* and *Crazy Rich Asians* landscape, and I wasn't anything special in the looks department; my work ethic was my only X factor, my secret sauce. Without that hustle, I'd still be in Toronto flirting with the poverty line, waiting for someone to give me my big break.

As time went on, my attempts to hide my career from my parents were growing increasingly more futile; family friends who had tuned in to watch my national commercial were asking questions, and my parents didn't have any answers. They pressed me for details, asking how I was doing all this stuff.

When I speak at colleges and events in Canada and the US today, the question of parents comes up constantly. How did they feel about my decision? Was it hard defying their wishes? How much money did it take for them to love me again? I look into the eyes of the students asking these questions and I see how scared they are of disappointing their own parents. The pressure to conform to their parents' will is so strong that many openly admit to pursuing fields of study they weren't passionate about simply because it was what their parents wanted.

I think about those kids often—the graphic designers, architects and artists masquerading as accountants, engineers or bio majors—and I wish I could help them all find their greater purpose. But not everyone is ready to be unplugged from the Matrix. I don't think I was either, until my life hit rock bottom after getting laid off. Looking back, the decision to pursue acting felt more like a series of happy accidents than a premeditated plan; it was anything but graceful. But, thanks to the most fortunate misfortune of all time, I still stumbled through it. I hope these kids will too, and while I can't force the red pill down their throats, I hope that I can at the very least plant a seed in their minds that will spark a curiosity. To them I would say that there's no harm in tasting different things—you never know what part of yourself you might awaken. Your parents did not defy destiny and settle halfway around the world so you could live a miserable and empty life. They want you to be happy doing what you love . . . they just might not know it yet.

Truthfully, I didn't grow up with much of a sense of filial piety; there wasn't much of a relationship to lose in the first place, considering how often we were fighting. Even if that hadn't been the case, though, I suspect I wouldn't have changed anything. I was a chronic slacker who had finally discovered his purpose; I was applying myself for the first time in my life, and I wouldn't have given that up for anything. I knew my lie wouldn't last forever, but it would buy me precious time to keep acting.

During this time, I was cast in a couple of projects that were absolutely instrumental in forming my mentality toward the industry today. I feel like I could easily have adopted a passive mindset, simply waiting by the phone for my agent to call and give me my big break. Had I done that, I guarantee you I would not be here today. Thanks to these projects, I learned the value of being a multi-hyphenate and a hustler.

In June, I was cast in a short film called *Summer Child* from—what else—an ad on Craigslist. The film itself was nothing special, but it introduced me to the Reel Asian Film Festival in Toronto and a program known as Unsung Voices, which funded young aspiring filmmakers and helped them workshop and produce their first short films. The following year I would apply and get into the program as a filmmaker, which was how I produced and directed my first short, called *Open Gym*. The experience of learning how to put a film together from the ground up has continued to pay dividends for me, allowing me to produce my own work when others were not giving me the opportunities I needed. I've written and produced short films (you can watch *Meeting Mommy* on YouTube!), optioned scripts and developed series ideas with networks. If I hadn't gotten cast in *Shang-Chi*, I would still be hustling every single day like it was 2012.

A few months later in September I answered an online ad and auditioned for a web series for the Machinima company, a gaming-focused YouTube channel with millions of subscribers that was just starting to dip into original content. The creator, Jared, was a young kid like me with big dreams. We clicked right away, and I was cast in one of the main roles. The show was called *Omega* and marked the first time I played a character with a name and across multiple episodes. *Omega* had a healthy budget and all the trappings of a potential hit; a cool post-apocalyptic invasion premise, solid VFX and a channel with good exposure. Jared and I would talk excitedly about where this show would take us. We were for sure going to get a season two, and then Comic-Con, then a movie, then we were going to make millions of dollars and buy mansions next to each other in the Hollywood Hills . . . it was a done deal!

The fact that Machinima no longer exists should tell you everything you need to know about how that all panned out for us.

Jared and I continued to keep in touch in the coming years; every time I saw him there would always be a project just over the horizon that was going to be a game changer. Every time, he would promise that I would have some role in it, only to go relatively silent after our meetings. Then, inevitably, the project would fizzle out. Of course it was frustrating to feel like I was constantly being strung along, but I'm extremely grateful to have known Jared because he gave me my first glimpse at the behemoth that is "Hollywood." Through his dealings with Machinima I came to understand the difference in scale between the US and smaller markets like Canada. Even though I loved being Canadian, I knew that I wanted to eventually play in the big leagues.

Jared himself radiated a different energy than anybody else I had worked with; as a young film-school grad in Canada, he directed a fan film based on a popular video game franchise that caught the attention of various agents and executives in Hollywood. It was a smart move, piggybacking off of existing IP to get your name out there. A subsequent cease-and-desist order from Microsoft only fueled his hype train more. He was incredibly entrepreneurial and had a commercial sensibility that resonated with my business school background. He would show me his pitch decks and series bibles, and then encourage me to start creating my own.

"You have to create opportunities instead of waiting for them, Simu."

I got to work immediately, creating a show in which I would play my dream role—a Marvel superhero.

I'm embarrassed to admit that Shang-Chi didn't even come across my radar. Instead, I read everything I could about Shiro Yoshida, or Sunfire. Sunfire was actually a member of the very first team of X-Men, but eventually left the team because of creative differences that I'm sure had nothing to do with the fact that he was Asian. He was a badass mutant that could harness solar radiation to propel himself through the air and rain hellfire on his enemies.

Shiro was raised by a villainous parental figure (his uncle) to be a master assassin. When he begins to express his mutant gene, the uncle sends him to America to wreak havoc as a terrorist. There, he is confronted by his real father, who is stationed there as a Japanese diplomat, and who he had presumed to be dead. When his father is subsequently killed by the treacherous uncle, Shiro renounces his upbringing and vows to become a force for good.

I wrote out a treatment for a ten-episode season that outlined Sunfire's redemptive arc and ended with an after-credit phone call from Professor Xavier. I even wrote out a beat sheet for an epic trailer that tied the character's mutant origins to the Fukushima reactor disaster in 2008, modernizing it from the original comics. Of course there was no chance in hell that this was ever going to get made, but it didn't matter; Jared had taught me the value of swinging for the fences and being the master of my own destiny.

Sooner or later, I'd hit my home run.

CHAPTER NINETEEN

SIMU THE STARVING ARTIST

After an incredible 2012 that saw me rebounding from absolute rock bottom and discovering my true purpose, the following couple of years sent me hurtling back to reality.

To start, my parents had grown increasingly panicked as months passed without any news of my employment. They demanded to know what I was doing with my life, and so, we hastily set up a lunch on a weekend in February where I broke the news that I was not going back to work as an accountant; I was going to give the whole acting thing a try.

"This is something that I'm really passionate about now," I stammered. "I know this is a lot to take in, but my mind is made up. I'm going to keep acting for a little bit."

"Oh."

Then . . . silence.

As I watched their gazes fall to the table I felt the full force of the shame that I had been putting off since April 12th. I was my parents' greatest failure, the colossal asterisk in their legacy of greatness. I was *Wild Wild West* in Will Smith's career, Jordan's two years in minor-league baseball.

You could even say that I was Jar Jar Binks.

On the one hand, I felt sort of vindicated. In refusing to bend to their wishes at least I could claim some sort of moral victory against them. On the other hand . . . I was keenly aware of the amount of time and money they invested in me from birth—immigration, day care, extracurriculars, tuition, a freaking mortgage—all for me to spit in their faces by throwing it all away.

Even faced with being a disappointment of the highest degree, I knew I couldn't go back to a job in the office. Not only would I be betraying the only dream I ever had—but I wouldn't even be *good* at it. The way I saw it, there was no other choice; I had to press onward and carve out my own definition of success. Although I did not agree with my parents on how to get there, I was unquestionably motivated by the same desire to be great.

It didn't happen right away.

If my 2012 was like Linsanity with the Knicks, my next couple of years were Jeremy's mediocre seasons with the Rockets, during which his hype level gradually came back down to earth. Following my initial success, I had expected my career to continue to make massive strides forward. What I got in 2013, though, was more of the same—commercials, some unpaid indie stuff and a one-liner on a Syfy show called *Warehouse 13*. A year ago, I would have been over the moon, but that was no longer enough. I needed more—I needed to be *great*. The high of simply working on set was starting to wear off; I wanted more than to just be "Friend #1" in a restaurant, or "Bartender #3" at the pool. I was playing in a tougher league now, auditioning for meatier roles against more seasoned actors, and I quickly came to the realization that I was out of my depth.

To be specific, two Toronto actors of Asian descent absolutely dominated me in the audition room: Patrick Kwok-Choon, who you can watch on CBS's *Star Trek: Discovery*, and Shannon Kook, a *Degrassi* alum who is currently killing it on CW's *The 100*. These guys (who I would later learn were actually cousins) were right in my demographic of tall, Asian and approachably handsome, but had degrees from renowned theater programs across the nation and resumes that completely eclipsed mine. If I saw their names on the sign-in sheet of a casting I knew I had no chance of booking; I could only scavenge what they were either unavailable for or too experienced to bother with.

To say that I was a competitive person would be the most titanic understatement in the history of understatements. I once forced Peter into a *Super Smash Bros.* marathon and refused to stop playing until I had won. Unfortunately, he was objectively *much* better than me. It was three hours before my Pikachu would taste sweet, sweet victory, our dinner plans having long since evaporated. Maybe it was playing sports from a young age or constantly being compared to other kids by my parents, but I always had a hard time with accepting defeat. I manifested many rivalries in my life, be it with my peers in academics or popularity or sports. If I surpassed them, I would look up and find another rival to beat.

To be clear, I didn't wish any ill will on these people; rather, I used them to motivate myself to be better. After all, there would be no Magic without Bird, no Federer without Nadal, no Fox News without fact-based journalism. I made Patrick and Shannon my rivals and vowed that I would soon get to their level.

Those people who watch TV and think, *Gee, I could do that*, are not necessarily wrong; anyone could convincingly deliver a single line or perform a single action on-screen. However, the same cannot be said for characters bearing the responsibility of carrying multiple arcs and conveying nuance and subtext in their work. In order to get to that level, I needed to get my butt to class. I signed up for all of the most renowned acting classes in Toronto, reinvesting almost all of the money I had made so far, and soaked up the information like a sponge. I learned how to break down scripts, and to identify each character's scene objectives and the tactics used to achieve them. I learned how to act to the characters' relationships—was I speaking to a lover, a mentor, a student, a best friend or a total stranger?

Whereas I had been operating on instinct alone, I was now learning a structured and consistent approach to my craft; in essence, I was graduating from being a hobbyist to becoming a professional.

A typical class was held once a week in groups of no more than ten students and was designed to mimic an audition environment. Some were even held in major casting offices. We would receive a scene to rehearse for each class and then perform it with a camera trained on us. I had the opportunity to play superheroes, police officers, drug addicts and a slew of characters I never would have gotten the chance to audition for. We got a copy of our footage after every class so that we could track our progress. I really loved the emphasis on play and self-discovery, in a space where it was safe to take risks and try new things. Acting, like life, gets a bit stale when you only make safe choices.

In addition to learning specific technique and theory, we were also slowly shaking off our nerves and dealing with *camera-brain*. Every single human being has camera-brain; I don't care how charismatic and charming you think you are, having a camera pointed at you will turn you into a bumbling idiot if you're not trained for it. You lose your thoughts midsentence, get caught up in your words and become hyper-aware of that twitchy thing you do with your lip. And don't even get me started about hands—I'm nearly a decade in and I still don't know what to do with them, like, ever.

Occasionally there would also be an opportunity to take an acting intensive, which would take place over a weekend and would usually involve performing in front of a casting director. It was basically like a class with a paid audition, which I had no idea had actually been outlawed in Hollywood. Too desperate for work to weigh the moral implications of pay-to-play, I signed up for everything.

There was just one small catch; I was now very, *very* broke.

According to data from the acting unions in the US and Canada, the average union member makes under $15,000 from acting work alone. I wasn't even a part of the union yet, and did not enjoy benefits like protected wages, overtime, and health insurance. I'd been able to get by until then without a joe job, but I couldn't keep it up with all of the extra expenditures piling on. The obvious choice was to serve or bartend somewhere, but I knew myself well enough to know that my pride would not be able to handle it. Once again I took to Craigslist, which I have plugged so much at this point they might as well sponsor me, and managed to get myself a job as a professional superhero.

Really, I'm not trying to be cute; the job I got was for My Perfect Superhero Party, which booked hero appearances for kids' birthday parties in the Toronto area. Because there were no Asian heroes at the time, I obviously couldn't be a hero with an unobstructed face—my only option was to don the Spidey-suit and become the friendly neighborhood Spider-Man to Canadian children ages four to eight. At $75 an hour it was a decent chunk of change, and I had the freedom to turn down gigs if I had an audition or something. Plus, it helped me get used to performing in front of people—even if the people in question were literal infants.

On the job, I quickly learned that five-year-olds were the best kids to deal with, on account of them being old enough not to poop their pants but too young to infer that the person standing in front of them was not *actually* Spider-Man. Six- and seven-year-olds started to get a little skeptical, and eights were just these little investigative journalists determined to expose your whole operation.

Every rule has its exceptions, though, and Trevor was the kid that broke me.

When I first got the call to do the party for Trevor Satan (just an educated guess), who was turning five, I was initially very excited. That excitement would soon turn to horror, however, as I would discover that Trevor was not a human child, but rather a being born of pure evil. Trevor was determined to ruin my day right from the get-go; he was sure I wasn't the real Spider-Man because I couldn't climb walls and shoot webs, and no amount of Spidey poses and backflips would change his mind. He screamed at me and physically assaulted me multiple times, then made sure his friends got in on the fun, too. He punched me in the eye and jumped me when I was kneeling down to help one of the other kids, having seen the zipper for my costume on the back of my neck.

"I see your zipper! I see your zipper! You're a fake!"

Knowing Trevor would not listen to the reasoned argument that even real Spidey-suits probably needed zippers, I looked over at the parents, pleading for help through my sweaty mask. But, unsurprisingly, Trevor's parents couldn't care less; they were just glad to have someone take him off their hands. They were relaxing on their deck with the other parents, beers in hand, and didn't look up a single time.

I practically snatched the cash out of the mother's hand when my hour had finished. On my way out, unable to help myself, I let out a little passive-aggressive jab:

"So, Trevor is . . . really something."

His mom laughed unapologetically.

"Well, what are you gonna do—he's five."

It took all of the self-control in the world not to just unleash on that lady in that moment. Instead, I simply said goodbye and walked away. I hung the mask up after that day, vowing never to don a superhero outfit ever again. Thankfully, the universe (and Marvel Studios president Kevin Feige) had other plans.

I'm sad to say that the destruction of my dignity in 2013 would not end with Trevor. I had also picked up work as a brand ambassador for an experiential marketing company, and that was also a doozy. We did branded activations all around the city, which is a fancy-feast way of saying we handed out samples on street corners. And that's *if* we were lucky, by the way; people are generally amenable to being bothered if they're being offered free swag but will be totally vile if you're just trying to catch their attention for free.

I was unfortunately roped into dancing in flash mobs on two separate occasions, for a bottled yogurt launch and to promote an exhibition rugby game. As I pranced around the streets, holding up traffic and drawing the ire of everyone around me, I silently cursed the white-collar marketing executives that came up with these ideas in a boardroom somewhere. They were woefully out of touch with reality, and my poor flash mob dancers and I were paying the price. I was further frustrated because I was probably just as qualified as they were; I had

At my parents' convocation in 1996. Despite arriving in North America
nearly a year apart, they managed to graduate on the same day.

My own convocation, fifteen years later. My mother appears
to have found the elixir of youth during this time.

Taking the stage during freshmen orientation week to claim my title as the Superfrosh of Western University!

Hip Hop Western prepares for the Ontario Universities' Competition for Hip-Hop (OUCH) in 2007. First (but not last) time wearing makeup.

Yéye and Năinai cozying up to my dog Barkley in 2013. We were finally able to bring them over to Canada permanently in 2008.

Before there was *Shang-Chi* ... there was *Crimson Defender vs. The Slightly Racist Family*, a short film about an Asian superhero I wrote, directed, and starred in back in 2014. Please don't go looking for it.

Power napping on the set of CBC's *Kim's Convenience* in Season 1. Word of advice: never fall asleep around Andrew Phung (Kimchee)!

On the set of ABC's *Dr. Ken* with Albert Tsai, Krista Marie Yu, Suzy Nakamura, and Ken Jeong in 2017. Ken let me visit the set and hang out anytime I wanted; an incredible friend.

2018—The cast of *Kim's Convenience* gathers to talk about the groundbreaking nature of the show and the importance of representation.

Smoking a fake doobie onstage for the Canadian premiere of *Vietgone* at the Royal Manitoba Theatre Centre in 2018.

2019–Singing the national anthem at the Staples Center in front of legendary head coach Doc Rivers. You can't tell in the photo, but I am pooping myself.

Guest starring on the 100th episode of ABC's *Fresh Off the Boat*, opposite the unreasonably tall Hudson Yang aka Yao Ming Jr.

When Asian American icon Jeremy Lin invites you to ride with him in the Toronto Raptors' championship parade, you don't say no.

Screen cap of my first self-tape audition for *Shang-Chi* in May of 2019. I was 98 percent sure I would never hear back from Marvel.

Draining a free throw at the CCYAA Celebrity Classic. Bart Kwan (*left*) and Phil Wang (*middle*) are two of the most prominent Asian YouTubers in the game.

I wasn't allowed out of my hotel room at Comic-Con without a security escort and a disguise. This was moments before the big announcement that would change my life forever.

The moment I walked onstage in front of eight thousand cheering fans, I felt my phone begin to vibrate. Ten minutes later, my battery was completely drained.

Minutes after my *Shang-Chi* announcement, I am invited to take the most insane group photo of all time. I have not washed my shoulder since.

On the set of *Shang-Chi and The Legend of The Ten Rings* in Sydney, Australia. It turns out that getting the role was the easy part; getting through the movie and its seventeen action sequences was the real mountain!

a top business school pedigree and completed a summer internship in consumer packaged goods. I mean, can you remember a single time you walked by a branded flash mob and thought, *Gee, I think I'd like to get to know that product better?*

Once, dressed up in all black to perform a haka in the middle of the most crowded intersection in Toronto, I felt a tap on my shoulder.

"Simu? Is that you?"

My heart sank.

One of my former coworkers at Deloitte had recognized me. He stood there in front of me dressed in a crisp suit and tie, sporting the same ID badge that once hung from my belt. He was probably well on his way to making six figures now, whereas I was a full-fledged starving artist and currently appropriating a traditional cultural ritual in order to promote a rugby game. I swear to you, I have never acted better in my life than I did in that moment; I greeted him with an enthusiastic smile and talked about how happy I was in my new life. Inside, all I wanted to do was bury my head in the sand and disappear from the world.

I had many long nights in 2013 where I would sit in front of my computer tweaking my website or cutting a new demo reel, just doing *anything* to feel like I had some modicum of control in my career. My girlfriend at the time—let's just call her Shelley—very patiently helped me work through a lot of my anxious thoughts; but still, they never fully went away.

Meanwhile, my relationship with my parents was quickly deteriorating. All correspondence between us was passive-aggressive at best, and overtly hostile at worst. When I emailed them to let them know I had booked a commercial for a chain of steakhouses, my mother responded:

> If this is the quality and dignity that you like after 16 years of school,
> then this is your choice.

I fired back that it was; I was building toward a career that brought me happiness. I made a last-ditch impassioned plea:

You know what's worth it in this life? Doing something you can be truly
proud of. Pursuing the things that matter. That's the ONLY thing that
matters. Too many people today "trade" their ambitions and dreams
in favor of a substandard life. Do you want to know why they wake up
unhappy, why they find life meaningless and monotonous? Because
they made the wrong trade. I wake up every day full of purpose. It's
so exciting I can't even begin to describe it. The rest will fall into place,
because true wealth and true happiness are reserved in this world for
the people who are willing to risk it all in order to capture it.

I can't help but laugh at the email I wrote after digging it up for this
book. I mean sure, it was a nice little piece, but who in the *hell* did this
kid think he was to make such sweeping statements about fulfillment
and happiness? What gave him the right to act like such a self-righteous
prick?

My mother's answer was so effortlessly savage I can practically hear
the mic dropping as I read it:

Some people like to take challenges . . . some others are afraid of
challenges. They do everything to avoid taking challenges, to choose
simple and easier lives which make them feel happy.

You may wonder at this point how badly my spirit was battered by
everything that was going on in my life. The truth is that I had more
than my fair share of days where I felt like giving up. I'd spend weeks
without booking a single acting gig, and then go on Instagram to see
all of my friends going on vacations, buying houses and otherwise just
doing regular adult things that I couldn't because I was so goddamn
poor.

If it weren't for my incredible one-woman support system, I honestly don't know if I would have made it through. Shelley was a real
bright spot in my life in 2013. We met celebrating a friend's birthday
and wound up in her bathroom later that night, giggling and kissing in
the pitch dark while our friend lay passed out on her bed just a few feet

away. A few weeks later, after pretending like I had to cancel our Valentine's Day date because of work, I showed up at her workplace with a bouquet of roses and asked her to be my girlfriend. Shelley and I were both going through transitional periods in our lives when we met, and we gave each other the love and understanding needed to take our next steps forward. She loved me at my most unlovable. Her family was also extremely supportive and nurturing in ways that my parents were not; they came to every screening I invited them to, bought tickets to every play, and donated to every crowdfund campaign I ever launched. Shelley and I would ultimately grow in separate directions, but I remain endlessly grateful for our time together and for all the times she shouldered the baggage I carried.

It took a certain amount of delusional confidence to fuel my insane decision to pursue acting. Something in my mind operated outside of the boundaries of reality and believed that I could be a successful actor as a twenty-three-year-old Asian kid in Toronto with absolutely no training. This was no time for pragmatic thinking; I had to believe beyond a shadow of a doubt that every shitty commercial I did, every birthday party I worked at and every dog food sample I handed out on the sidewalk brought me closer to my eventual success.

In my darkest night, I clung desperately to the belief that my salvation was just around the corner—I just had to hang on and keep fighting. And so I endured my parents' scathing disapproval and scraped together what money I could from my odd jobs so I could continue to act. As I toiled away, the light inside me growing progressively dimmer, I kept telling myself over and over again that my glory would come. I had to protect my dream, and it would endure all hardship and blossom into the most incredible reality I could possibly imagine.

Deep down, in the recesses of my mind, I wondered if I had gone completely mad.

CHAPTER TWENTY

BACK TO CORPORATE

Everybody who has ever ventured boldly into the unknown knows the feeling of crippling self-doubt, especially in the moments when the losses are piling up faster than the wins. You feel your dream slipping further and further away, and you begin to wonder whether you made the right decision to pursue it in the first place.

Maybe you were too stupid and naive to see that you had no chance to begin with; maybe you were just wasting your time, carried away by daydreams and delusions of grandeur, while all of your friends graduated from medical school and actually built careers for themselves. Maybe your parents actually *did* know best and were just trying to stop you from throwing your life away. As your thoughts begin to spiral deeper and deeper into the depths of negativity, you feel sick to your stomach as you ask yourself, *What have I done??*

It's in those moments that you think back to the life you gave up, and you wonder if it was really so bad to begin with. In 2014, a moment of weakness nearly caused me to give up my dream entirely and brought me back into the world of accounting.

Aw shit, here we go again . . .

It's gonna be a bit of a slog as we return to the land of bank reconciliations and payroll runs, but hey—if you think *reading* about accounting is tough, imagine actually having to do it for a living.

• • •

On a night out with some old friends from Western, my friend Elaine had casually mentioned that she was looking for someone to fill an entry-level accounting position at the architecture firm that her family owned. Meanwhile, my latest role of the last few months had been calling out bingo numbers while dressed in a bathing suit for an app called *Beach Bingo* that you definitely should NOT download.

"Hey, maybe we can help each other out," I found myself saying to Elaine. I was in the midst of seriously reevaluating my priorities, and my self-esteem was so beaten down that I actually felt myself yearning for the stable nine-to-five office lifestyle I once had.

Elaine, not privy to any of my internal monologue, loved the idea and promised to follow up. The only thing I asked for in return was the flexibility to leave work to audition from time to time, which was very rare in that line of work. She agreed and offered me the job.

When I told my parents the news, they acted like I had just gotten out of rehab.

"We're so glad you've come to your senses, Máomao."

"Yes—no more distraction."

To them, Elaine was my savior, sent from the heavens to redeem my troubled soul and steer me away from vile concepts like being an artist, or pursuing one's interests. With a rapidly declining bank balance and not a lot of options on the table, I was beginning to think the same—that is, until I actually *started* the job.

Through no fault of Elaine's at all, I was immediately reminded of how much I absolutely *loathed* accounting. As soon as I opened up my very first expense report, my head started to spin and I began to feel physically ill. I began to fall into old habits again, waking up late and prolonging my breaks just so I wouldn't have to work, while turning in spreadsheets that were riddled with errors. All the while, I would be fixated on the clock like a hawk, waiting to be able to leave. One time, as Elaine's mother was explaining some of their reporting practices to me, I actually fell asleep right in front of her. My head suddenly snapped back up and my eyes flew open as I realized what had happened, and I could only apologize profusely and blame a bad sleep the night before.

What little joy I got from the job came from the side projects that had nothing to do with accounting. I took great pleasure in revamping the company website, editing proposals for language and grammar, and going gift shopping for the company's closest customers. I also made a friend at the office who could talk NBA with me. That helped a bit.

Precisely three months in, Elaine and I sat down and mutually agreed to part ways, ending my second and final stint as an accountant. I was now utterly and completely sure that I was not meant for life in an office—it was misery and torture of the worst possible degree. I was incredibly grateful to Elaine, though, for giving me a brief moment of stability during a volatile time of my life and taking a chance on me (not to mention giving me flexibility for auditions). By the time I turned twenty-five in April of 2014, I was once again a happy—albeit starving—actor.

My parents and I went back to not speaking to each other.

I genuinely feel bad that I couldn't be a better accountant for Elaine, but I could not force myself to like it any more than you could force a lactose-intolerant person to digest a milkshake. I was indescribably relieved knowing that I would never have to record a time sheet, update a ledger or build a pivot table ever again. Nothing—no accolades, no parental love, no amount of money—was worth spending my life shackled to a job that I hated that much. That is no way to live, and if you are reading this paragraph with that sinking feeling in your stomach because I have just described *your* life, I implore you to begin taking the steps to find an occupation that leaves you with a sense of joy and accomplishment when you come home every day. At the very least start looking at ways you can get a side hustle going. The unknown is always scary, but not nearly as much as waking up one morning realizing you have wasted your precious life in pursuit of someone else's idea of success. I choose the unknown, every time.

• • •

Although I was back to starving artist status in 2014, I resolved to work harder than ever before. That meant more classes and, yes, more expenditures. Luckily, thanks to a few major bookings in rapid succession, I was able to join ACTRA, the Canadian equivalent of getting my SAG card, which entitled me to higher wages and overtime when I was working as an extra. It wasn't glamorous work, but very few other jobs would net me the same amount of money per hour. When my background agent called I would show up to set, do my work and keep my head down, afraid that the camera would pick up my face and I would subsequently be barred from auditioning for that show as a principal character (we called that "burning your face" in the industry).

I actually became quite the little union expert during this time, using my affinity with numbers to figure out exactly what our base rate was for the day (it was different between television, film and commercial), when we hit a meal penalty (when a meal was not served after six hours of consecutive shooting), or when we hit a new overtime multiplier (on a sixteen-hour-shoot day your incremental hourly earnings are triple their normal scale, for example). Funnily enough, my name is still in a lot of background agency databases. I still get texts checking my availability to be an extra on a show shooting in Toronto. One of these days I think I'll show up, just for funsies!

My union knowledge served me well when I was cast as a paramedic on a CW show called *Beauty and the Beast* later that year. According to the rulebook, characters who spoke less than five lines of dialogue were deemed less important and therefore paid significantly less. My paramedic character had exactly five scripted lines, which meant that I was right on the edge of a huge pay raise (and a *principal* acting credit, which was far more prestigious). On set I made sure to improvise as much as I could at the beginning and end of the scenes, adding some background chatter in the hopes that the director would like my work in the editing room. I waited eagerly for the episode to come out a few months later and, as luck would have it, the director *did* end up using a bunch of my unscripted lines! I phoned my union rep to request a pay adjustment and then promptly treated myself to some Uber Eats.

As time went on, my investment in classes began to pay off. I became more confident in the audition room, even edging out my nemeses Patrick and Shannon on occasion. My work was evolving beyond simple one-dimensional roles—playing a character that was "mad," or "sad," or "happy"—to playing fleshed-out characters full of nuance and subtext. Up until that point I, like so many new actors, believed that my job was to *present* feelings and emotions. For me, this was rooted in my own insecurity; I thought that in order to perform I had to *do* something to show the audience what my character was thinking. My biggest breakthrough came with the realization that in life, we often go to extreme lengths to hide how we feel. We go through life putting on different masks, only breaking our composure when something truly challenges us. Great actors can move us to tears barely moving a single muscle, because we naturally understand all of the emotions that are bubbling just beneath the surface. Conversely, we often roll our eyes at actors that we deem are "overacting" or "trying too hard."

The best training I would ever get as a performer came with the opportunity to do theater. I was cast in a tiny play called *About Allegra* for the 2014 Fringe Festival, which marked the first time I had ever done stage acting. Up until then my understanding of acting only spanned from "action" to "cut"; I would stand on a mark, deliver some lines, and then do the same scene a bunch of times until we moved on. I was suddenly being asked to memorize an entire script and then perform it from beginning to end with no margin for error. I wasn't paid a dime for *About Allegra,* but going through the rehearsal process was easily more useful than any class I had ever attended. I had to track a character chronologically through a story and to fully live in each moment, beat by beat. I learned the importance of physicality on the stage, where the audience was too far away to read facial expressions. I cultivated a chemistry with my costar and learned how to react off of her instead of delivering my lines the same way every time. The production itself performed very modestly—we struggled to fill even half of our seats on any given night—but it was truly an invaluable experience. To this day I've experienced very few highs like the one that comes from the sound of applause at curtain call.

After our play closed I was back on the hunt for the next gig. Any thoughts of giving up or returning to my old life were now firmly behind me. My parents had thought my dreams were the signs of a total loss of critical thinking and reasoning, but the opposite was true; I was only going mad when I had managed to convince myself that I had to give up on them. I had doubled down, kept grinding away and fought to keep the doubt and anxiety at bay.

My skills had risen sharply, and I knew I was poised for a breakthrough, if I could just get the right opportunity. Little did I know, it was waiting for me just around the corner.

Our acting union in Toronto had a subcommittee for young actors called the Young Emerging Actors' Assembly, or YEAA. They held monthly meetings to talk about being a working professional in the union, and would throw the occasional mixer for its members.

The thing that drew me to YEAA was an annual short-film program that gave the young actors a chance to produce their own work and have it screened at a film festival. In the fall of 2014, I saw a post on the Facebook group calling for applications for the program spearheads. What really drew me to apply for the position was the fact that the spearheads' films were automatically selected to be in the program; I would get the chance to develop a story of my own and show it to an audience. I felt like I was pretty qualified on account of an intensive program I had done the year before, so I applied. After a pretty quick interview process, I got the job—I was going to get to make my second short film. This time, with a bit more budget to work with, I could take a stab at the role I had always dreamed of. You guessed it . . . I wanted to play a superhero.

Talk about a broken record.

With my goal clearly laid out in front of me, I got to work, and in one single night fueled only by passion and diet soda I wrote *Crimson Defender vs. The Slightly Racist Family*. It was a short but hilarious script in which the Crimson Defender rescues a family being held hostage by a criminal syndicate only to have the family question his validity as a superhero because of his ethnicity. At one point a member of the rescued family, struggling to comprehend the presence of an Asian superhero, asks me: "Are you maybe somebody's sidekick? Like a Robin, or a Watson, or Joe Biden?"

The absurd premise reflected the equally absurd thoughts of a twenty-five-year-old kid who was just starting to become woke to issues of diversity and representation, who was also looking for ANY excuse to dress up in tights. It was half social commentary and half wish fulfillment.

Okay, 40 percent social commentary. *Definitely* not less than 25 percent social commentary. That's right, not a hair less than 10 percent social commentary.

I reached deep into my network and found a fashion student at the nearby Ryerson University who was willing to work on the super-suit. We designed it together, he took my measurements and then he made the whole thing from scratch. I was in disbelief the entire time; was it really that easy? Who needed Marvel when I just had my custom suit made for five hundred bucks!

I wish I could say the suit fit like magic and that I had an out-of-body experience while a light shone down on me from the heavens and the doves sang . . . but it was actually pretty underwhelming. I looked like I was going scuba diving in a wetsuit that was too small for me. A word of advice for all the hobbyists and aspiring superheroes out there: ALWAYS PAD THE MUSCLES. My body compressed into the neoprene, removing all my curves and definition, and left me as kind of just this blob. Even then, I didn't care; I was going to make this movie!

As I was prepping for *Crimson Defender*, I would also get the call to audition for a small Canadian drama called *Blood and Water*. I knew right away that my big breakthrough was here; the show was centered on a Chinese Canadian family, and my character was required to speak fluent Mandarin. Knowing I was perhaps the only actor in the country who possessed the language skills for the role, I prepared like crazy and absolutely killed my audition. Sharon Forrest, the casting director on the project, looked up from her paper after we cut.

"How come I haven't seen you before, Simu? Are you new in town?"

Confidence and swagger coursing through my veins, I replied: "No, ma'am, I've been here this whole time. You just haven't called me in."

"Hm." She nodded and looked down thoughtfully. "That's gonna change."

I walked out of the room already knowing that I had booked the gig. Days before we were meant to start shooting *Crimson,* I got the formal offer for my first role as a series regular.

Although I knew the show and my short film were two completely unrelated projects, I took this as another sign from the universe that good things happened to those who *did the work*. I cannot stress enough that without *Blood and Water,* or *Taken,* or *Kim's Convenience,* or Marvel, I would not simply be waiting for someone to give me my next break. I was and am the master of my own destiny, with full ownership and accountability. I would have made more short films, written more scripts, or found more programs and classes and conservatories to be a part of.

We shot *Crimson Defender* that November, in a barn over an hour north of Toronto. It was absolutely *freezing*; the pizza we ordered for our crew lunch emitted a single plume of warm steam when we opened the box, and then froze almost immediately. I made my amazingly tolerant cast and crew shoot for sixteen hours in horrible conditions from 5 p.m. until almost 10 a.m. the next day. Most of the crew were working for free, as was typical for these passion projects where everyone was just trying to make something good with no money. I powered through the night, went home and promptly got shingles.

Spoiler alert: it was the wooooorst.

The version of *Crimson Defender vs. The Slightly Racist Family* that I had in my head could probably only have been done with a million dollars and a far better actor than I. Still, everyone on the crew gave it their all, from the gaffers and grips to the stuntmen who definitely had better things to be doing with their weekend. I owe so many people from that set an unpayable debt—perhaps most of all to Angel Navarro III, my director of photography, who kept my brain from completely panicking once I realized I did not know the first thing about directing a film. Angel and I continued to collaborate in the years that followed, and he never once asked for a dime. "I believe in you, man!" was all he kept saying.

(Peter also deserves a shout-out here because I roped him into shuttling the cast and crew back and forth for sixteen hours straight. I know, I know, I sound like an awful friend, but I *was* the best man at his wedding five years later, and gave a pretty phenomenal speech that made his mother cry, so I'd like to think I've almost paid him back.)

If you're reading this and thinking you want to actually watch *Crimson Defender*, allow me to make something crystal clear—this was *not* a well-made film; my acting was horrendous, my "fight scene" looked awful, and the plot made no sense. To top it all off, I also edited, color graded and sound mixed the movie to save on costs. My only qualification was watching a few Final Cut Pro tutorials on YouTube. Unsurprisingly the final product had "amateur" written all over it. Despite all of that, it ended up being accepted into some smaller film festivals around the US and would get me my first professional writing gig in the industry. The experience cemented in me perhaps the most important lesson I've ever learned; that it is one thing to have a dream and another altogether to own it—boldly, fearlessly—in its entirety.

Owning a dream to me consists of two key components—declaring it to the world, and taking action. When you put your dream out into the universe you will attract those who dream the same thing, and who understand its struggles. These people will become your allies, your collaborators, your mentors and your guides. But it's not enough to simply pay lip service to your dreams—you've got to walk that walk and act on your ambitions. You've got to *DO*. Without taking action, your best ideas are just random neurons firing in your brain, like lost ships passing through an endless ocean of consciousness, doomed to be forgotten.

I had all the highest hopes in the world for *Crimson Defender*, but when I first dreamed it up, even I knew it was somewhat ridiculous. Still—perhaps because I just didn't know what else to do—I pushed on. I mean, come on; if this book were written at any time before this, I'd laugh at the sheer naivete of my younger self, the kid who wanted to be a superhero so badly that he wrote it into a short film. Instead, all I can do as I type this is shake my head in utter disbelief; *the son of a bitch actually did it.*

As the year drew to a close, so too did an era that I would look back on quite fondly. It was a time of my life defined by scarcity, desperation and self-doubt—but also of the pure and untainted joy of discovering one's true purpose. Like a child I felt free to run and jump and scrape my knees without giving any thought to the bigger questions, like *where is this all going?* or *what is your plan?* My plan up until that point had been to do whatever it took to get back on set. It was chaotic and unstructured, yet totally focused at the same time; I had no idea what would work, so I just . . . did everything.

Life is a bit different for me now—I don't check Craigslist unless I'm looking for a good deal on furniture, the characters I play actually have names, and my parents only mildly wish that I was a doctor—yet there are days where I catch myself reminiscing about a time when life was simpler. Not so long ago, success meant a few hundred bucks and a chance to work on a film set, twelve likes on my latest Instagram post felt amazing and Hollywood seemed as far away as the stars shimmering in the night sky.

CHAPTER TWENTY-ONE

BLOOD AND WATER

Before *Crazy Rich Asians* . . . there was Paul Xie in *Blood and Water*.

Prior to shooting my first show as a lead character, the entirety of my on-screen experience, accumulated over two and a half years, pretty much amounted to three speaking roles on network television, four or five national commercials, a handful of short films, a web series, a smattering of music videos and—of course—*Beach Bingo*, that app that you *really* should not download. Suddenly I had a character with a name, a backstory and an arc that carried over an entire season of television!

Like our favorite Singaporean pretty boy, Paul was the oldest son in a family of billionaire Chinese real estate developers. The similarities would end there, though; you've seen Henry Golding's face, right?

Our season began with the sudden murder of Paul's younger brother Charlie, and focused on the subsequent investigation led by Detective Jo Bradley. Over the first few episodes we revealed key bits of information on each of the Xie family members and gave possible motives for wanting Charlie dead. But suddenly, out of left field, Paul's sordid past reveals itself in the penultimate episode—it turned out that Paul molested Charlie frequently when they were both younger, and then murdered Charlie years later when he threatened to leak the information and ruin Paul's career.

That's right; my first substantial acting gig was playing a murderous pedophile.

While it was not quite what I had imagined for my big breakout role, I was still committed to seizing the most of this opportunity. We shot the show over five weeks in early 2015, in Toronto and Vancouver, on an absolutely skeletal budget. The majority of the funding for *Blood and Water* came from the CRTC (the Canadian Radio and Television Commission) in an attempt to cater to non-English-speaking families. One of the stipulations of the money was that no more than 50 percent of the show could be in English. It was well-intentioned for sure, but horribly misguided—many of the actors were crippled by the language requirement by virtue of them having grown up in Canada, and as a result were not able to perform their best work. For a Chinese-born kid like myself, though, it was a chance to shine.

But I also knew I couldn't do it alone.

Despite all of the summers spent back in China during my teenage years, my Mandarin skills had slowly eroded after years of barely communicating with my Chinese relatives. Even at my most fluent, I couldn't read most Chinese words. I almost had an aneurism at our first table read when I was presented with pages upon pages of Chinese dialogue that I would have to master. If I was to get this character right, I knew I'd have to ask for help. So, I called the last two people in the world I'd ever ask for acting advice—and unbeknownst to me at the time, took the first steps in reconciling with my parents.

For my mom and dad, who had been racking their brains for over two years on a way to dissuade me from continuing to pursue acting, *Blood and Water* was a mixed bag of emotions. On the one hand, I had been validated as a working actor, proving that I was not *completely* out to lunch; on the other hand, it meant that I was falling even deeper into the artist life, and it would be that much harder to pull me out. Still, they were on the phone with me every night while I was in my hotel room prepping for the next day, coaching me meticulously through every line.

"Make sure you get some sleep," my dad said to me after one of our late rehearsals. *"Don't overwork yourself."*

I sat with his words for a long time after we got off the phone. In his tone I sensed his recognition of the hard work that I put into my craft, and—just maybe—a hint of pride as well. That was huge for me; I knew what I had put my parents through the last twenty-odd years, and it finally felt like the tide was starting to turn. I promised myself I would make the most of this opportunity.

Months later *Blood and Water* premiered to virtually no fanfare on OMNI 2, one of Ontario's multicultural channels. Nobody even watched OMNI 1, so we were *waaay* deep down the TV rabbit hole. A lot of us felt like the show was never put in a position to succeed; instead, it felt like a half-assed PR move to virtue signal a network's commitment to "diversity" without putting any real money on the line. Before I knew it, I was back on the audition grind in Toronto, going out for the typical day-player roles. Still—who was I to complain? I was just happy I was able to go to work.

For all of the bureaucratic mess that surrounded *Blood and Water*— both in its production and its airing—it was still a show that employed over a hundred people and featured an all-Asian cast at a time when Asian shows in North America did not exist. Furthermore, our show-runner Diane Boehme had fostered a fun and collaborative work environment on set; as I've continued to work for other shows, I've really come to realize how rare that is.

Working with Diane made me feel like I was much more than just an actor brought in to say some lines; she placed a tremendous amount of trust in me and made me feel like a creative equal. Diane would also call me into her office after watching my superhero short film to offer me a job as a writer for the show's second season. Paul had thrown himself off of a bridge in the first season climax, so I really wasn't expecting to come back. Thanks to Diane I got to participate in a writing room, pitch ideas and even write an episode of the show. What she did for me went beyond just paying me to do a job; Diane saw something in me, and her belief in me helped me believe in myself.

In life, I've come to realize that all big breaks come from a small handful of people who are willing to stick their neck out for you. You can't control how or when they come into your life; you can only control your own professionalism and preparation level. I didn't know when that next opportunity would come, but I knew it was worth any amount of time, money or rejection; I returned to Toronto ready to hustle like never before.

Had I not produced a short film in the previous year, or done a Fringe play for free, or networked with my friends in stunts, I probably would have spent the rest of my year waiting for my next audition to come, while doing the same old odd jobs like dressing up as fake Spider-Man or handing out samples on the side of the street. Instead, the seeds that I had planted years ago began to open up new pathways for me in 2015.

In May, the stuntmen I had been networking and training with suddenly called with a job—I was to get the shit kicked out of me in a fight scene for the NBC reboot of *Heroes*. Of course, I jumped at the opportunity. I loved being on set more than anything, and as far as I was concerned it was easy money. And so, I showed up on set for my first day as a stuntman, wide-eyed and ready to take a fake punch to the face, or maybe a little kick to the chest . . .

"We need somebody to do a gainer breakfall."

Wait. What?

"Yeah. Director thinks the fight scene is too bland. We need to just spice it up a little bit. Who's it gonna be?"

A gainer breakfall was no joke; it meant launching yourself into a backflip off of one foot, flailing in the air and then landing on your face. I looked around at the other performers in the scene, who were in turn eyeing me back. Their gaze told me everything I needed to know: the new guy needed to earn his stripes. Never one to back down from a challenge, I stepped forward and volunteered with as much false confidence as I could muster.

There was only one problem; I had never done a gainer breakfall before.

I mean, my friends and I would mess around at our local gymnastics gym, where every fall was cushioned by a sprung floor and as many mats as we wanted, but this was completely different; I'd be fighting in the lobby of an office building with tile floors in full costume. If I lost my aerial awareness in midair, I'd risk breaking an arm or splitting my head open. My heart was beating out of my chest as our camera rolled for our first take. As the director yelled "ACTION," the first few stuntmen charged at the main actress of the show. I waited anxiously for my cue, ran at her with my fist raised, then hurled myself toward the sky, life flashing before my eyes . . .

. . . and landed on my chest with a loud WHUMPH!

"CUT! That was great! Let's go again!"

I sprang to my feet in an instant, relieved to be alive. I'd have to repeat the stunt another fifteen times before we got all the coverage we needed, but at the end of our long day there was no question whether or not I had earned my paycheck. Our fight coordinator Tommy Chang, a no-nonsense taekwondo grandmaster from Korea, shook my hand and promised there would be other calls. He was true to his word; thanks to Tommy I've been shot in the chest, nearly set on fire, thrown down stairs and knocked out in every way you could possibly imagine. Not bad for a guy whose entire martial arts experience amounted to doing flips in his backyard!

Meanwhile, an Asian Canadian theater company had been keeping tabs on me since *About Allegra,* the Fringe play I had done the previous summer. In the early fall I was asked to audition for a play called *Banana Boys,* about a group of five Asian Canadian students navigating girls, school, drugs and (of course) racism. I did, and booked the part of Rick, the high-functioning drug-addicted lead character. *Banana Boys* was mounted at the Factory, one of Toronto's more well-known theaters. This was a massive step up from the Fringe, where we only did about seven shows; *Banana Boys* would run for over a month, with a five-week rehearsal period. It was an artist's dream.

Independent theater in Toronto was anything but lucrative, but it made me a far better actor. Under the guidance of our director Nina Lee Aquino and our dramaturge David Yee, we took the time to break down every single piece of dialogue and stage direction during our rehearsal process. By the time we opened in October, I had the entire 110-page play in my head backward and forward.

To this day I'll never forget the feeling of seeing the audience in hysterics after a couple of our best sequences. One sketch, "Battlefield of Love," had the five of us running and diving around like soldiers caught in a massive firestorm of love. One by one, my costars were "taken down" by unfair dating stereotypes associated with Asian men. In a climactic moment, a "small-penis grenade" is thrown onstage and one of the characters bravely sacrifices himself by falling on the exploding weapon with his groin.

The remaining soldiers look on in despair; "Is there no hope for us?"

Suddenly (and I'm not making this up), I emerge from the bottom of the stage completely topless with a cocky smirk on my face. Bullets ricochet off of me as I flex my muscles, implying that some of us were capable of transcending the stereotype. It wasn't Shakespeare by any means, but tell me a time when an audience erupted in howling laughter and cheers at the end of a scene in *The Tempest*; I'll wait.

In another scene, I was the host of a game show called "Doctor, Lawyer, Businessman, or Engineer" in which Asian mothers confronted their children with a multiple-choice career ultimatum.

One of the characters, Michael (played by Matthew Gin), attempts to protest that he wants to be a writer, causing the mother character (played by Philip Nozuka, who also played one of the boys) to unleash a hilarious beatdown on her son. I could barely keep a straight face as Phil dragged Matt all around the stage, finally getting him in a painful headlock.

"DOCTOR DOCTOR I'LL BE A DOCTOR JUST MAKE IT STOP!"

Phil pauses for a split second and then, on a dime, turns into the sweetest and most loving mother imaginable. Even his headlock morphed seamlessly into a tender caress of the face.

"We love you, Michael," Phil would say softly, kissing Matt's forehead ever so gently.

Seriously, it was a privilege to get to do this weird, demented, and brilliant play that was specifically written for Asian Canadian performers.

I was hitting a nice stride in Toronto, earning income as an actor both on stage and on TV, and also as a stuntman and screenwriter. Yet still, even on my busiest days, I could not bring myself to be satisfied. As much as I loved the city that raised me, I knew that I had to venture out; what I truly yearned for could not be satiated by a small market.

An artist's success is predicated on their ability to jump from one project to the next—but what was next for me after *Blood and Water* if I chose to stay? How long would it be before another substantial role for an Asian male in my age range came up in Toronto? What about after that? I wasn't willing to waste my prime years waiting for a job that might never come. I had no intention of begging for scraps from the gatekeepers in my little pond—living in perpetual poverty, no less—while the true wielders of power in the industry were completely oblivious to my existence.

The film industry in Canada was a mixture of homegrown Canadian series like *Kim's Convenience* or *Schitt's Creek,* and American shows such as *Suits, The Boys, Star Trek: Discovery* or any show on the CW. Occasionally we'd get a big-budget movie like a *Pacific Rim* or a *Suicide Squad.* Crew shortages were not uncommon during our busy season because the demand for them was so high. Unfortunately, that was never really the case for the actors—most of us were stuck counting the days since our last audition and wondering when we'd get another chance to play a small unnamed role on a network television show.

Between Toronto and Vancouver, our main shooting hubs, roughly fifteen casting directors controlled which actors would audition for various supporting roles. My livelihood rested in the hands of these fifteen people, who themselves were often hired by a larger US casting office to fill the roles that they deemed unimportant. The leads were almost always cast out of Hollywood, even for the Canadian shows, in some attempt to capitalize on the American star's fan base. In many ways it was the perfect place to start a career—there was much less competition for the roles compared to Los Angeles—but the economic reality for Canadian actors was that most would make less than minimum wage doing the thing they love.

Any semblance of a star system—that one thing that actors could rely on for some modicum of job security—did not exist in Canada. If I was lucky enough to be cast as the lead of a show, there was no infrastructure in place for me to become . . . well, famous. Without the possibility of "breaking out" in Canada, Canadian performers had to adjust their career expectations. I found that many of us adopted a self-defeating mentality—most were just grateful to get the chance to be on set a couple of times a year. For me, a business school grad who was taught from day one to *build* and *grow*, that was unacceptable.

Even playing outside of the box and doing everything I could to take matters into my own hands, I knew that staying in Toronto meant that I was essentially treading water—I really had no choice but to leave. I had to invest in myself, dream BIG; and if I was going to fail, I would do so in the only way I knew how—spectacularly, dramatically and without any regret whatsoever.

I'd always had the idea to move to Hollywood someday, but my Canadian citizenship made it a little more difficult than packing my bags and hopping a plane. I had to prove that I was an "alien with an extraordinary ability" to the United States Customs and Immigration Services, by showing that I was a successful working actor in my home country. Luckily, though its ratings were effectively zero, *Blood and Water* was getting some critical acclaim in industry circles; it was as good a ticket to the major leagues as any. In the middle of another restless night in the fall of 2015, shortly after the show came out, I went down an IMDb rabbit hole and found the names of about twenty-five US-based managers who represented Asian actors I recognized. I figured it would help to have a manager that knew what to do with someone who looked like me. I crafted a customized cover letter for each of them and sent them out at around 4 a.m., after which I was finally able to drift off to sleep.

When I awoke the next morning, there was just a single message waiting for me in my inbox:

Hi, Simu,
Let's schedule a call this week. Let me know your avails and I'll match one.

Blessings,
Chris Lee
Talent Manager | East West Artists (EWA)

I did let Chris know my avails (I had a lot of avails back then), and four years later, he would be backstage at San Diego Comic-Con watching as I was introduced to the world as Shang-Chi.

CHAPTER TWENTY-TWO

AN INCONVENIENT SUMMER

After communicating back and forth with Chris over email, I decided that it'd be a good idea to meet. Those of you who have ever hit it off with someone on a dating app ought to know what I mean. Sometimes you just need to see it for yourself, you know?

I scraped together what little money I had, bought a discount flight to meet up with my new manager and booked a couple of nights in a cheap hostel off of Hollywood and Schrader. I fell in love with the city the moment I looked up out of the airport and saw the palm fronds swaying in the wind.

I naively thought that being on Hollywood Boulevard meant that I would be close to, well, Hollywood—but as it turned out, it just made me more likely to get scammed on the street.

Upon landing I made a beeline for the TCL Chinese Theatre, wanting to soak in the glitz and glamour from the City of Stars. I had completely romanticized Los Angeles—in my head it was this magical fairyland where dreams bloomed as easily as flowers in a garden. As I was taking photos, a gentleman dressed as Spider-Man came up to me and snatched the phone out of my hand.

"Come on, man! I'll take a photo of you!"

Americans, I thought cheerily. *They're just as friendly as we are!*

"Sure!" I happily posed for some photos, after which Mr. Spider-Man also took a couple of selfies of the two of us. I think I had a soft spot for him because I knew what it was like to wear that costume (Hint: TOIGHT). I stuck my hand out for my phone, and he hesitated. Uh-oh.

"Twenty dollars for Spider-Man, please!"

Son of a bitch.

"Are you kidding me? You snatched the phone out of my hand."

"You let me take the photo."

"SERIOUSLY?! I thought you were just—you know what? Never mind." I reached into my pocket and dug up a five that I had gotten as change. "This is all I got. Now please get away from me."

That was my LA welcome right there. I wish I could say that it was about more than just money, but I really, *really* hated losing that five dollars.

The next day I met Chris at a Starbucks next to the hostel. I couldn't afford to rent a car or anything, so he had graciously agreed to drive all the way over to meet me. I had run the scenario a hundred thousand times in my head and imagined Chris as Ari Gold from HBO's *Entourage*—a fast-talking man in a suit driving a Benz who was going to tell me that I was going to be a star. When a beat-up Civic coupe rolled up into the parking lot, and a guy wearing flip-flops and a polo walked out, I thought it couldn't *possibly* be him.

"Hey, Simu!" He looked over at me and waved. I smiled sheepishly and waved back, wondering what I had gotten myself into.

As we sat and talked about my life and career, it was obvious that I was not Vincent Chase and Chris would not be my Ari Gold. He made no promises or guarantees, and told me that a very long road lay ahead of me. He would submit me for projects when he could but would be actively pushing for his more established clients. Essentially, I'd have to prove that I was worth his time first—otherwise, I wasn't really a priority.

There was also the tricky issue of my Canadian citizenship. I needed a US visa if I was serious about coming down for pilot seasons, and in order to get a visa I'd need to pay thousands of dollars I didn't have in legal fees.

"You guys . . . don't cover those?"

"Uh . . . no."

Chris would happily corroborate my version of the events if you asked him today. There was simply no such thing as discovering someone from obscurity and staking your whole career on that one person because you "believed in them." I wasn't entitled to Chris's time and energy if I couldn't prove to him that I was a marketable asset, and he was too good at his job to risk it all for a complete unknown. Nobody was going to hold my hand and take me straight to the top of Hollywood.

In retrospect, it was a reality check that I needed very badly. Besides, *Entourage* has aged *terribly*.

I gave Chris a DVD of all my *Blood and Water* episodes, and then we shook hands and went our separate ways. I'll be honest here—I really wasn't sure about him at the start. I think I was hoping for an ego stroke and some easy answers.

I flew back home to Toronto the next day a little beaten, but not defeated. Come hell or high water, I promised myself that I would find a way to make my mark in Hollywood. I would give Chris a reason to fight for me.

Midway through our run of *Banana Boys* in the fall, we had gotten a tip that a big shot playwright was coming to attend one of our shows. His name was Ins Choi, and he had written an incredibly successful play called *Kim's Convenience*. I, still being fairly new to the industry and also a relatively uncultured person in general, had no idea who he was; my costars, however, spoke of him with a deep reverence.

I met Ins when he came backstage to introduce himself to us before our show. He was a quiet and stoic man whose voice never went above a very moderate indoor level, with a presence (and a beard) that would suggest a spoken-word poet or a Jedi Master. We were polite to each other, but really didn't talk that much. On his way out, Ins wished us all good luck, and then paused for a second.

"You know, the play that I wrote is getting turned into a TV show. We are going to be holding auditions soon."

Maybe it was the way that he said it, or maybe it was the Force calling out to me, but I swear to you that I felt a chill go up my spine as he turned and left.

I got the chance to watch *Kim's Convenience* onstage in Toronto just a couple of months before my first audition for the show, and it had a profound impact on me. My impression of theater had up until that point been like going to a museum or an art gallery, where you looked at pieces of artwork or history at arm's length and then moved on with your life. Watching Paul Sun-Hyung Lee and Jean Yoon onstage made me feel like I was seeing into the minds of my own parents, and viewing my own life through their eyes. I had never cried so much watching anything in my life—and let me tell you, Bing Bong's sacrifice in *Inside Out* left me an emotional wreck. I felt each and every word on a raw and visceral level. It's no surprise that Paul and Jean would both reprise their roles as Appa and Umma for the show.

The play—which was very different than what the show became—took place over the course of a single day and focused on the lives of Appa; Umma; their daughter, Janet; the convenience store that the family owned; and their estranged son, Jung, who nobody ever talked about. I loved the many familiar moments of Janet bickering with her parents about her life, her dating choices and her career, but my heart would just stop every time I saw Jung. The once-prodigal Kim son appeared only in two scenes throughout the play, but I was immediately taken by the richness and complexity of his character. The final scene involved Jung walking into the store to see his father for the first time in fifteen years, and to date is still my favorite moment that I've ever witnessed on a stage (and I've seen *Hamilton* twice!). It was a perfect mix of humor and pathos wrapped in a distinctly Asian Canadian story.

I had some very rudimentary understanding of the importance of representation in media and arts before, but watching *Kim's Convenience* really hit home the value of seeing yourself reflected in the world you live in. I promised that I would write something of my own one day that I could share with the world, and that is why you're reading this book right now.

Over the next few months I auditioned quite a bit, both in person in

Canada and on tape for Chris in LA. I could tell that I was being trusted with more complicated material, which was a surefire sign that I was getting solid feedback from the other side of casting. In February of 2016, when the call to audition for *Kim's* finally came, I found myself in the most unlikely predicament of already being cast on another project!

The show in question was NBC's *Taken*, based on the action movie franchise starring Liam Neeson's ominously deep telephone voice. It was just the latest in a long line of ill-fated reboots and rehashes that were greenlit by some unimaginative executive in an effort to leverage some built-in fan base. Did you like the Jack Bauer Power Hour? Well then, you'll love *24: Legacy*! How about Jackie Chan and the Rush Hour movies? Partner, I've got just the show for you—it's *Rush Hour: The Series*—and no, Jackie Chan isn't in it. Weren't Mel Gibson and Danny Glover great together in *Lethal Weapon*? Why not watch the exact same story unfold on TV with two lead actors that absolutely detest each other? I honestly didn't have high hopes regarding the longevity of the show, but I was far from picky—if someone was going to pay money for me to be on TV, I was pretty much on board.

My American management had been a virtual nonfactor up until this point—I would get an occasional self-tape or a single-sentence email from Chris here and there, but nothing ever came of them. I was beginning to wonder if he even watched the tapes (he did). When the offer from *Taken* came through, Chris indeed got to work. He pulled some strings and got the news announced on Deadline, a site that reported on Hollywood. That recognition would prove useful in the coming months, when the time came to apply for a US visa.

I auditioned for *Kim's Convenience* with cautious optimism. There was little doubt in my mind that I would be going up against my usual suspects Patrick and Shannon, the former of which played Jung when I saw the play (quite well, I might add), but I was pretty confident going in. I had taken some comedy and improv classes in preparation for this role and had also accumulated some on-set experience in the last year or so; I was ready for battle.

I ended up acing my audition—perhaps having another job lined up also helped to mask the stench of desperation that so many actors reek of when they go in the room—and was immediately called back. After my second session, my agent told me that they wanted the specific details of my contract with *Taken*. For a brief moment, it seemed like I would have to choose between the two shows. The answer may seem painfully obvious to you now, but consider that *Taken* had a guaranteed US-wide broadcast run with a primetime slot while *Kim's Convenience* was on the CBC, the Canadian public broadcaster, with no guarantee of ever airing anywhere else. While I think in the end I would still have chosen *Kim's Convenience*, it would have been a very hard decision to make.

Thankfully, it never came to that. After going back and reviewing the contract, we realized that I was clear to do both shows—and I had my very good friends at NBC to thank!

You see, of the ten regular cast members who were hired for the show, I was the *only* Canadian. The others had signed big fat series option deals through the show's American casting director and were making a (rather large) flat sum per episode. I, on the other hand, was brought on as a local hire through a local casting office—that meant that I made barely more than the union scale, which worked out to about $1,500 a day before overtime. My entire salary was a tiny, inconsequential drop in NBC's bucket; they did not allocate anything more than the absolute bare minimum for a Canadian hire because, quite frankly, we're not respected until we prove ourselves south of the border. Therefore, because the network couldn't be bothered to *option* me—that is, to offer me an exclusive multi-season contract—I could not be legally prevented from accepting a regular role on another show.

Days before my twenty-seventh birthday, I was brought in for a screen test.

A screen test, or chemistry read, is an audition typically involving all the key decision makers of a show, as well as any actors already cast to determine compatibility. It's usually the final round before a major casting decision is made. You may have seen some famous tests floating around on YouTube—Marvel tends to release them, so you may even see mine one day—but my personal gem is Steve Carell's hysterical audition for *Anchorman*; without giving too much away, I think it's a pretty good example of why he is one of the greatest actors of our time.

It's standard in the industry to sign your deal prior to going in for your test; for me, it was a four-year series option with a built-in raise for every season the show was renewed. It was more money than I had ever seen in my life, and I bragged to my parents without having even booked the part.

"See? I'm finally making a living doing what I love!"

"That's nice. Did you know that Cheryl recently bought a house with her fiancé, Ernest? He's a urology resident and will make minimum $400,000 a year once he becomes a full doctor."

Well shit, Mom.

I would later learn that my father had recurring nightmares for a week that I didn't get the role, which was actually kind of sweet. It definitely showed that he cared, although I suppose it also kind of revealed his level of confidence in my abilities.

The day of my test I walked into an eerily empty waiting room and felt immediately on edge—I had fully expected to see either Patrick or Shannon (or both) sitting there, pacing back and forth and running their lines. Their absence was very unsettling. I went over to the reception desk to sign in, and saw that the sheet was completely empty; there was nobody else coming in.

At this point, I started to get very, *very* nervous.

A few moments later Paul, who played Appa, came out and warmly shook my hand. He was a large, jovial man—kind of like a Korean Santa. His warm and engaging presence put me at ease a little, but that wouldn't last long—within a few minutes we were called in to the main room where a dozen executives, producers and casting agents all sat in a row, waiting for me.

"Hey, Simu! Thanks so much for coming in. How are you feeling?"

Like evacuating all of my orifices at once, ma'am. "Great, thanks for bringing me in!"

I may not have had conservatory-level training as an actor, but

I could work a room; it was one of the accidentally relevant skills I picked up in business school. We used to mock interview each other ad nauseam in preparation for recruiting season, refining our soft skills and drilling our answers until they were perfect. Put plainly, I could bullshit my way through a professional setting. I marched through the door of the audition room and shook everyone's hand, the whole time fighting the urge to collapse in a fit of nervous body spasms, and then took my place in front of the camera.

"Aaaaand, ACTION!"

I performed two scenes in total—a comedic one with a reader, and then a more dramatic one with Paul set in a hospital room—over the course of about a half hour. The most important piece of mental clarity I gained was not to treat an audition room as a place of judgment, but rather of collaboration and play. I think that directing my own work and sitting in on other auditions as a reader was what really drove it home for me. In studying other actors, I had seen so many instances where they had defeated themselves before even uttering a single line. Conversely, I had also seen incredibly talented performers who simply weren't right for the specific role they were reading for. At the end of the day, I learned that—contrary to what most actors would like to believe—it really wasn't about *us*. So, why not try to have some fun instead of worrying about things we couldn't control?

Easier said than done, I know. Trust me, if I never had to audition again in my lifetime, I would be a very happy man.

Still, on the day, I tried as hard as I could to disregard the power dynamics of the room and simply focused on having a nice back-and-forth with my director and scene partner. When I got a request to do a scene again with notes and adjustments, I would take it as an opportunity to show more of my range, rather than as a criticism of my acting skill. While I knew that I couldn't necessarily force anybody to cast me, I also knew that I wouldn't be in my own way.

Afterward, I went home and tried to pass the time doing literally *anything* to take my mind off of the job. I napped often and slept in as long as I could, as every waking minute I was wondering why my agent hadn't called yet.

After two excruciating days of waiting, I was officially offered the part of Jung Kim on *Kim's Convenience*. I cried for a long time that day, thinking about all of the nights of self-doubt and severe anxiety I'd had over the past four years. I'd pushed my parents to the limits of their tolerance, invested years of my life in a venture that had landed me right on the poverty line and in debt. Now, *finally*, it was all starting to pay off.

There was just one catch—getting cast in two shows was great and all, but I still had to physically *shoot* both of them. Looking at their respective schedules, I was facing about two months of overlap between the two shows. I asked my agent how it was going to be possible.

"It's possible. But you're not gonna like it."

Thus began the busiest summer of my life.

On a clear, balmy day in June, production of season one of *Kim's Convenience* commenced with a scene between myself, Andrea Bang (playing my sister, Janet) and Andrew Phung (playing my best friend Kimchee). We were all so convinced that we were going to suck, and then the director and the network would realize they had made a terrible mistake and swiftly replace us.

We were shooting an episode tag (ending scene), where Janet would sneak up to Kimchee and *dongjeem* him (basically ramming two hands folded in prayer position right up the butt crack) while he was bent over cleaning a car. It was a hilarious scene, but there was very little laughter; we were all sweating profusely, terrified that we weren't being funny enough.

"Kevin . . . was it shit? Am I shit?" I asked one of our showrunners anxiously after the first take.

"It's not shit, Simu."

"Okay. But you'll tell me if it is, right?"

"Sure, buddy."

It was pretty unheard of to have a show built around so many unknown faces, but that burden fell on us because of the times—there were very few Asian Canadian actors working at all, let alone with any name recognition whatsoever. We could either fumble the golden opportunity that was given to us, or rise to meet the challenge.

By no means am I saying that I was where I needed to be right away ... but after five successful seasons, I'd say we definitely seized our moment.

Then in mid-July, production began on *Taken*. I was a minor character, an office tech that never went into the field, so the producers from each show were able to coordinate a sustainable shooting schedule for me. It wasn't necessarily the most fulfilling work in the world (especially knowing that the Americans were being paid exponentially more for doing the same job), but I learned a tremendous amount about how the industry worked in the States through talking with my costars. Hanging with them was great; I never got the sense that they looked down on me for being Canadian, and they were always willing to help.

Once, in the middle of an all-night shoot, Gaius Charles (one of the regular actors) pulled me aside for a pep talk.

"I've been thinking about your situation, and I think you really gotta go for it," he said to me as we sat in our cast chairs. "There's a lot of opportunities opening up for people like us, so you gotta swing BIG."

As an actor of color himself, I think Gaius really understood that a massive paradigm shift was about to reverberate throughout Hollywood. His words really cemented in my mind what I was already feeling, and I felt more committed than ever to blazing a path from Toronto to Hollywood sooner rather than later. I can't say how thankful I was for his words. I immediately called Chris and told him to set me up with an immigration lawyer to help me get a US work visa.

My shoot schedules between the shows did not always blend together harmoniously. I remember one week in particular I worked seven "days" between Monday and Friday; I'd get picked up at 5:30 a.m. to be on the *Kim's* set, work thirteen hours until 6:30 p.m., and then hop onto the transport shuttle for *Taken*, which would already be waiting for me. I would cease to be Jung Kim, the lovable assistant manager at Handy Car Rental, and would become Faaron (first name only . . . or was it a last name?), the ex-CIA tech operative on lead character Bryan Mills's support team. I'd work another eight hours hacking mainframes, creating GUI interfaces and saying "enhance" a bunch of times, and then head home at 3:00 a.m. to lay my head on a pillow for a few minutes just to start it all over again. Pretty much anytime we changed camera setups, I was in my trailer trying to give my body an ounce of the sleep it so desperately needed.

Even at my peak level of exhaustion, though, there was a little voice in the back of my head reminding me how fortunate I was to be in this position. I was just grateful to be working.

Kim's Convenience would air on the CBC in mid-October, while I was still shooting pickups for *Taken*. Even though we believed in the show and our story, I don't think any of us expected it to hit the way it did. My parents bought a massive 90-inch TV, turned their basement into a screening room and invited their friends to come over every week to watch the newest episode. They had been the laughingstocks of their friend group for a long time because of me—now, their son was on a hit show on a major Canadian network. Finally, they could hold their heads up high.

In the fall, as I was finishing up my shooting, I received word from US Customs and Immigration that my visa had been approved; I was now legally able to audition in the States as an "alien of extraordinary ability." I had spent hours (and thousands of dollars) building up a strong application with my lawyer, consolidating everything from press accolades to award nominations, to the bewilderment of my parents.

"You've only just gotten on your feet. What's wrong with you?" My dad lost his temper on me over the phone one night. *"You're totally unestablished. What makes you think you'd have any credibility in LA? You need to focus on doing a good job* here *and appreciating the opportunity you've been given. Stop dreaming things that are unrealistic."*

I was so irate I hung up on him. Years later, after hearing my father's own unbelievable tale of coming over to Canada, I had to ask him:

"You realize the irony, right, Dad? You defied the odds to come here and build a life and then told me to do the exact opposite."

My dad laughed. "It's exactly because I had been through it already that I knew how hard it would be. Plus, I had a master's degree in a technical field; you were just a guy on TV! Where's the stability in that?"

He had a point, but I'm glad I didn't listen to him.

Although I had been hoping to escape to someplace tropical and slow roast on a beach after a hectic summer, I immediately booked a trip to Los Angeles and told Chris that I would take any audition, meeting, coffee chat or anything that he could throw my way. I went through all of my materials—cleaned up my resume, spruced up my demo reel—and even assembled a business-style pitch package that spoke to my marketability and return on investment. I think my b-school professors would have been proud.

Any doubt that I had harbored about Chris completely evaporated at this point. With the ammunition that I had given him, my manager picked up the phone and got to work. Within a few days I had a jam-packed schedule of agency meetings, auditions and even a go-see with the producer of the Disney remake of *Mulan* (despite the fact that I obviously didn't get the part, the meeting actually went really well). Chris had seen how all-in I was, and he was finally ready to go all-in with me.

Hollywood was no longer a faraway fairy tale, an unobtainable fantasy—it was close enough to touch. This time, I would be ready—this time, I would steer clear of the tourist traps, stay in an actual Airbnb and rent a car to get around. I was ready for a rematch.

CHAPTER TWENTY-THREE

CITY OF SHATTERED DREAMS

I actually almost booked the very first audition I was ever sent on in America.

I was in Sharon Bialy's casting office to read for a major role on HBO's *Here and Now*, created by visionary screenwriter Alan Ball—just names and words for this Canadian fresh off a plane. I remember apologizing to Sharon that I hadn't had time to read the entire pilot yet, thinking that I had blown my chance with her. Chris rang me the next day with a callback appointment.

"Make sure you read the pilot this time, bro."

I was incredulous; this would be even easier than I had thought! Soon after, I had the opportunity to audition for Alan (who I had realized by then was a pretty big deal) on a lot in West Hollywood. We got incredible feedback and were told a screen test deal was imminent. I was all set to make big moves in California!

Between the fall of 2016 and the end of 2018, I visited LA eight separate times in intervals ranging from one week to four months. That first audition in Sharon's office was proof to me that I was where I needed to be. *Kim's Convenience* had been swiftly renewed for more seasons in the wake of its success, so I would still return to Toronto for the summers, or to do any other work that I was offered—otherwise, I would try to be in California as much as I could.

It was a tough sell to my girlfriend at the time, who did not know she was signing up for a quasi-long-distance relationship. As an actor herself, though, she ultimately understood putting career first and striking while the iron was hot—if our positions were reversed and she were the one with the visa, I'd have expected her to do the same thing. She's still out there today, fighting the good fight as one of the most talented actresses I've ever had the pleasure of watching.

With my partner's blessing, I proceeded to wholeheartedly commit to becoming a working actor in Hollywood. My plan was simply to start at the bottom of the pile again and work my way up—this time, I'd be armed with a chunky resume and a manager who knew his way around—and see what would stick. I figured that at the very least I could nail down a couple of small roles to warm myself up and establish my name, and then work my way up slowly. At most . . . well, who could say? The beauty of the city was that there was no limit to what could happen.

As I eagerly awaited news about *Here and Now*, we finally got word that HBO's business affairs department killed the whole deal because of my multiyear contract with *Kim's Convenience*. The terms of my deal with *Kim's* and the CBC meant that they possessed *first position*, meaning that they had a legal right to request my availability at any point throughout the year. Thus, even if the shoot dates for *Here and Now* were totally clear of our show's, HBO wouldn't want to put themselves in a position where they could potentially be screwed if dates shifted for any reason.

It hurt to hear Chris explain the situation to me, but I remained pretty encouraged. *Maybe this wasn't meant to be,* I thought. *Maybe something better lies just around the corner.*

"Just around the corner" turned out to be a lot longer than I thought. Over the next couple of years I would sink tens of thousands of dollars into my LA venture—in airfare, accommodations, car rentals and living expenses—and make absolutely nothing. I was burning money so quickly I might as well have been day-trading crypto. Every time

I would think I had finally caught a break, something would happen and the opportunity would be yanked out from under me.

Chris and I had been hoping to sign with a top-tier US agency that would further bolster our team. Agents were more plugged in to the studio system than the managers, who tended to be more client focused. In a smaller market like Canada, there was no need for anyone to have more than a single point person—in the States, you needed a full team behind you if you wanted coverage across all the casting offices for the hundreds of studios, networks and streaming platforms that were out there. After hitting up all the contacts he had, Chris set up a slew of meetings at some very strong shops around town. I did the rounds and received a lot of offers for representation, but I always had Gaius's words in the back of my head—*swing big*. I wanted to hold out for a major agency, the type that represented *movie stars*.

The opportunity came with a meeting with a partner (let's call her Linda Williams) at United Talent Agency. UTA was the same agency that built the careers of A-listers like Channing Tatum, Kevin Hart and Chris Pratt—definitely the big swing that I had imagined. My manager had worked with Linda back in the day and had used his connection to set up a little get-together.

Linda was waiting for me as I walked into the massive lobby of the UTA campus. She radiated a power and confidence with every step that she took. I, by comparison, was a fidgety little boy who still could not believe how high the ceilings were. She introduced herself to me with a firm handshake, and I remember thinking—*damn . . . this is my person.*

Linda asked if I wanted a water. I stammered a yes, and she procured me one from a nearby fridge.

"Remember this moment—Linda Williams just brought you water."

Brilliant, I thought. *This is going really, really well.*

And then . . . she just left.

I was confused—weren't we supposed to meet to talk about representation? Instead, I was ushered into a boardroom where a junior agent made small talk with me for a few minutes and then quickly ended our meeting. When Chris followed up with Linda later, she said that there was already an Asian man on her roster that she was trying to build, and it wouldn't be fair to take us both on. Fair enough, but then why tell me to even show up? I figured that she had probably sized me up and immediately decided that I wasn't worth her time.

I promised myself that one day, I would prove her wrong.

With UTA now off the table, and none of the other major agencies even bothering to return a call, our search for top-tier representation had ended in total failure. In the meantime we were constantly running into issues with my visa; I had originally thought that having work papers would mean that I could work in the States like any other actor, but it turned out not to be the case; many studios refused to accept O-1 visas as valid work permits or had very specific rules about hiring O-1 actors. In April of 2017, I was cast in a short film as part of a Warner Bros. accelerator program for directors. It was a small-scale project that paid a hundred bucks a day, but I jumped at the chance to get my feet wet and work on the famous Warner's lot. I excitedly booked a round-trip flight to LA and waited for the director to get back to me about a rehearsal day.

She never did.

Instead, I got a call from Chris telling me that the studio had told her they weren't willing to hire O-1 actors for this project. With all my tickets and hotels already booked, I ended up flying down for a week and spent my days networking and eating Thai food.

Later in the year, I was offered a four-line role on an hour-long legal procedural on ABC called *For the People*. I had auditioned for a bigger guest star role initially, but I could not have cared less; this was going to be my first American credit, and I wasn't opposed to starting small. Like a basketball player riding a cold streak, I just needed to see the ball go through the net. This time, the deal had closed, the contract was signed, and a script had been mailed to me—surely nothing could go wrong?

As I was preparing to leave my place to go to my wardrobe fitting, I felt my phone buzz. I reached into my pocket with a knowing sense of dread and, lo and behold, it was the show's wardrobe department:

> Hello Simu,
> Your fitting today with Costumes for For The People has been cancelled. Linda Lowy Casting has reached out to your agents and they will be able to explain the situation further.
>
> Best,
> Jackie

It was against the network's policy to hire foreign actors to play smaller roles. Once again, I had been screwed by bureaucracy.

It was all beginning to feel like some cruel joke, but my misfortunes would not end there. One month I'd get put on hold for a massive commercial campaign and then get released. Another month, a show would express interest in offering a test deal, but we would run into the same issue with the *Kim's Convenience* contract. One night I sat at home with a plane ticket and a test deal in my hand, waiting for the two networks to agree on legal terms so that I could fly out and audition. The green light would never come, and the plane ticket went to waste.

One of my greatest heartbreaks of all would come when I auditioned for a little movie called *Crazy Rich Asians*. The casting director reacted positively to my audition for Nick Young, but suggested that I try for one of the other roles as they had just found their lead in a relatively unknown Malaysian TV host by the name of Henry Golding. With Nick already spoken for—Henry was just about the most suave and gorgeous man I had ever laid eyes on, by the way—we went down the list of other crazy rich characters hoping that I would catch director Jon Chu's eye.

After a few weeks of sending tapes back and forth and crossing my fingers, articles on *Deadline* and *Variety* began to pop up announcing that each of the roles had been cast. I reached out to my manager to get some form of closure.

"Hey, man... so we did talk to Jon, but—uh... are you sure you want to hear this?"

I felt my chest tighten up. What choice did I have at this point? I told him to tell me.

"He said you were a good actor... but you just didn't have that *it* factor."

Boom.

And there it was, a ton of bricks being dropped right on top of me. *Well shit*, I thought, *that's gonna be inside my head for a while.*

Chris would go on and say that it was just *one* opinion, and that I shouldn't get too hung up on it—but I could already feel the truth in the words. The mental dams that I had constructed to keep my insecurities at bay finally collapsed, and my mind was overcome with a wave of anxiety and paranoia. I replayed my auditions endlessly in my head, dissecting them and feeling bad despite there being nothing I could do. I thought back to all of these lost opportunities and found a way to pin the blame back on myself. I was, after all, the common denominator in all of this. Maybe if I had been better, I would have turned some of those nos into yesses. If I had been better, maybe the networks would have been more willing to take a chance on me, and maybe Linda Williams would have stayed to chat. There was no end to my downward mental spiral.

When *Crazy Rich Asians* was released in 2018, I was in a far better place mentally and was able to fully celebrate the importance of the moment. It was a resounding victory for Asian American representation, featuring an ensemble of actors who were *perfectly* cast, from the painfully handsome Henry Golding and the intensely vulnerable Constance Wu to a disarmingly elegant Gemma Chan, a hilariously quirky Awkwafina, the simply amazing Ken Jeong and so many more. Jon's words (at least as they were relayed to me) motivated me to continue to perfect my craft and be a better actor. I can't deny that it still hurt like hell back then, but life has a way of bringing things full circle, and Jon and I had already become friends by the time this book was being written. He remembers his words very differently, and we now think it was just a case of broken telephone that happens all too often in Hollywood, where most everything is filtered through an agent, assistant, publicist, manager, therapist or golf caddy; something always gets lost in translation. At the end of the day, the reality was that I just wasn't right for any of the roles.

We agreed to keep the words in this book as I originally heard them, though, because of how deeply I was affected by them. It's a testament to Jon's thoughtful and compassionate nature—definitely not the type of guy that would throw around phrases like "it factor"—and I remain extremely grateful to have gotten that feedback, even if it didn't directly come from him.

The anguish that I faced then was vastly different than in my early years as an actor—I was no longer fighting just to keep myself out of credit card debt, but that didn't mean that the stakes were any lower. In LA, I met actors driving Ubers whose careers I would have *killed* to have had. Ultimately, an actor was only as good as their next project, and there was never any guarantee that there would even *be* a "next"— especially for actors who looked like me. My job with *Kim's Convenience* was paying the bills, but how long would it last? What would happen after the show finished? If I couldn't springboard myself to my next opportunity while my show was still relevant, then I risked falling back into total obscurity and starting all over again. At the time, those felt like life-and-death stakes to me.

I had come down with guns blazing hoping to take the city by storm with my talent and hard work; but the longer I stayed, the more I started to doubt myself.

Amid all the rejection and heartbreak I was experiencing in Hollywood, *Kim's Convenience* should have been a silver lining, a respite from the anguish and uncertainty. Our show became a bona fide global hit in 2017 when it was licensed by Netflix and released in dozens of countries worldwide. With accolades coming left and right, we should have been on top of the world. Regrettably, however, this was not the case—at least for me. As the years went on, the show began to feel less like a big break and more like a dead end.

My anxiety toward our show was rooted in more than the restrictive nature of my contract with the producers. Season after season, Jung's screen time was becoming more and more scarce, his story lines progressively less consequential. It was like he had become a supporting character in his own story—a feeling that I'm sure will resonate with many people of color reading this. I remember blinking back tears during a season three table read in which Jung did not appear until the nineteenth page of the script. Selfishly, I was worried that my career was tanking before it even really took off—but on a broader level, it broke my heart to see my character relegated to the background while many non-Asian characters were given more and more opportunities to shine. In general, I felt our show veering away from the authentic immigrant narratives that gave us our unique voice; instead, we were embracing slapstick comedy, quippy one-liners, and story lines that didn't carry past a singular episode.

I wasn't the only cast member to feel this way, and many of us attempted to voice our concerns to the show's producers to little avail. The message we got back was loud and clear: we were *actors*, not writers, and we ought to be grateful to even have a seat at the table. Hell, even my parents echoed the same sentiment when I tried to voice my frustrations.

"You owe that show everything! Put your head down and show some gratitude!"

I want to be crystal clear here—I was, and am, endlessly grateful for all that *Kim's Convenience* gave to me. But I refused to let that gratitude silence my voice or cloud my desire to demand better for myself. I put my heart and soul into our show, but I knew that it did not love me the same way. The salvation of my career would lie elsewhere—in the place where my shining star was washed out by the blinding lights of a million other dreamers who wanted the same thing. In Hollywood, there was always someone taller, smarter, funnier, better looking, and with more followers on Instagram . . . and even *that* person was probably serving tables to make ends meet. Frustrated both at home and abroad, and seemingly thwarted at every turn, my path to success seemed unfathomably narrow. Yet, as abysmal as my odds were, I knew that I could not let up; if I failed, it would mean that the producers and my parents were all right about me. It would mean that I really was a fool for believing that I deserved more.

Fool or not, I had to prove them all wrong.

Fool or not, I had to bet on myself.

CHAPTER TWENTY-FOUR

BIG ASIAN ENERGY

For most of my life I've thought of myself as a bit of a lone wolf—real self-important, me-against-the-world type stuff.

Having changed families at age five, I think I learned about the impermanence of all things early on. Despite always dreaming of being a part of a loving family, I only ever knew the feeling of being alone. I grew up bouncing around cities and schools (and friend groups), never settling into any one community. I didn't feel safe at home with my parents, who were aloof and distant at best, and abusive at worst. I didn't even have any brothers and sisters to talk to and go through it all with; I had no choice but to rely on myself.

I carried this mentality with me throughout my career as an actor, where it served me well. It was very much me against the world, fighting against whatever or whomever stood in my way. I remembered every time I was passed over, second-guessed or outright rejected, and used it to fuel myself to work harder. I refused to accept any status quo that the world attempted to impose on me, whether it was a casting director, a schoolteacher, a classmate or my own parents. I always liked that about myself—it made me scrappy, hungry, self-motivated and maybe even a little mysterious?

In Hollywood, however, I would see the limits of where that chip on my shoulder could take me. I would experience frustration and helplessness like I had never felt before, as the so-called city of dreams served me one defeat after another. I was beaten down and losing my will to keep going. Alone in the big city, I would have been swallowed whole by the monstrosity of the Hollywood machine and ultimately defeated by my own sense of anxiety, failure and isolation.

In order to survive, I had to learn how to embrace something greater than just myself.

It all started with the kindness and generosity of one man: the incredible Ken Jeong.

When I landed in LA in 2017 for my first pilot season, I didn't know a single soul aside from my manager Chris. Ken had heard about our show—before we even got a US Netflix deal, no less—and had followed all of us on Twitter, which meant his DMs were open to me. Figuring I had nothing to lose, I shot him a message and asked if he'd be down to meet for a coffee or something (advice for any DM-sliders out there—keep it as easy and noncommittal as possible).

I was not prepared for the tsunami of generosity that was about to hit me.

Ken responded within minutes:

Ken Jeong (@kenjeong):

Hey Simu!
My email is [redacted] let's figure out a time to hang
I am working on Dr Ken all month at Sony in Culver City

My brain exploded; someone as famous as Ken wanted to email with *me*?! I quickly obliged and, within minutes again, I received parking instructions and a drive-on pass to the Sony Pictures lot in Culver City. I was told to visit anytime—whether it was a rehearsal, a table read, or an episode taping.

Did I have anything better to do than to visit my new friend Ken Jeong on his set? Surely not; this was the opportunity of a *lifetime* and I made myself entirely available, slinking around rehearsals and stuffing my face with craft services during episode tapings. Every time he saw me, Ken would wrap me up in a big hug and tell me how much he loved my show. After live audience tapings, Ken would retreat to his dressing room to take a break from working all night and from the large crowds that formed each and every week. I'd always get a call or text from his assistant asking if I wanted to go over and say hi. I've never told him this, but Ken was a shining beacon of kindness during some of my toughest days in LA.

Getting to know Ken emboldened me to reach out to more people within the Asian American community. I got to know Michelle Sugihara and all of the incredible work she did with CAPE (the Coalition of Asian Pacifics in Entertainment), from dinners with major network executives to mentorship programs for emerging screenwriters. Michelle connected me to Jeff Yang, a writer whose son Hudson played Eddie Huang on *Fresh Off the Boat*. Through Jeff, I was able to visit the set of *Fresh* and meet Randall Park, another hugely famous Asian American actor, who was also incredibly kind and generous with his advice and connections. Soon, my schedule was packed with meetings and my network had grown to a considerable size.

I realized that the reason any of those people gave me the time of day was because they knew firsthand the struggle of being Asian in this line of work. Like me, they had wrestled with identity their whole lives, constantly fighting to be seen as equal to everyone else. Having laid down roots in a city that exports culture all over the world, they understood that representation on-screen did not come easy, and needed to be supported.

I had wanted to meet Philip Wang from Wong Fu Productions for many years before I ever became an actor. Phil had started Wong Fu as a hobby while he was still in college at UCSD with his friends Wes and Ted. The three of them made lip-sync videos and funny sketches that went viral, leading them to build a massive YouTube channel that boasts over three million subscribers today. At a time when there were very few Asian people in the traditional system, Phil went ahead and made his own system. Wong Fu became a household name among Asian kids raised in the West, and I was beyond excited when we got connected through a mutual friend.

From the moment I sat down with Phil at the Wong Fu office, I could tell how deeply he believed in what he was doing. He was one of the first people I had ever met who spoke of being Asian as an *advantage*. He believed that our community, of which he had been an important custodian, was actually our superpower. Phil's willingness to lean into his Asianness had allowed him to build a massive and dedicated audience, made up of the very people who needed a voice. I told him I wanted to be a part of that in any way possible.

Phil would introduce me to an entire ecosystem of Asian American YouTubers, musicians and influencers who did not rely on any network or studio to give them a job. They existed in a fully self-sufficient system directly supported by their fan bases, just like Wong Fu. It was absolutely awe-inspiring to be in the presence of so many people who owed their success to leaning into their communities and being proud of who they were.

I came to a massive epiphany right when I was at my most discouraged state, and it has defined my life and guided every decision I have made ever since.

Having been a part of two television series with all-Asian casts, I was already a very vocal proponent of diversity and inclusion. But I realized in talking with Phil and his friends that I had only begun to scratch the surface of what that truly meant. It was more than just being able to see yourself reflected on a screen somewhere—it was about building out our culture through our shared experiences and reflections. It didn't matter if you were raised by Chinese parents in Toronto, or Vietnamese parents in Melbourne, or Korean parents in Los Angeles; there was a common DNA between all of us, and it was imperative that we fought to create content that captured our collective voices.

In 2018, Phil would ask me to play a character in *YAPPIE*, a web series Wong Fu was developing that centered around young Asian professionals in California. I could not have said "YES!" any faster or louder. Being plugged in to Wong Fu's audience base immediately skyrocketed my platform, but I knew that this was about more than just growing Instagram followers. I had a responsibility to make each and every one of them feel like they were represented and that they *belonged*.

If you think about it, Asian diasporic life is still so sparsely covered in mainstream media. I'm not talking about Chinese culture, or Japanese, Indian, Korean or Vietnamese; those countries produce their own media and culture which represents them just fine. But what about the experiences of second-generation kids like us—like feeling ashamed of the lunches our parents packed us because they were too "ethnic"? Or having to translate things for our parents because our English was better than theirs? Or struggling to communicate with our relatives in our home country because our Mandarin/Cantonese/Hindi/Korean/Viet was absolute horseshit?

How about being home alone at a far younger age than was legally permissible because our parents worked so much, and actually *loving* it because it meant we got to watch cartoons without guilt? Or having a dishwasher at home that never ran because your parents weren't accustomed to using one? I could do this all day.

I don't know where you typically go to grab a drink with your friends, but for me, it's neither Starbucks nor the Irish Pub—I stopped drinking alcohol when I graduated from college (although I'm partial to a delicious pumpkin spice latte once in a while, 'cause I'm basic like that). For me, it's the Go For Tea in Markham, Ontario, Boba Guys in the Bay Area, Bopomofo in the San Gabriel Valley or Machi Machi on George Street in Sydney's CBD. When I sip the sugary goodness of bubble tea through my oversize straw, I'm drinking not only the tastiest beverage ever made, but also an *insanely* popular one that has been completely ignored by Hollywood and other mainstream media.

Ever tried to get a table at a Korean barbecue joint on a Friday night in K-town? Good luck—without a hookup or a reservation, you'll be waiting hours! The same goes for hot pot, a delicious cook-it-yourself experience where slices of meat are dipped in broths like a fondue right in front of you. These restaurants are more than places to eat dinner; they are a way of life.

Watching television, though, you'd never even know that these places existed. It so perfectly exemplifies the racism that we continue to feel every day—not necessarily of outright hostility (although the COVID-19 pandemic certainly brought that out in people), but of invisibility and erasure.

The roots of anti-Asian racism in the West can be traced all the way back to the Chinese Exclusion Act of 1882, signed by American president Chester A. Arthur to systematically prevent prospective Chinese immigrants and migrant workers from obtaining American citizenship. In the late nineteenth century, tens of thousands of Chinese migrant workers had come to America and Canada to help build the infrastructures of the respective countries, primarily in mining and railway construction. While this was initially welcomed by the general population, public opinion of the Chinese waned in the coming years as white nationalists began to spread propaganda that painted all Chinese as threats to national security. These horrendous drawings depicted all Chinese people as rat-like, bucktoothed devils who were out to take white people's jobs and women.

Just to be clear, America invited the Chinese people to work on their railroads because they did better work for a lower wage, and then turned on them . . . because they did better work for a lower wage.

This xenophobia was so pervasive that it infected every level of American society, from the working class to the elites. US Supreme Court judge John Marshall Harlan once said that Chinese people were "a race so different from our own that we do not permit those belonging to it to become citizens of the United States." And so, to make it official, the Exclusion Act was passed in 1882 and would not be struck down until 1942, after which the ever-benevolent government was "kind" enough to permit a whopping 105 Chinese immigrants to enter the country each year.

That's . . . not even enough people to staff an Apple Store.

Similar pieces of racist legislation passed in Australia and Canada in the coming years, all with the express objective of limiting the flow of Chinese immigrants entering their borders. The Canadian government imposed a Chinese head tax in 1885, which forced hopeful immigrants to pay a preposterous amount of money ($50, or the equivalent of almost $2,000 today) in order to get into the country. Fifteen years later, the amount was doubled to $100 (almost $4,000 today) per head. Three years after that, the government increased the fee fivefold to $500. Finally, two decades after *that,* someone in the House of Commons straight up said, "You know what, why do we even need Chinese people at *all*?" and banned immigration, which should tell you all you need to know about how Westerners viewed Asian people at the time.

"They are unfit for full citizenship and are permitted to take no part in municipal or provincial government. Upon this point there was entire unanimity. They are not and will not become citizens in any sense of the term, as we understand it. They are so nearly allied to a servile class that they are obnoxious to a free community and dangerous to the state."

The point I'm trying to make through all this is that even though Western countries like America, Canada and Australia have leaned on and benefited greatly from Asian immigrants for over 150 years, our place in the Western world has always had an asterisk beside it. For some (maybe even *most*) white people, those who look like me and my family will never truly belong. Just ask the tens of thousands of Asian people who have suffered verbal and physical harassment in the wake of COVID-19, empowered by Donald Trump's never-ending (and scientifically unsupported) stream of "China virus" rhetoric. The perception of all Asian people as perpetual foreigners meant that no matter where we grew up, claimed citizenship, or paid our taxes, we would always be seen as "other." Perhaps that's why every time I scrolled through my phone, I'd see countless instances of Asian people being pushed to the ground, or punched, or stabbed, or shot.

Enough was enough.

Our culture deserved to be normalized and celebrated without being made into a punchline in movies and on television. We, in turn, needed to fight for our right to be treated as human beings. As my platform grew, I began to realize that I had a responsibility to be an outspoken representative of our community. When it seemed that our world was being consumed by xenophobia and hate, a sea of voices emerged and pushed back with an equal and opposing force of love and pride in our cultural heritage. Alongside others, I joined this rallying cry. I wrote an op-ed piece that was featured in *Variety*, filmed public service announcements with other prominent Asian figures, spoke out in interviews with major news outlets, and even participated in a roundtable discussion about AAPI issues with Hillary Clinton.

(In case you're wondering, yes—I was very, *very* nervous.)

As I began to shift my social messaging to become more outspoken on issues of culture and race, I received invitations to speak at corporations and colleges across North America. Often, I was brought in by culturally specific student unions or AAPI employee groups.

I spoke about growing up in an immigrant household and butting heads with my parents, whose lives were so fundamentally different from mine that it made conflict almost inevitable. I spoke about growing up ashamed of my Asianness, from the food I ate to the shape of my eyes and the color of my hair, and wishing that I was white. I spoke about the echoes of racism still felt from the Chinese Exclusion Laws and the internment of Japanese families in America and Canada.

I've since traveled all across the continent—and logged on to many a Zoom session—to speak at colleges and universities about finding my purpose, following my dreams and reclaiming my cultural pride. Afterward, I always try to stick around and chat a bit. I've heard countless stories from students who felt like they were in the wrong program but were scared to tell their parents that they wanted to be an actor, or musician, or graphic designer, or anything except what their parents deemed acceptable. More still wanted to know how my own parents dealt with my sudden decision to pursue acting. I've also heard from employees who want to feel more empowered to speak out in the workplace, whether it be for equal opportunities and pay or to call out microaggressions and cultural blind spots. It really cemented for me the idea that there was a connective tissue that defined what it meant to be Asian American or Canadian or Australian, much of which was passed down from our mothers and fathers. Contrary to what I had often felt in my adolescence, I was not alone; my experience was one that was shared by countless other people struggling with parental pressure, cultural barriers and internalized self-hatred. What I hoped to impart to everyone I spoke to was that while we need to be grateful for the wisdom of our parents, we also need to forge our own path in this society. Many of our parents told us to keep our heads down, but I wanted us to stand up, to not be afraid of taking up space in the room, and to understand how powerful we could be if we banded together.

I'm truly happy to have met so many people and impacted their lives, if only in a small way; they've certainly impacted mine.

As the audience for *Kim's Convenience* grew larger and the cast attained a small slice of celebrity, we found ourselves the unwitting spokespeople for diversity in Canada. In every round of press that we did and every red carpet that we attended we were constantly asked to comment on the show's social significance. The idea of speaking on behalf of an entire race of people used to make me uncomfortable, but I would happily attack that question now, boldly, for every Asian boy or girl who has ever felt like they were less than.

I want to stare right at them through their screens and let them know that their Asianness is a part of what makes them *amazing*, that they are a part of a rich and vibrant culture, that their parents moved mountains to be able to settle in a new country, and that they should always hold their heads high and NEVER apologize for who they are.

By the time my career is done, and I'm a washed-up has-been hosting the 83rd season of *Family Feud*, I hope I'll be remembered for my off-screen accomplishments as much as my work as an actor. These days my team and I are fighting across all fronts, whether it's working with Asian creatives to develop culturally specific projects that celebrate our people, implementing inclusion riders whenever we can to ensure adequate representation across all levels of cast and crew, or chasing after parts that were not written Asian and persuading producers to change their minds. I also try to use my platform to spotlight Asian-owned non-profit and for-profit businesses, organize large-scale cultural celebrations, and work with advocacy groups like RUN AAPI to activate diasporic Asian youth and get them fired up about political participation. I'm still a small fry in the business, and I don't expect I'll always get the win, but know that I will always be fighting the good fight in one way or another.

In December of 2018, on the heels of a wildly successful premiere of *Black Panther* that shattered box office records as well as the notion that people of color could not carry big-budget tentpoles, Marvel Studios announced that they were fast-tracking a movie about an Asian superhero.

Gee, I thought, *wouldn't it be great if it were me?* I facetiously tweeted:

Simu Liu (@SimuLiu):
OK @Marvel, are we gonna talk or what #ShangChi
7:54 AM—Dec 4, 2018

It's not like I actually believed that I could book the job—I was just cracking a joke, in the way that ordinary people talk about winning the lottery, or dating Cate Blanchett. Just one year later, though, and despite my lack of confidence in my abilities, I would find myself in Sydney, Australia, gearing up to play the role of a lifetime.

CHAPTER TWENTY-FIVE

A DATE WITH DESTINY

When I was eleven, I somehow scored the winning goal in the championship game of my house soccer league.

I was far from the best player on my team, but I was a reliable midfielder because I could hustle up and down the field like my life depended on it. I may have been a scrawny little kid with next to no muscle mass, but I could *run*.

After two scoreless halves, the game was in sudden-death overtime; whoever scored the first goal would win the championship trophy for their team. We kept trying to get the ball to our star striker, Matt, but the defense was all over him.

We were battling it out on offense when it happened: amid the chaos of a pack of muddy preteens chasing one another around a field, the ball ricocheted to me and I saw a straight shot into the opposing team's net. I knew immediately what I had to do. Time slowed to a crawl as my foot connected with the ball, and for one *perfect* moment, I knew that it was going in before anybody else in the world.

The goalie reacted just a bit too late, and the ball sailed effortlessly past the goal line into the net. Boom. Championship.

As the referee blew the whistle and everyone stormed the field to scream and dogpile on top of me, I closed my eyes and tried to imagine the looks on my parents' faces as they watched from the sidelines. It must have been so surreal for two immigrant parents to see their son hoisted on his coach's shoulders and celebrated as a hero.

In that moment, my parents' dreams were realized.

In that moment, we were no longer foreigners . . . we were home.

I had no idea that 2019 would mark the moment that my life would be irrevocably changed, forever altering my family's destiny and catapulting us into a stratosphere we never imagined in our wildest dreams.

My whirlwind year began with all the chaotic energy of a preteen soccer match; as dozens of little opportunities began to pop up from all over, I scrambled and tripped over myself trying to leverage all of them. I was busier than ever with speaking engagements. My growing social media presence opened the door to brand deals for the first time. I even booked my first major acting job in the US.

If all of that wasn't enough, 2019 was also the year that the Toronto Raptors won the NBA championship, and I met my number one hero of all time, Jeremy Lin. Becoming a minor Canadian celebrity was great and all, but *nothing* could match the excitement of seeing my Raps overcome a 0-2 deficit to eliminate the Milwaukee Bucks in the Eastern Conference Finals, before besting Steph Curry and the Golden State Warriors in a tense NBA Finals series. I was so happy; booking my first US role and riding in the Raptors' championship parade with my new friend felt like a damn good place to call it for the year. Nothing could have prepared me for what came next.

But let's back up a bit first, shall we?

Early on in January, a few days before I was set to travel down to LA for another pilot season, my friend Clement asked if I wanted to meet Jeremy—*THE* Jeremy Lin, who scored 38 on Kobe, dunked all over John Wall and sparked a global phenomenon in 2012 forever known as Linsanity. Every Asian person remembers where they were during this crazy two-week stretch, and they sure as hell remember the way Jeremy made them feel: like they were finally *seen*. Jeremy was more than a prolific basketball player—he was a cultural hero.

I answered in a manner that was appropriate for any grown-ass man, which of course meant screaming yes and then immediately bursting into tears of happiness.

Clem ran a community organization in Toronto called the Chinese Canadian Youth Athletics Association (CCYAA), which provided athletics programs for Asian youth in the Toronto area, and frequently worked with Jeremy to organize meetups and fan events when he came into town to play games. I had spoken to his kids and his volunteers in the past, and we became good friends through our recognition of our shared goals. Knowing that Jeremy was perhaps my biggest hero of all time, Clem organized an on-camera roundtable discussion with the two of us where we would talk about our paths in our respective industries.

Yes, Clem is a keeper, and no, you can't have him.

We met Jeremy at the Ritz-Carlton as the Atlanta Hawks arrived straight from the airport. I was anxious to make a good impression and had at least eight different flavors of bubble tea delivered to our room (because of *course* he would drink bubble tea, right?). We had all the drinks laid out when Jeremy came through the door rocking socks and flip-flops; he took one look at them, smiled sheepishly and explained that he was on a strict diet during the season.

I drank a *looot* of sugar that night.

Jeremy was incredibly nice and welcoming from the moment he introduced himself, and even said that he watched the show. I never told him this, but I held myself together with the utmost professionalism throughout our nearly thirty-minute discussion, waited until he left the room, then promptly collapsed in a fit of giddiness.

"I just had a first date with Jeremy freaking Lin!!!!!!"

We were just a couple of milk teas and one NBA diet away from a perfect meet-cute.

Meanwhile, the non-Jeremy aspects of my life were developing just as quickly. It was as if I had been pushing a boulder up a hill for seven years, and had suddenly hit the peak; now, the boulder was starting to move on its own, picking up so much downhill speed I started to have trouble controlling it.

For two excruciating years, my time in the States had mostly amounted to a small fortune in Airbnb fees and lots of close-but-no-cigar opportunities. Still, I kept on, building and creating wherever I could, all the while holding on to a blind faith that my next big break lay just beyond the horizon. What I got in early 2019 was not a single break but a stream of little ones, the first of which was a guest-star role on ABC's *Fresh Off the Boat*. It seemed like the drought had finally ended, but I had been so beaten down that I didn't want to believe it at first. It wasn't until I was on set that Chris and I finally shared a moment of relief over the phone:

"Holy shit, you finally did it, bro! Now that you've cracked the seal, more is gonna come our way. I can feel it!"

How fitting, too, that my very first opportunity in America would be given to me by another network sitcom featuring an all-Asian main cast. It is such a testament to the importance of creating environments for diverse talent to develop; just think of how many Asian American actors, writers, directors and extras were able to work because of that one show about a Taiwanese American family!

Chris was totally right, by the way; immediately after shooting *Fresh Off the Boat*, I was tapped to do a little indie movie in San Francisco. Then, as if on cue, my mailbox began to flood with requests to speak at colleges and events—not only Canadian schools, but all over the States as well: UCLA, Berkeley, Boston College and even Harvard. (My mother was incredulous when I told her the news. "Harvard wants *you* to speak? But . . . *why?*")

I suddenly found myself gasping for air during breaks in my schedule—the constant traveling, while very gratifying, was starting to take its toll on me. I was on a plane almost every other day, flying from shoots to speaking engagements and then home to present at an awards show, then back to LA to regroup for a few nights before doing it all over again. For a period of a few months, I think I spent more nights on an airplane than in my bed. I actually spent my thirtieth birthday in upstate New York speaking to students at Syracuse University. They were even nice enough to get me a cake!

That night, alone in my hotel room, I reflected on my extremely privileged thirty years of existence. As a child who immigrated to Canada, I'd enjoyed a very high quality of life thanks to the efforts of my parents. Despite our tempestuous relationship during my adolescence, I was still raised with the fundamental belief that what I did *mattered*. I was fortunate enough to drastically alter the course of my life not once but *twice*; first in becoming an actor, and then by working with my parents to repair our relationship. Otherwise, I'd still be a miserable accountant harboring a deep resentment for the people who raised him.

It seems like such a paradox to me that human beings are both great adapters to change and terrified by it at the same time. So often we drift through life bound by the poor decisions we've made in the past, too afraid of the uncertainty that comes with challenging our status quo. We find ourselves stuck on a ship that is headed full speed to a place we're pretty sure we don't want to go, but we also don't want to deal with the discomfort of jumping. So we say nothing, watching helplessly as we sail toward our doom like silent prisoners of our own past.

Luckily I didn't have a choice—rather, change was forced upon me against my will, in the form of a pink slip from my employers at Deloitte. Only when faced with nothing else to lose was I finally able to muster up the courage to make the decision to pursue acting. Thanks to the lucky fluke of losing my job, I became the person I was always meant to be.

The thing is, once you detach yourself from the status quo, whether by conscious effort or sheer stroke of dumb luck, you kind of develop a knack for it. The more I learned not to take my world for what it was, the more I saw the way things should be. Sometimes you have to rock the boat a little bit, and other times . . . well, you've just gotta ditch the boat and find a new one. It took thirty years, but I finally knew that I was on the right ship.

I came back home to Toronto in the spring to shoot the fourth season of *Kim's Convenience*. I had hoped that it would be something of a denouement, a break in the crazy whirlwind that was my life—in the end, though, I would be my own greatest obstacle. In the span of a month, I landed my first major commercial endorsement with Old Spice, received a development offer for a digital series I had optioned, began drafting a blueprint for a basketball charity event with Clem, and started working on a manuscript that would eventually become this book.

At dinner with my parents one night, I confided in them that life was getting busier than I could keep up with.

"Your eyes look tired." My mother, once my greatest adversary, regarded me now with great sympathy.

"I feel like every three months my life shifts into another gear. I don't know how much more of this I can handle."

"You push yourself this hard because it's what we taught you," she responded. "Please don't forget to be good to yourself."

Of course, it made sense that I would inherit my parents' words as my internal monologue. I was extremely hard on myself all the time, constantly berating myself for taking too much time off, or being distracted by social media (to be fair, I *am* constantly distracted by social media; it's a problem). I placed my personal well-being dead last on my list of priorities, behind my career—something I had most definitely inherited from my immigrant parents. I wish I could tell you I've since resolved to be kinder to myself, but undoing my programming has proven to be difficult; it's definitely still a work in progress.

When my manager sent an audition request for an *Untitled Marvel Studios Project* in May, I was knee-deep in shooting our show while simultaneously planning for the inaugural CCYAA Celebrity Classic, a charity basketball game that would feature prominent Asian Canadian and Asian American celebrities and influencers. Despite the typical

Marvel-level secrecy, everyone knew what the project was. I couldn't even begin to imagine the number of people going out for the role. As with countless auditions before, I taped my audition, forgot about it, and promptly went on with my life.

In June, the Raptors vanquished the Warriors in six games and won the championship. Pandemonium swept through the streets of Toronto—it was our first NBA championship and first major sports win since the Blue Jays won the World Series in 1993. Cars would just randomly honk on the street and all the nearby pedestrians would cheer. Strangers hugged each other spontaneously. It was an incredible time to be in the city, and I allowed myself to be swept away by its energy. Jeremy, whom I had grown a lot closer to during his time in Toronto, invited me to ride on his float for their victory parade.

Up on the float with my biggest hero, surrounded by two million rampant fans and a highly intoxicated Marc Gasol—who I swear to God made our bus sway every time he waved his ginormous arms back and forth—I thought that it couldn't possibly get any better than this. Then, impossibly, it did.

I got a call from Chris while I was on the set of *Kim's Convenience*, which I of course declined because I was a consummate professional.

He called again. I pressed *Sorry, I can't talk right now*!

Again, my phone buzzed. This dude *really* needed to get ahold of me. We were in between setups, so I quickly excused myself to retire to my room and take my manager's call. Chris wasted no time:

"How fast can you get to LA?"

In the timeless words of Martin Lawrence in *Bad Boys II*, shit just got real.

I took advantage of a shooting break and the Canada Day long weekend (that's July 1 for non-Canucks) to slink off to California for my callback. I spent the whole time trying to temper my expectations and keep my cool. I don't think I need to tell you how badly I wanted to be a Marvel superhero, but it still seemed so insanely far-fetched a thought to entertain that I forced it out of my mind as hard as I could.

The audition took place at Sarah Finn's office in Larchmont Village. Sarah, of course, is the legendary casting director responsible for virtually every face in the entire MCU. I walked nervously up the stairs to her waiting area, past signed posters of the Avengers movies mounted on the wall, imagining the footprints of the great actors who walked before me, signed in and waited for my name to be called.

After about ten minutes, I heard a voice outside.

"Let me just go in and say hi to him real quick."

A moment later, Destin Daniel Cretton, who I would later come to know intimately as my director and fearless leader, walked in with a huge smile on his face. I was immediately put at ease—it was just one of Destin's many remarkable talents—before I was led into the audition room.

Thirty minutes later, I stumbled out of Sarah's office on the verge of having a panic attack.

I can recall pieces of what happened in the room—my reader Molly's auburn hair, Sarah's smile, Destin nodding his head in approval—but it all went by in a blur. I think at some point I threw my pages away and just invented a scene in my head. I did know one thing, however, beyond a reasonable doubt: it was the best audition I had ever done.

My mind went apoplectic, showing me every possible scenario a hundred times per second. I shook all over, no longer able to contain my expectations. I was beginning to believe that I could *actually* do this.

Eventually I was able to calm myself down, fly back to Toronto and continue on with my life. Although I yearned for someone to help me share my emotional burden, I knew I couldn't tell my parents—each time I had ever shared information about an audition, they had always lost sleep thinking about it. They never suspected anything, and I threw myself into work yet again.

A week later, I got another call from Chris; Sarah and Destin wanted to set up a screen test. The date was, of all days, the one that we had set for our celebrity basketball game.

Inspired by what I had seen in LA, I was determined to spread a bit of that same cultural pride and infectious energy to my home city of Toronto. I knew right away that Clem was the guy who would help turn my idea into a reality; he worked tirelessly for his community, whether it was organizing career mentorship programs or running summer sports camps for Asian Canadian youth. I hardly had to sell Clem on the idea when I brought it to him; he was all too ready to jump into the deep end with me and create something truly unique and special.

By mid-July Clem and I had been prepping for our big event for over three months, lining up community sponsors, booking venues and selling tickets. We had assembled a roster of some of the most famous Asian personalities in North America, including first-generation YouTube sensations like Wong Fu Productions, the Fung Brothers, Bart Kwan, AJ Rafael and Jason Chen, as well as television personalities like Hudson Yang from *Fresh Off the Boat* and my *Kim's Convenience* costar Andrew Phung. Proceeds from the event would be donated to the Jeremy Lin Foundation, which gave financial support to community organizations in the cities that Jeremy played in. I knew that the event could theoretically run without me, but also that I would forever regret missing it. And so, impossibly, I said no to Marvel Studios.

Okay, fine, it was more like a gentle suggestion to move the date—maybe even a little begging. Thankfully, Destin and Sarah acquiesced, and the test was pushed a day later; it meant that I would be able to attend the game, but also that I'd have to hop on a plane to New York at 5 a.m. the next morning.

The night before my friends were set to fly in for the game, I began to fall apart. A faint whisper of doubt in my mind grew to a deafening echo that repeated itself in my mind:

Why me? What makes me worthy?

I honestly didn't know how to answer that; I was neither the tallest, the most handsome, the buffest, nor the best martial artist of any of the Asian actors I knew. What gave me the right to believe that I could play the Master of Kung Fu in the greatest franchise in the history of Hollywood? I had been clawing my way to the top of a small market for the last seven years, faking the part of a trained actor as best I could. But I could not fool Sarah or Destin; surely, they would see straight through my false confidence and expose me as a total fraud.

Unable to hold in my anxiety any longer, I called my parents and explained the situation to them.

"I know that you'll lose sleep over this and I'm sorry for putting that on you, but I really need you," I said. "This is the most important audition of my life."

"We understand. We will always be here to support you," my dad replied.

"No matter what happens, we will be by your side," my mother emphasized. *"Whether it is this opportunity or another one down the road, it's just a matter of time."*

My mother's words pierced deep into the inner reaches of my soul and obliterated any lingering self-doubt I had. What they said wasn't anything particularly groundbreaking—they were Chinese immigrants after all, not Aaron Sorkin—but I had experienced my parents' reassurance and unconditional love for perhaps the first time in my life . . . and it made me feel invincible. Our family was no stranger to life's high-stakes, buzzer-beating moments. From Harbin to Beijing, Tempe to Kingston, we had triumphed and persevered over impossible odds time after time.

Maybe it was time for us to take Hollywood too.

On Saturday, July 13, I walked out onto a completely packed outdoor court with my friends. We held our event alongside the Toronto Night Market, a massive celebration of Asian food and culture that ran all weekend and brought in over 100,000 people. Our tickets had sold out within minutes of going on sale, and those who weren't able to scoop them up had crowded around the boundaries, hoping to get a peek at the action.

My team was trailing by one with the seconds winding down when YouTube musician Jason Chen sliced in between two defenders and laid the ball in for an easy two. The opposing team missed on their possession, and I grabbed the rebound; we were in the lead, but only barely so. With twenty seconds left I took the ball down the court, spotted up at the three-point line, and let fly just about the ugliest jumper you had ever seen.

The ball clanked loudly off the backboard . . . and through the net. Home team up three (my foot was on the line)!

The crowd EXPLODED. Our announcer was yelling my name over and over again. The opposing team had barely five seconds to scramble together a play, but the shot would go way off as the final buzzer sounded. We shook hands and presented a check for $15,000 to the Jeremy Lin Foundation.

Later that night, I met all the players in our hotel lobby as they prepared to head out to the after-party. I of course had to be up early in the morning and wouldn't be joining them. One by one, my friends embraced me and wished me luck for my big day. Phil and I held each other for a long time—I knew how long he had been fighting for us, waiting for the day that we would get our seat at Hollywood's table.

"The community is with you, brother."

Those words meant the world to me. I woke up the next morning with the adrenaline from the game still coursing through me. I had initially thought that my hectic schedule would put me at a disadvantage for my audition, but I was so wrong—everything that had happened had cemented in me the belief that I was going to do this.

On the plane, too amped to sleep, I closed my eyes and listened to the *Avengers: Endgame* soundtrack on repeat. I felt the heroic notes permeate through every cell in my body, preparing me for the task at hand.

It's now or never, Simu.

When I land at LaGuardia I am swiftly picked up and taken to a soundstage in Brooklyn where Destin and executive producer Jonathan Schwartz are waiting for me. The screen test is set up like the full shoot, complete with hair, makeup and wardrobe—the whole nine yards. I am processed and then led onto a set, where my scene partner is waiting for me. My heart suddenly stops as I recognize who this actress is:

"Holy shit, Awkwafina?!"

"It's so good to meet you, Simu! You're gonna fuckin' rock it, dude."

God, she's so cool.

"Camera rolling."

As the crew begins to set up for the first take of the day, time begins to slow. I am right back on that soccer field again, a skinny little twelve-year-old who nobody expected to take the game-winning shot. I have been running for years, fighting and clawing just to be here in this exact spot, with the ball coming right at me.

"Sound Speed."

In this moment, there is no longer any doubt in my mind that I am the one who is meant to play this character. By myself, I was a force to be reckoned with—I had broken from my predetermined path, discovered my true passion and then pursued it with absolute conviction. With the full support of my friends, my community and my *family* behind me . . . I was completely unstoppable.

"Scene 1 Take 1, Mark."

I stare through space and time to when I was a little boy living in China with his grandparents, watching tiny superheroes with calabashes on their heads fighting to save the world.

I see my parents in Kingston thirty years ago, huddled around a tiny dinner table they had scavenged off the street, eating the ground beef they had bought from the discount section of the supermarket, dreaming of a day when they wouldn't have to fight so hard just to survive.

I see a confused boy, desperate for the love and affection his parents never gave him, who hated the skin he was in and wished that he was anybody else in the world.

I see the three of us today, our little family of dreamers, smiling back at me. My parents are beaming with pride at the son who has disobeyed practically every single order they had ever given. My own reflection stares back at me stoically, calming me, as if telling me that this is my time.

Every step of our shared journey that spanned two continents and sixty years has led me to this moment. This was the point that my parents and I, despite our insatiable ambition, had never dared to dream beyond . . . until now.

Now, *together*, we would take the next step forward, and make history.

"Camera set."

I take a deep breath, fill my heart with gratitude . . . and prepare to face my destiny.

"ACTION."

ACKNOWLEDGMENTS

I'd like to begin by thanking my friend, LX4 bandmate and editor Adrian Lee, who not only helped craft the bones and the structure of this story, but also interviewed my parents and me over many painstaking hours. When Adrian was working at *Maclean's* in 2017, he approached me to write a letter for a column called "Before You Go," which was meant to be a way to share unsaid words with loved ones. That letter, which you can still find online, became the catalyst for everything that came after. Love you, buddy; let's get the band back together sometime.

In early 2018, I received a Facebook message from a woman claiming to be a literary agent. She had read my letter in *Maclean's,* and was positive that I could take its essence and turn it into a memoir. That woman was the legendary Jackie Kaiser at Westwood Creative Artists, who waited patiently for a whole year until I was actually ready to put pen to paper.

(I mean, I was twenty-nine years old; I didn't think I had lived a memoir-worthy life!)

Jackie helped me craft my initial proposal into something worth bringing to a publisher, made a sale, and then worked in tandem with my agent at CAA to sell the book *again* in the US after my Marvel news broke. It's thanks to Jackie's patience and gentle guidance that you're reading these pages right now.

To my editors Iris Tupholme at HarperCollins Canada and Mauro

DiPreta at HarperCollins/William Morrow (and all of the marketing and sales staff), my agent Cindy Uh and my team at CAA, my publicists Charlene Young and Stephen Huvane at Slate PR, my attorney Shelby Weiser and my managers Chris Lee and Kyle Pak: thank you for putting up with me during our many Zoom calls, and for helping to shepherd this book from inception to release. I'm more grateful for you than you will ever know. You are the *ultimate* dream team.

Tragically my yéye and năinai both passed away over the course of producing this book. They both lived full lives of over ninety years, during which they witnessed the Japanese occupation of Shanghai, the liberation of China, the Cultural Revolution, and the birth of one very stubborn grandson. Although they never got to hold this book in their hands, or watch their grandson play a superhero on the big screen, I can feel their presence and eternal love always. I can't overstate how instrumental they were in my early development; all of my decency and kindness come from my sweet, nurturing năinai, while what little intelligence I possess is from the brilliant analytical mind of my yéye. 爷爷, 奶奶, you are my guardian angels, my everything, and I miss you every day.

To my dog Barkley, who came into my life at my most desperate time of need and held on until the moment he knew I would be okay: I hope you're wagging your tail up there on the Rainbow Bridge. I miss you every day, my boy.

Finally—with all the love that I have in this world—I want to thank my parents, whose struggles and triumphs are the true heart and soul of this book. 爸爸, 妈妈, everything I am and everything I have achieved is because of you. Thank you for driving me to every swimming lesson, soccer practice, and piano lesson and for picking me up from the GO Transit station every day for six years. Thank you for your willingness to revisit the bad memories with me, and for allowing me to tell our story honestly and openly in the hopes that families today could learn from us and steer themselves from the same mistakes. You continue to inspire me in all that you do, and I love you with all my heart. You have most *certainly* lived a memoir-worthy life.

Along that same vein, I'm sorry I was (and continue to be) such a damn headache. I wish I had been an easier kid to raise, but we've got every day from here on out to make happy memories full of love and laughter. I can't promise not to do dumb things like crashing the car into the garage, but I will always help to clean up the mess. You're in my heart no matter what I do, no matter where I go.

Well, that's all, folks! Thanks for reading, hug your families and your dogs, and be well. I'll see you on the big screen.